D1575503

Gloria Deák is a writer and independent scholar, specializing in American art and cultural affairs. Her books include *Picturing New York: The City from Its Beginnings to the Present*; *Picturing America, Volumes I* and *II*; *Profiles of American Artists* and *American Views: Prospects and Vistas*.

PASSAGE TO AMERICA

Celebrated European Visitors

in Search of the

American Adventure

GLORIA DEÁK

I.B. TAURIS

LONDON · NEW YORK

Published in 2013 by I.B.Tauris & Co. Ltd
6 Salem Road, London W2 4BU
175 Fifth Avenue, New York NY 10010
www.ibtauris.com

Distributed in the United States and Canada
Exclusively by Palgrave Macmillan
175 Fifth Avenue, New York NY 10010

Copyright © 2013 Gloria Deák

The right of Gloria Deák to be identified as the author of this work has
been asserted by her in accordance with the
Copyright, Designs and Patents Act 1988.

All rights reserved. Except for brief quotations in a review, this book, or
any part thereof, may not be reproduced, stored in or introduced into a
retrieval system, or transmitted, in any form or by any means, electronic,
mechanical, photocopying, recording or otherwise, without the prior
written permission of the publisher.

ISBN: 978 1 78076 075 9

A full CIP record for this book is available from the British Library
A full CIP record is available from the Library of Congress

Library of Congress Catalog Card Number: available

Text design, typesetting and eBook by Tetragon, London
Printed and bound in Great Britain by T.J. International, Padstow, Cornwall

MIX
Paper from
responsible sources
FSC
www.fsc.org   FSC® C013056

CONTENTS

# LIST OF ILLUSTRATIONS

Where copyright is not attributed, the image is in the public domain.

To my beloved husband István,
with ever increasing affection

 ACKNOWLEDGMENTS

WHAT GOOD FORTUNE for me that I was able to attract the help of two astute and willing readers who followed the progress of this work and made informed comments. I am highly indebted to Ella Milbank Foshay, an American art historian, and to Sanford Malter, an architect steeped in American history, for their unfaltering readiness to help. Each of them read every chapter carefully as they crossed the Atlantic once again in the accounts of the fifteen travelers whose trips to the New World are here recorded. They never failed to catch errors en route, nor to make astute observations. Each of them read every chapter carefully, three of which – recording the travels of Hyde de Neuville, Frances Trollope and Charles Dickens – appeared in an earlier form in *The Magazine Antiques*.

I also had the good fortune, at the start, to find my manuscript in the hands of Joanna Godfrey, senior editor of History and Politics at I.B.Tauris, who accepted it for publication and with whom I had an engaging exchange of correspondence. I salute her with enthusiasm. Ellie Robins and Alex Middleton edited and proofread the manuscript with remarkable perspicacity while Alex Billington, managing director of Tetragon, astutely guided the text into the final stages of design and printing. To all three, I extend a robust *thank you*.

There were others who were of help in various ways, and I am delighted to record their names: Tarik Amar, James Brust, Sally Carr, David Combs, Zöe Kaplan and Alison Petretti. Let me not neglect to mention the names of my husband István Deák, my daughter Éva Peck and her husband Thomas Peck, who were all helpful in ways small, large, and ever affectionate.

GLORIA DEÁK

 FOREWORD

A MERICA WAS a proud province in the nineteenth century. After their revolution, Americans knew they were no longer living in Europe. It was this knowledge that had provoked the American Revolution in the first place – the sense of America's local connection to destiny, of its local traditions and local forms of government. Nor, in the nineteenth century, did America have anything resembling Europe's historic grandeur. It lacked the metropolitan sophistication of Paris and London, the musical magnificence of Germany and Austria, the endless artistic achievements of Italy. America was one of many provincial non-European places, though for a province its self-confidence was strange. Its muddy, unspectacular capital city was being built according to a grand architectural blueprint. New York was extending its urban chaos steadily up the island of Manhattan. Fantastic areas of territory were being annexed to the American republic, purchased, negotiated for or simply grabbed. Expansion was only the physical pretext for Americans' 'constant habit of praising themselves', as Basil Hall put it, summing up his 1827 journey (see Chapter 3). The true source of their pride was political, not commercial or territorial. Americans believed themselves pioneers in the art of self-governance. If self-governance was at the heart of modern politics, then Europe might be the real province and America the unacknowledged center. American pride was counter-intuitive – especially to the nineteenth-century Europeans who encountered it – one of the many interesting novelties on display in the United States.

In *Passage to America*, Gloria Deák brings these surprised Europeans beautifully to life. Each of Deák's travelers is the Columbus of a different America. The eye of the beholder is not objective, and the country to which these Europeans were voyaging, in the nineteenth century, was enmeshed in ceaseless change. It began the century an agrarian republic in thrall to the austere figure of George Washington, robustly committed to slavery and with no real image of what its culture was going to be. It concluded the century almost on a par with the European great powers, still coming to grips with Lincoln's Civil War promises of freedom for African-Americans and of a new home for millions upon millions of European immigrants. Deák ends her book with Henry James returning to America in 1904, after twenty years in Europe and hardly able to recognize the country of his childhood. More than Europe, America was stepping decisively toward the future, in James's Europhilic estimation. James starkly separated America from Europe. Deák writes of a key question among James's contemporaries, that 'of whether the American nation represented a decided advance on European inequalities, or whether it had taken a giant step backwards'. To ask this question is to ponder a world apart.

The answers were contradictory. Some found genuine liberty and progress in America, with suffrage and education more widely available than in Europe. Behind political excellence might lay generosity of character – the hospitality, for example, that Tchaikovsky enjoyed during his 1891 visit. The equation could also be more complicated. Some saw vulgarity as the political norm in America, and some admired America's political system while wondering about the status of American culture, or – to use a word more resonant of the nineteenth century – of American manners. There was often some 'tincture of the barbaric' about America, in Thomas Hamilton's words, and this could make Americans' outspoken pride baffling as well as annoying (see Chapter 5). The obvious American barbarism was slavery. It rarely escaped European notice, giving a salutary prick to the antebellum American conscience. Frances Trollope said little of politics in her scathing and scathingly funny *Domestic Manners of the Americans* (1832). Charles Dickens registered a similar skepticism about American manners after his 1842 trip. It is interesting to note that the critical commentaries of Trollope and Dickens earned them small fortunes back at home. If the literary marketplace was any measure, Europeans wanted America to disappoint them. Overseas barbarism confirmed civilization at home. Nevertheless, the will to European superiority, the mirror image of American pride, is at the periphery of Deák's story.

The central story in *Passage to America* is of a political–cultural map on which the borders are bracingly unclear. To go to America was to remain somehow in Europe. The grids common to so many American cities have their origin, Deák tells us, in the architectural thinking of Vitruvius. Americans spoke English, a bridge to Europe's literature, which nineteenth-century Americans avidly read and which was not then under copyright in America – one reason for Dickens's frustration with a country that adored him. Boston, Philadelphia, New York and Washington, DC, all echoed the European city, a claim advanced in Edward Dicey's amusingly inaccurate description of New York as 'Venice without canals' (see Chapter 12). Americans' touching eagerness to lionize such heroes of European culture as Dickens and Tchaikovsky (invited to New York to celebrate the opening of Carnegie Hall) illustrates the proximity of Europe to America in this century of European hegemony. Even American democracy had its roots in European antiquity and in the European Enlightenment, which is why so many Europeans were willing to make the arduous sea voyage, to endure the often terrible travel conditions in America and to suffer through the locals' long monologues of self-praise. They wanted to see what American democracy would mean to them: it was this curiosity that distinguished their travels from mere tourism. Broadly speaking, they had a share in creating American democracy, and in the twentieth century, as nineteenth-century Europeans seemed to anticipate, American democracy would have a share in the recreation of Europe.

MICHAEL KIMMAGE
The Catholic University of America
Washington, DC

 PREFACE

Passage to America

'NOWADAYS COUNTRIES are always being discovered that were never in the old geography books,' avowed Thomas More in sheer wonderment as news circulated of the extraordinary findings across the Atlantic reported by Columbus, Vespucci and a host of successive explorers. That sense of wonder, recorded in the year 1516 in the opening pages of More's *Utopia*, would continue as two large continents gradually revealed themselves, shattering Old World cosmography and undermining some of the long-revered interpretations of the Bible. With one society after another proceeding over time to take its place among the world's long-established nations, artists and poets rivaled mapmakers in making sense of their newly expanded universe. Christopher Marlowe, Edmund Spenser, Martin Waldseemüller, Gerardus Mercator and Abraham Ortelius were among those who ventured during the course of the sixteenth century – along with Thomas More – to interpret the new findings to a world long incredulous and awed. It was Mercator's map of 1538 that named the two Western continents for the first time, while the Mannerist artist Maarten de Vos personified America in a widely circulated drawing of 1594 as a majestic and beguiling female, proud of her destiny.

Over the next several centuries, perhaps no emerging country west of the Atlantic would excite as much curiosity as that vast expanse of territory that would become known as the United States. Here came into view a country of extraordinary natural resources, eminently accessible by sea via both its Atlantic and its Pacific ports. Here, too, was a country whose early population would prove to be an unprecedented mixture of Native American, European and African cultures. Indeed, the continuing fascination of those casting a glance overseas from Europe can be said to have been augmented throughout the nineteenth century as the original thirteen colonies steadily blossomed into a full-fledged nation, based on a representative government and heralding democratic principles. Though initially dependent on Britain for her language as well as for many of her cultural institutions, the new nation was determined on her own path. Would there be lessons, in time, to be learned here by Europe's often disquieted societies? More's *Utopia* suggests no less than the expectation of a spirited exchange between the Old World and the New.

A host of questions continually loomed as it became manifest that, in expanding its geographical borders, the United States had staked out a new social order. What exactly was this new social order? What was meant by the dictum in its Declaration of Independence that all men were created 'equal'? How could this possibly be, when long-established world traditions had decreed otherwise? What would be the implications for the European societies from which Americans were descendent? Would not America, with her brash ideas, find herself a pariah among the very nations she sought to rival? How should she dare impose her new concepts on countries with longer histories? Indeed, when would she be mature enough to make significant contributions to global advancements in the sciences and the arts? A gallimaufry of such reactions filled the air as the new nation across the Atlantic sought her place in the line-up of historical societies. By the outbreak of the First World War, the United States would no longer loom as an evolving country, for by then it had not only taken its place among the league of the world's nations, but had boldly charted its role as a formidable leader.

As an author, my interest in nineteenth-century European reactions to the still-evolving American way of life was sparked on reading the memoirs of an aristocratic couple who had been banished abroad by the newly ascendant Napoleon. Of English–French ancestry, the Baron and Baroness Hyde de Neuville recorded their seven-year stay in the New World, beginning in 1807, in three volumes of memoirs as well as in a series of drawings made by the Baroness. These diminutive drawings, so appealing in their spontaneity, capture the mood of a new and ever-expanding society. Assigned by *Antiques Magazine* to prepare an illustrated article on the de Neuville banishment for one of their monthly issues, I became intrigued by the story of the exiled couple and their laudable adaptation to a rhythm of life totally alien to their upbringing. Although the Baron and Baroness unceasingly looked forward to their return to Europe, they permitted themselves while in America to become immersed in a truly foreign atmosphere and wrote of the experience with candor and charm. As this led to my interest in other European visitors, a book then slowly took shape with advice from my publisher to give preference to the reports of British travelers by way of establishing a consistent voice. Many of the latter visitors saw much that met with their disapproval while yet acknowledging that there were social and political innovations that could be applied to the reform of European society. It was More's conviction in *Utopia* that while the New World had 'immediately adopted all the best ideas that Europe has produced', the reverse would probably never be true; this despite the fact that the New World was so much ahead 'politically and economically'.

Most Europeans who successively found their way to nineteenth-century America were seeking new economic opportunities largely as immigrants, but there were those who came as eager investors, particularly before 1850. A sizeable group came out of curiosity. This last group invariably meant visitors who had both the leisure to make the transatlantic crossing and the education to render a detailed account of their stay. Over the decades of that century, hundreds of books accordingly appeared by travelers who registered varied interests in making so remarkable a journey. The fifteen accounts chosen for this volume cover not only the steady geographical expansion of the new nation but reactions to the major upheavals in her young history.

Few visitors who crossed the Atlantic as observers, it would develop, were shy of being candid in their reports; no one, however, can be said to have been as vituperative as the fulminating Frances Trollope. Her book proved to be truly offensive to the emerging nation, for Americans were not always as certain of their country's political, economic and social achievements as they often professed. Yet Trollope was right in many of her judgments, and I have made no

attempt in rendering her account, or any other, to soften harsh criticism. Some fifteen years later, when Charles Dickens followed Mrs.
Trollope, he had his own reasons to be displeased with the New World
(namely the lack of copyright to protect his income from reprinted
books). While Dickens did author a published account of his visit,
he preferred to register his true reaction to America through his
novel *Martin Chuzzlewit*: this work of fiction permitted more candor
than would a straightforward report. The impressions of William
Makepeace Thackeray can be learned from the many letters that this
prominent author wrote, rather than from a book, which he purposely
declined to write. Still, there is a reliable account of the trip prepared
by his young assistant Eyre Crowe, who was an artist and who, like
the earlier Baroness de Neuville, made a series of reportorial drawings. Peter Ilich Tchaikovsky also did not write an account when he
came to inaugurate Carnegie Hall, but he did leave a diary and letters;
in addition, the press in America reported on all his movements. All
other travelers in this volume left published accounts.

Perhaps no early-nineteenth-century visitor was more unusual
than Frances Wright – young, beautiful, rich and a zealous reformer –
who was certain she had the answer to no less a New World problem
than slavery. With unwavering belief in the course she was taking,
Wright accordingly set up a bold experiment in the wilds of Tennessee.
Though she had the support and friendship of such eminent personalities as the Marquis de Lafayette and Thomas Jefferson, the experiment
failed. Fanny Trollope was asked to be a participant in that astounding
undertaking, but fled in horror at so primitive a scene. Visiting in the
first half of the century were two other remarkable women: Fanny
Kemble, the actress, and Harriet Martineau, the political scientist.
Kemble charmed American audiences with her acting while being truly
convinced that, before long, America would revert to a monarchy. This,
she claimed, was because 'the feeling of rank, of inequality, is inherent
in us, a part of the veneration of our natures.' It was surely not a view
taken by the astute and ever-deferential Martineau, who traveled widely
and supported the dangerous notion of abolitionism. Though she was
profoundly deaf, her observations of the country's mores and politics
were astonishingly keen; indeed, her many volumes eventually led to
the scholarly discipline of modern sociology.

A young Scottish captain named Basil Hall arrived in the New World in the year 1827 with a distinctive set of opinions. The United States, in his view, did not represent a new and audacious experiment in equality but was one of England's 'occasional failures'. He rued America's renunciation of the practice of entail, as well as the repeal of the law of primogeniture, both being judged unwise abandonments of English tradition. In the year 1830, when Captain Thomas Hamilton arrived attended by a personal manservant, reform was in the air in the British Isles of a kind disturbing to any of that country's elite. This had been provoked in part by tremendous national debt following the Napoleonic Wars and a wave of poverty accompanying the Industrial Revolution. As a confirmed Tory, Hamilton was bent on discovering for himself whether or not democracy was in effect nothing short of mob rule. It became the purpose of his two-volume account to discourage the exportation of democracy to England and, while he recognized that his views were unfavorable, he was nonetheless certain that they were educational and to the new country's benefit. Young Charles Augustus Murray crossed the Atlantic in the first half of the century with an inexhaustible supply of goodwill. It was his determination to gain a better understanding of America and its indigenous culture by living for a while among a tribe of natives in the West. His two-volume memoir was to reflect his Eton and Oxford training by bringing erudition and sparkle to the record of his unusual experience. Thomas Colley Grattan arrived in the United States in the year 1839 as an official visitor with the rank of British consul to the state of Massachusetts; he would hold the post for seven years. So long a residence in the New World, he became convinced, must be felt by a man of European tastes and habits as a 'banishment'.

During the middle years of the nineteenth century, the specter of a war dividing the states of the new nation could not escape the attention of visitors continuing to cross the Atlantic westward. When war finally erupted, many reporters were sent to cover the course of the devastating conflict. Firm in the grasp of the journalist Edward Dicey was a thoroughgoing professionalism, which he would bring to bear while reporting on the Civil War for the London *Spectator* and *Macmillan's Magazine*. His pro-Union stand set him apart from most British journalists and was in distinct opposition to the anti-Union cause adopted by the British government. Yet, it was Dicey's prescient conviction that the success of the North could only be viewed as being in the interests of the countries on both sides of the Atlantic. The written portrait he drew of Abraham Lincoln, after making the acquaintance of America's sixteenth president, has left historians forever in his debt.

And what was the nature of the visit of young Oscar Wilde in 1882? It was like no other to be sure, both in its purpose and in its unfolding over the course of an entire year. His mission was to introduce the 'new aestheticism' to American audiences, ranging from New York to obscure towns in the far West. Though such a rarefied concept, to be sure, was enigmatic to the majority of his listeners, Wilde did not fail to attract attention wherever he went. Accumulating fame during his tour was an unspoken goal for the colorful visitor, and it was grandly achieved. Though Wilde and the 'new aestheticism' were often ridiculed as he lectured from place to place, it was the conviction of the young Oxford graduate that 'satire was the tribute paid by mediocrity to genius'.

The final selection of Henry James for this book requires some explanation, as the question will be asked: Was he not an American? Indeed he was, but he lived mostly abroad and became a British subject. We therefore have the advantage, in his voluminous report, of an insider–outsider point of view that is as revealing as it is perspicacious.

 CHAPTER 1

The New World Sojourn of Baron and Baroness Hyde de Neuville

'A PRODIGIOUS VITALITY animates this still developing but already potent republic,' declared Baron Hyde de Neuville with ebullience shortly after he took up residence in the New World following his banishment from France. The year was 1807. It had now been four years since the Baron had been forced to live a nomadic existence, first in Europe and then in America, as a result of eviction by the newly triumphant Napoleon Bonaparte. Always with him was his talented and ever-optimistic wife, Anne-Marguerite-Henriette Rouillé de Marigny, who shared his political views as well as a willingness to undergo the vicissitudes of banishment from a life that had been cherished by generations of her family.

It was in the very year that Maximilien François Marie Isidore de Robespierre lost his head to the guillotine that Anne-Marguerite had married the wealthy royalist Jean Guillaume Hyde de Neuville. The wedding took place in France shortly after Robespierre's execution, or as the Baron recorded in his memoirs, it was *'peu après le 9 thermidor'*.[1] The coupling of the happy event with one of the more resonant dates in the French Revolutionary calendar – 27 July 1794 – is a reflection of the future Baron's total immersion in the political life of his country as a defender of Bourbon rule.

Political reverberations of one kind or another echoed throughout the duration of the de Neuville marriage and profoundly affected their lives. Born in La Charité-sur-Loire of both English and French noble ancestry, Hyde de Neuville was all of eighteen years old when he went to the altar; his wife, born in Sancerre, was apparently a good bit older than her husband.[2] The Baron was handsome, beguiling, hotheaded, adventuresome and affectionate; his bride sweet-tempered, rich and talented. And she adored him. Whenever the tumult of the Revolution required it, she gladly let him pose as her son, rarely questioning his motives when he engaged in frequent conspiracies to support the ill-fated Bourbon monarchy. More than once they were forced to live under assumed names; more than once they changed their residence in fear for their lives. The enforced sojourn in America was to be one of the most peaceful interludes they would encounter in an existence dominated by politics. A pivotal turn in the couple's destiny had taken place in 1803, when Hyde de Neuville was condemned as an outlaw for his alleged part in an attempt to assassinate Napoleon. It was a bitter moment for the two royalists: they faced proscription by the government, including the sequestration of all their properties. Anne-Marguerite showed implacable courage by journeying from place to place during 1803 and 1804 seeking an audience with influential French officials to disprove the charge of conspiracy and to have the proscription overturned. She was unsuccessful until she took her cause to Napoleon himself. Her odyssey in 1805 by horse-drawn coach, crossing Germany and Austria in the wake of the French army in an attempt to be heard by Napoleon, is a tale of real heroics. Impressed by her pluck, Napoleon allowed the de Neuvilles to retain their properties on condition that they leave France.

Banishment from France saved Hyde de Neuville's life, but it was without doubt a harsh sentence imposed on him and his wife. During a dalliance of more than a year in Spain, they formed a lifelong friendship with Chateaubriand, who had been to the New World over a decade earlier and had achieved fame with his novel *Atala*, based on his experience with Native American culture. Not without trepidation, the de Neuvilles embarked for America from the Spanish port of Cadiz. The transatlantic crossing aboard the American vessel *Golden Age* took an exhausting fifty days: they arrived in New York in June of 1807, with the fervent hope that their exile would be brief. No one could have convinced them that they would remain all of seven years on American soil.

A diminutive watercolor of New York Harbor records the arrival of the de Neuvilles in America and introduces us to the guileless art of Anne-Marguerite. The Baroness often made drawings of places she visited, and her delightfully spontaneous, if naive, style has endowed the small collection of American sketches she executed with great documentary appeal.[3] They tell us much pictorially about American life in the opening decades of the nineteenth century and of her response to a New World setting: there is an appealing lack of hauteur in the things that attracted her. With a population approaching ninety thousand, New York City in 1807 presented a colorful scene of busy waterways filled with a forest of tall-masted ships and a line of eager faces at the Battery watching the vessels come in at the southern tip of Manhattan. But the mournful fact that 'neither relative nor friend' awaited the arrival of the exiled couple was duly noted in the Baron's journal. European advice to the couple had been to travel for a while in the new nation before fixing on a permanent residence. Accordingly, after three weeks in New York, they journeyed up the Hudson River toward their final destination of Niagara Falls and, like so many visitors before and after them, they were enchanted by the Palisades and other wonders of the river that define the western shore of New York. 'The Hudson is very beautiful, of an imposing immensity,' wrote the Baron, 'and its two shores continually offer a panorama that is as picturesque as it is romantic.'

Populating the Hudson River region were various tribes of Native Americans, in which the exiles took a great interest, stimulated as much by their own natural curiosity about all aspects of the New World as by the conversations they had held in Cadiz with Chateaubriand. The latter had engaged the recently deposed couple with riveting descriptions of sparsely settled areas in America as well as recounting stories of his encounters with the native population. Yet the properties he assigned to the 'Indians' in his *Atala* of 1801 did not accord with the character of the Oneida tribe the Baron encountered near Utica; the latter observed in his memoirs that many of them were inebriated and indolent, and their lodgings unkempt. Nor did that unflattering characterization accord with one of the earliest encounters reported by the English explorer Martin Pring. Upon landing in Plymouth Harbor in 1601, one of Pring's seamen took to strumming his guitar: the sound so enchanted the Native Americans that they came in large numbers to dance to the music. Such a beguiling image was more in accord with the figure of the noble savage romanticized by Chateaubriand in his writings; there he challenges the portrayal of Western and Native American cultures as ethical opposites. The negative impression gained by the de Neuvilles was later partially reversed after the French couple passed through Geneva, Batavia and Buffalo in the state of New York, where the Baron wrote, '*Nous avons trouvé de plus beaux sauvages.*'[4] Clearly these 'more handsome' natives had not been contaminated by prolonged contact with European settlers and taken to drink. They may have been part of the five tribes that constituted the strong Iroquois League peopling the New York State area. Most of these tribes were agricultural, village-dwelling natives who lived in long, bark houses.

A stop in Utica, New York, was the occasion for a long letter from the Baron to his sister commenting on his new American experiences. He wrote that he found the naming of towns in America after Roman and Greek cities rather amusing – an attempted historical link between the New World and the Old – even if the freshly emerged Utica (consisting of a dismal cluster of houses in 1807) had little to do with the celebrated city of the ancient world. He commented on the pioneer settlements fast rising out of forests, on the different 'Indian' tribes he had been able to observe, on the general industriousness of Americans, on the dignity accorded to labor and, above all, on the lack of 'false' social ideas of the kind often prevalent in class-conscious Europe. He wrote as well of the country's drawbacks – particularly underlining its materialism ('Americans like money too much') and the frequent abuse of nature in settling the land – yet he was able to say with unrestrained wonder, 'This is a land truly full of miracles.' When they finally reached Niagara in September, the thunderous falls had the predictable impact: incredulity and awe. Unfortunately, no watercolor by the Baroness survives to give us her artistic impressions of this natural wonder, though it seems unlikely that she was not moved to sketch so magnificent a spectacle. There was rarely a visitor, beginning at the end of the seventeenth century, who was not inspired to render a drawing or a written account of what was termed, in 1697 by the French chaplain Louis Hennepin, 'a prodigious cadence of water'. Nothing in the early nineteenth century interfered with the pristine beauty of the cataract or its surroundings: it may be that the Baroness found the cascading rapids too overpowering a subject for one of her diminutive watercolors.

The return to New York City was fixed for the winter of 1807–8, as the émigrés were encouraged to feel that their constant dream of returning home might soon be a possibility following the news that Napoleon had signed peace treaties with Russia and Prussia at Tilsit. But when they heard via influential friends that Joseph Fouché, Duc d'Otrante, the French Minister of Police, had decreed against the Baron's return, that dream was shattered. The exiles thereupon determined to relieve the sorrow of their exile by plunging into useful and rewarding occupations in their new country. They were to spend the next three winters in New York City and summer in upstate Angelica, near the Genessee River in Genessee (now Allegheny) County, where they found a host of compatible neighbors. The hamlet of Angelica, founded by the English settler Philip Church in 1800 and named for his mother, had recently taken on a lively air with the arrival of a number of French émigrés dislocated both by the French Revolution and by recent uprisings in the West Indies. Prominent among the Angelica group were Victor Marie du Pont, the elder brother of Éleuthère Irénée du Pont, and members of the family of Madame Marie Jeanne d'Autremont. In this agreeable pastoral refuge, the de Neuvilles purchased land and set up a farm, which they called La Bergerie. The tranquility of Angelica's surroundings and the proximity of congenial friends did prove to offer a certain surcease from the bitterness of exile;

the Arcadian repose permitted the Baron to take up the study of agriculture and medicine and to engage in voluminous correspondence. In a letter to Madame la Princesse de la Trémoille, we find a remarkable prescience in his evaluation of life in America:

> We have no clear notions in France of what is happening on this continent, certainly my own were far from the truth. Since my arrival in the United States I have become convinced that these rebel Colonists are on the way to forming a strong and powerful nation. Only let the Americans be prudent, let them calmly, without revolution, inject a little more strength into their administration; let them remedy certain abuses, and we shall see them one day the astonishment of Europe. I don't know if I am deceiving myself but, from this close vantage point, one feels as if something unknown were stirring in the future; as if the tyranny that presses down on our unhappy country were not the last word of this beginning century; as if a fresh wind had passed over the world, at once the cause and the effect of our Revolution.[5]

That the 'rebel colonists' were in the process of forming a strong nation was particularly evident under the leadership of Thomas Jefferson, who was at that time American president and who was continually proving himself an enlightened leader of the developing nation. He had strong French connections, having served as United States minister to France and, as the de Neuvilles came to appreciate, was a passionate participant in Enlightenment ideas stemming from his interests in philosophy, science, architecture and religion. Just a few years before the arrival of the French exiles, Jefferson had negotiated through shrewd diplomacy a major land acquisition from Napoleon that doubled the size of the United States at the time. Known as the Louisiana Purchase, this amazing territorial acquisition of the year 1803 had been handled for Jefferson by Pierre Samuel du Pont de Nemours, a French nobleman with close ties to both Napoleon and the American President. The staggering purchase ran from south to north in the central portion of the country, constituting the equivalent of one third of the United States today. Then, not long after this historic event, Jefferson arranged for an expedition to explore not only the newly acquired territory but well beyond it, across vast stretches of unclaimed land leading to the Western coast. This expedition, headed by Meriwether Lewis and William Clark, was conceived by the President for a multitude of scientific purposes, but was also intended to document the United States' presence there before any European nation could claim the land. After traveling more than four thousand miles, the explorers reached the Pacific Ocean, having been rewarded with invaluable information pertaining to unknown Native American tribes as well as to scientific and natural phenomena they had carefully observed as they made their way – often with great difficulties – west. Accompanying the expedition was a young native (whom they referred to as a 'squaw') named Sacajawea, married to a French Canadian trader, who acted as one of the interpreters while crossing thousands of miles of wilderness in what can only be described as an heroic chapter in human achievement.

Two years after the de Neuvilles had begun their enforced stay in America, Jefferson was succeeded as American president by James Madison, whom the exiles would come to know during a sojourn in Washington. Meanwhile, for their home in New York City the French couple had chosen a residence on or near Warren Street with a view of the Hudson River. Here they were within walking distance of much that was of interest: the Merchants' Exchange, the Vauxhall Gardens, the French Église du Saint Esprit, Trinity Church, the Park Theatre, and the busy quays of the East River where varieties of merchandise from Europe were constantly unloaded. A short distance east of their residence lay Broadway and the as yet unfinished City Hall, which provided at the time a lively topic for discussion. The competition for the design of the Hall had been won by a French architect named Joseph François Mangin together with John McComb, Jr., an American designer. (Mangin had earlier assisted with the plans of the Place de la Concorde in Paris.) The design originally presented by the two winners, based on French Renaissance motifs, was considered too costly and the size of the building was accordingly somewhat reduced. But the finished structure could still boast of an elaborate pavilion with a dome, rotunda and cupola flanked by two projecting wings. Attention was given to an elaborate interior as well, with a pair of flying marble staircases that culminate in a second-story gallery ringed by Corinthian columns. With its commanding view of the surrounding countryside, the Hall became one of the city's architectural splendors and is so considered to this day. Another major event involving the profile of the city being hotly discussed during the tenure of the exiles was the laying out of the city's streets. This resulted in the Commissioners' Plan of 1811, which made a grid of most of the city by creating twelve avenues running north–south, paralleling the two embracing rivers; the avenues were then crisscrossed by streets every two hundred feet at right angles. Although the notion of a grid-designed city dates as far back as the era of the Roman architect Vitruvius, many New Yorkers bemoaned the aesthetic absence of interrupting circles, squares and ovals. These were deemed not to serve real-estate purposes, however, as much as would the neat parcels of land carved out geometrically. The city was therefore bereft of some of the magnificence that would be accorded to the layout of Paris by Baron Haussmann during the second half of the nineteenth century; Haussmann would be allowed to have relatively unfettered control in directing the embellishment of the French capital.

The Warren Street residence of the de Neuvilles in New York was well below the grid layout of the city and allowed for a leisurely excursion from one shore to the other. Directly south of their house was Columbia College, then occupying a handsome pre-Revolutionary edifice on a hill rising from the Hudson River; the French couple must have often encountered college students during the course of their stay in New York and undoubtedly met some of the scholars teaching there. Their immediate neighborhood consisted of two- and three-story houses built close together, a fair number of them serving typically as both a residence and a place of business. The area had all the earmarks of an idyllic village when Anne-Marguerite made a watercolor of the scene. New Yorkers can be seen busily going about their daily business in her rendering – pumping water, sawing firewood, sweeping the sidewalk or just strolling. Private moments captured in a public situation constitute one of the main characteristics of the Baroness's drawings, giving her topographic projections a warm, human dimension.

During this early-nineteenth-century exile of the Baron and Baroness, the popularity of French culture was at its height in America, often surpassing the influence of England. Enlightenment ideas, promulgated by the *philosophes* and *encyclopédistes*, had had a great impact on the young republic, which sought substantiation for a host of principles in which it believed. French influence had not abated as prominent travelers from France found their way to America and recorded their impressions, in numerous publications, of an extraordinary new experiment in democratic government. Among the more prominent of the recent travelers was Chateaubriand, the friend of the de Neuvilles whose novella *Atala*, published in 1801, went through five editions in its first year and was translated into many languages. A much earlier visitor had been François-Jean, Marquis de Chastellux, who had been assigned by Louis XVI to serve in the American army and was to profess unbounded admiration for America's earliest leaders. Four of the many whom he came to know personally during his extended sojourn (from 1780 to 1783) were George Washington, Benjamin Franklin, Samuel Adams, and Thomas Jefferson. The de Neuvilles were well aware of the works of the Marquis, who was one the forty 'immortals' of the Académie Française and who published two volumes of his experiences in the New World entitled *Travels in North America*, a publication that was found by Thomas Jefferson to be the most flattering account of America thus far written. Chastellux was profoundly concerned with philosophical questions that centered on the wellbeing of mankind, always seeking an answer to the question of whether society was capable of true happiness. The ideas provoked by this profound inquiry led him to a consideration of the rising American nation as a testing ground wherein its leaders would be inspired to work for the happiness of the greatest number. Here in the new nation, he felt, was a unique opportunity to pursue a course that would distance itself from what could only be described as the essentially tragic history of mankind up to that time. During the three years he had spent in America, he was led to entertain so optimistic a vision because he viewed the nation's earliest leaders with the greatest respect and felt they were capable of guiding the country in its goal of social equality. This would certainly not be accomplished without problems, he was only too well aware, because it was to be expected that changes in social status would inevitably arise. While every citizen appeared to be equally well off at that time, or nearly so, success in trade and agriculture would predictably produce a wealthy class, the Marquis conjectured, which would inevitably exert an undue influence in the workings of the government. He pondered the question at some length:

> Now such is the present happiness of America that she has no poor, that every man there enjoys a certain ease and independence, and that if some individuals have been able to obtain a smaller portion than others, they are so surrounded by resources that their future status is considered more important than their present situation. It is important to foresee to what degree democracy is likely to prevail in America, and whether the spirit of this democracy tends to equality of fortunes, or is confined to equality of ranks.[6]

When marked differences in wealth inevitably occurred, he reasoned, would not the American striving for a real democracy be challenged? He raised questions of a similar nature not only theoretically but in discussion with important politicians whom he came to know. The major work of this extraordinary Frenchman, entitled *De la Félicité publique, ou Considérations sur le sort des hommes, dans les différentes époques de l'histoire*, presents the profound conundrum as to whether human society is truly capable of moral amelioration.

The de Neuvilles were, of course, thoroughly familiar with the philosophical preoccupations of the Marquis whose works they admired. They, too, held the rise of a new nation bent on democratic principles in a certain awe and determined to make the most of their exposure to this experience. As they were not without benevolent inclinations, they determined to make whatever kind of contribution was possible during their enforced New World stay. A plan was accordingly conceived whereby the couple would open a school for the large New York population of impoverished French émigrés who had fled the troubled islands of Santo Domingo and Cuba: this they went about with characteristic energy. Petitioning the city's Common Council for a building, they matched their request with their own successful fund-raising. The building that the Common Council allowed them to use was a long, low edifice known first as the Charity School; it was not far from the city's Bridewell prison nor from the building housing the Board of Health. The school inaugurated by the exiles soon began to hum with activity. An office and a press installed in the allotted building allowed all the school manuals to be printed on the premises and, with indefatigable zeal, the Baron also conceived the idea of publishing a monthly journal. Entitled *Journal des Dames*, the publication was intended to generate income for the school through subscriptions, as well as to engage the students in literary exercises. The Baron himself was its chief contributor, writing verse as well as prose under the name L'Hermite du Passaic. It was not before long that a committee appointed by the Common Council delivered – most deservedly – a highly laudatory report on the method of teaching at the French school. In March of 1810 the school inaugurated by the exiles, known as the École Économique, was incorporated as the Society of the Economical School of the City of New York. Benjamin Moore was named president; General Jean Victor Marie Moreau, vice president; and Baron Hyde de Neuville, secretary.[7] The Common Council subsequently gave the school (which operated until 1825) two lots and a liberal amount of money, with the declaration that

> the respectable character of the Trustees and the indefatigable philanthropy of Monsieur Neufville [sic], its principal conductor, excites a confidence that any grant made by this Board will be properly applied and extensively promote the wishes and views of the friends of literature.[8]

More than two hundred students were enrolled in the École, with the Baron and Baroness becoming extremely attached to some of them. A portfolio of nineteen sketches executed by the Baroness records the activities of the school and the extent to which the French couple was engaged in this eleemosynary effort. In one appealing sketch of a female student, she has carefully rendered her subject's coiffure and dress as she works with head bent studiously at her desk; she does not reveal the sitter's identity, as she did in some of the sketches.

The Baron was to take great personal pride in his election, on 24 January 1810, to the Philomedical Society of New York. He had no illusions about the extent of his command of medicine, which he had studied independently, but the election flattered him enormously.[9] Apart from his interest in science, he felt genuinely stimulated by his sustained exposure to the New World, writing enthusiastically to a friend, 'this country presents inexhaustible sources for worthy endeavors and excites my astonishment every day.'[10] Observations of this very nature were to be made more than twenty years later by another French visitor, when the young Alexis de Tocqueville visited America and soon wrote a letter to his mother exclaiming his amazement over the tempo of life in the New World:

> Here is where one must come to witness the most singular state of things imaginable. A people absolutely without precedents, without traditions, without habits, even without foundational ideas has cleared a new path for its civil, criminal, and political legislation and plunged ahead, indifferent to the wisdom of other peoples and all memory of the past. It is shaping its institutions the way it has built roads straight across the forests, secure in its knowledge that it will encounter no limits or impediments; a society that does not yet have any bonds, be they political, hierarchical, religious, or social; where each individual is what pleases him to be, regardless of his neighbor; a democracy devoid of limits or measures.[11]

As to the earlier astonishment of the Baron, it was surely promoted by the heightened activity that then marked the city, for New York at the time of his residence was taking a most dynamic lead in expanding the prosperity of the budding nation. American neutrality during the Napoleonic Wars allowed for expanded trade across the Atlantic and proved of great local advantage as it led to the transformation of the city into the nation's premier port and marketplace. French purchases of the most basic commodities were heightening the trade between the two nations, with the majority of goods passing through Manhattan's points of entry. Boasting one of the best harbors not only along the Atlantic but anywhere in the world, New York quickly replaced Philadelphia at this time as the leading port in the United States. Not only was Manhattan's harbor deep and directly accessible to the open sea but it also had a superior commercial infrastructure of ships and wharves.

It is evident from the Baron's memoirs that he felt himself not only a witness to but an engaged part of all this activity, and it is just as clear that he and the Baroness did not view themselves merely as impatient outsiders but were among those making contributions to America's rising profile. Sometime during 1811 the French couple had purchased property not far from New Brunswick, New Jersey, which they assiduously developed into an attractive farm; there they raised merino sheep. They sold wool to the family of Éleuthère Irénée du Pont, whose house and powder-works plant they visited in Wilmington, Delaware. They had fixed on the New Jersey countryside for a country haven because it was only 'twenty leagues' from New York and was increasingly accessible by the Hudson River ferryboats that were now becoming more frequent and more rapid thanks to the ingenuity of Robert Fulton, an artist and engineer. (Fulton had earlier designed the first working submarine while living in France.) By 1809 Fulton's *Raritan* was making a regular run between New York and New Brunswick via the Raritan River; it is duly recorded in the Baroness's sketch entitled *Vue d'Amboy et du Steam-boat 28 juillet 1809*, which has the distinction of being the earliest known representation of a steamboat in America. The Baron wrote of these crossings that they were often made in the company of 'most' amiable friends. Indeed, their social circle had become greatly enlarged not only through friendship with other émigrés but through increasing contact with local residents, among them the Louis Simons, John Wilkeses, and Philip Churches.[12]

Life on the farm in New Jersey and in the more elevated circles of New York was now giving the de Neuvilles a large measure of satisfaction, although in the Baron's memoirs he turns unceasingly, and not unexpectedly, to the scene in France. He was aware of every turn in politics there, of the machinations of Fouché, of the daring of Napoleon and, particularly, of the political destinies of those close to him and his wife. Throughout his exile he kept his contacts alive, addressing letters to the Comte d'Artois (a brother of Louis XVI and XVIII who was crowned Charles X in 1824), the Duc d'Angoulême, and a host of others, as well as to Louis XVIII himself, who, like the Baron, had been forced to live a peripatetic existence. What was most difficult for this last during the years of exile was the loss of family and friends; the most heart-rending loss was that of his beloved mother, who died in the winter of 1808. 'I had needed to hope that after so many trials and tribulations,' he wrote, 'I would find this revered mother again.'[13] In this unhappy circumstance he accepted the sympathies of General Moreau and his wife, who were the de Neuvilles' neighbors on Warren Street in New York City for a while and who were supportive friends throughout their years in America. Under the straitened circumstances of émigré life, Moreau, the staunch Republican who had fled the regime following his condemnation by Napoleon, and Hyde de Neuville, the ardent royalist, found common political ground in their distrust of Napoleon. In his memoirs, the Baron declared frankly of Moreau:

> He was cold and not very expansive and so an intimacy did not develop easily. But ultimately one could become very attached to him, through the respect he inspired rather than by his brilliant qualities which were concentrated on a single theme: his ambitions to be a military hero.[14]

The two found enough common ground for Moreau to ask the Baron to draw up a memorandum of principles constituting a summary of their political conversation. A few highlights from it disclose how the two French émigrés reconciled their differences. They also indicate the irrevocable attachment of the two men to the notion of a monarchy despite their favorable exposure to a democracy: they were led to advocate a monarchy that was to be 'restrained':

> The Republic and the ancient regime cannot be restored. The monarchy is the form of government suitable to France, but this monarchy, for the happiness of its people must be restrained. A usurper [Napoleon], no matter who he is, cannot hold on to power without despotism. A restrained monarchy, being the only desirable government worthy of being maintained through loyalty, courage and honor, Louis XVIII should, and can be the only one, to be restored to the throne.[15]

Moreau was to be the first of the two who returned to France, following Napoleon's humiliation with the defeat of the *grande armée* in Russia in 1812. The clouds were now lifting for the exiled French couple. Though the Baron's impulse was to join the general and return to France, the Baroness was too ill at the time to attempt the voyage, and his consideration for his wife was ever paramount. It was not until

May 1814, following the abdication of Napoleon, that the de Neuvilles sensed the proper time had finally come for their own return. On 21 May they embarked on the *Amigo Protector* bound for England, from where they would leave for France. When the couple was already on board the Portuguese vessel, a letter was delivered to the Baron in the name of the École Économique, expressing the profound appreciation of the students as well as of DeWitt Clinton (then president of the school) for the de Neuvilles' inestimable contribution to the cultural life of New York. The distinguished émigré was especially thanked for the time, talent, money and inexhaustible goodwill he had lavished on the school. It was a fitting tribute on the occasion of his leave-taking of a country for which he had accumulated a great affection: the letter moved the Baron deeply. On 9 July 1814, when the couple arrived in England, a sailor was heard shouting, 'Bonaparte is on the island of Elba and Louis XVIII is in Paris!' With that shout, reflected the Baron in his memoirs, uttered by a sailor ignorant of the momentousness of his words, their years of exile ended. Within a few days, the Baron and Baroness were, at last, in their beloved France.

The de Neuvilles returned to America once again, under circumstances somewhat more exalted than their enforced exile. In 1816, Louis XVIII rewarded the Baron's loyalty with an appointment as Minister Plenipotentiary to the United States; the French couple took up diplomatic residence in Washington, DC, and summered at their pastoral retreat in New Jersey. During this new chapter of their lives, the relationship between the Baron and his wife remained, as always, consistently close. In his memoirs the Baron wrote proudly that

> Madame Hyde de Neuville was truly the companion of her husband; no woman has ever given to this word [woman] an interpretation so complete and so lofty; the word meant for her obligations a little austere, no less than unwavering sentiments. One could say that she lived by this measure. Never was there one existence so entirely absorbed in another; her personality was therein dissolved.[16]

During the Washington period, between 1816 and 1822, the Baron continued to exhibit a fierce ardor in politics as well as in his writings. John Quincy Adams, the Secretary of State at the time, found his views on occasion extreme but he could also say of him, 'No foreign minister who has ever resided here has been so universally esteemed and loved; nor have I ever been in political relations with any foreign statesman of whose moral qualities I have formed so good an opinion.'[17] This was indeed a remarkable tribute from Adams, who was known to be a difficult if not a caustic politician. Still, Adams also enjoyed a reputation as a brilliant tactician, having negotiated several treaties during his tenure as secretary of state, all of which were of intense interest to the Baron; the latter was witness, during the course of his sojourn in Washington, to the continuing expansion of the young country and to its steady affirmations as a sovereign nation. Adams negotiated the terms leading to the treaty of 1819 whereby Spain formally ceded East and West Florida, an acquisition that allowed the United States to gain a number of highly desirable ports along the Gulf of Mexico. The same treaty also joined the western reaches of the Florida territory to the vast expanse of land within the boundaries of the Louisiana Purchase, which had been so deftly acquired from France in 1803 during the presidency of Jefferson. The Baron was aware that Napoleon believed that by concluding that latter monumental sale, he had built a mighty adversary against Britain, while in effect what it did was assure the rising nation across the Atlantic an independent and more secure position between France and Britain during the Napoleonic Wars; it also assured the country a sought-for dominance on the North American continent. Under Secretary of State Adams, the new nation would continue to underscore that dominance by issuing a political statement declaring that the New World and the Old were to remain separate and distinct spheres of influence. 'The American continents are henceforth not to be considered as subjects for future colonization,' was a declaration framed by Adams during the tenure of President James Monroe. That declaration would become part of the crucial Monroe Doctrine of 1823, which has since been repeatedly invoked.

The Baron was also witness to the efforts made by John Quincy Adams on behalf of the Native American population. Conscience-stricken by the plight of America's indigenous population as the country ruthlessly expanded, Adams had appealed to Congress for land in the West where they could settle peacefully and undisturbed. It was undoubtedly clear to the French exile, as it was to many others immersed in the politics of the country, that the admirably talented and ambitious Adams was destined for the presidency of the young nation. Indeed Adams (son of the country's second president) was eventually elected as the sixth president of the United States in 1825. By that time, the Baron and Baroness had long departed for the happy return to their beloved France.

CHAPTER 2

Frances Wright Brings Reform to America

S HE WAS BEAUTIFUL, she was rich, she was talented and she was a visionary. Of Scottish heritage and enlightened parents, Frances Wright was also very young when she came to the New World in 1818 – not as a wandering tourist but with the lofty purpose of witnessing the political dynamics of a country that had declared itself totally independent of Old World traditions. Fanny, as the 24-year-old was known, was not quite sure what she would find: Americans had been described to her either as a tribe of wild colts or as a race of shrewd artificers and plodding farmers. It was her inclination to insist on viewing the people of the New World as high-minded, enlightened and animated with the soul of liberty. The very fact that a new and independent nation was flourishing across the

Atlantic had wildly excited her imagination when she was a teenager. Before then, her childhood had been spent in the depressing days of Britain's role in the Napoleonic struggles, added to which she viewed all history books as uninspiring stories of subjugation. To learn that such a country as America existed had virtually the same effect on her as it had (so it would seem) on Thomas More in the sixteenth century when he wrote in the opening pages of his *Utopia*: 'Nowadays countries are always being discovered which were never mentioned in the old geography books.' It was assuredly with high expectations, then, that the lovely Fanny boarded the sailing packet *Amity*, which left Liverpool in August of 1818 and disembarked a month later in bustling New York.

Traveling with her was her younger sister Camilla, who not only shared Fanny's liberal views but found her older sibling a wondrous model to follow. In New York, the sisters were well connected and were accordingly entertained in the homes of many prominent New Yorkers, where their open and attractive personalities were welcomed during the several months of their sojourn. At every turn they found congenial company, having the good fortune to meet such leading lights of the city as Cadwallader Colden (soon to be mayor), David Hosack of Columbia College (which was then picturesquely located on the banks of the Hudson) and John Trumbull, the artist. It was in the ambiance of such congenial circles, then, that the wide-eyed visitor augmented her American contacts and steadily enlarged her impressions of a dynamic new world. Moreover, the talented Fanny soon felt very much encouraged to seek the production on a New York stage of one of several plays she had earlier written. Much to her delight the play, entitled *Altdorf*, was accepted and performed for three nights at the Park Theatre in February of 1819, with a visiting company of English actors interpreting the roles. It had earlier been turned down in London when the author had offered it to John Kemble, actor and part owner of Covent Garden Theatre; now it was performed with the name of the female author withheld. The plot, which centers on the fourteenth-century struggle of the forest cantons of Switzerland against the dominance of Austria, gained the sympathy of a reviewer for the *New-York Columbian*, who wrote:

> The author is unknown. He has trusted his work to its own merits
> and to the unprejudiced liberality of an American audience. He has
> trusted a tale of freedom to the feelings of the only nation where the
> cause of freedom dare be asserted.[1]

Those words, of course, echoed Fanny's own sentiments and subsequently led her to have the play published with her name divulged as
author. The book, well received, prompted the new and unexpected
delight of an admiring letter from none other than Thomas Jefferson,
now retired as the country's third president and living in Virginia.
His judgment was that the leading character of *Altdorf* was 'a model
of patriotism and virtue well worthy of the imitation of our republican
citizens.'[2] It was in continuing good spirits, then, that Fanny and her
sister undertook to travel north from New York throughout some of
the Northeastern states. Wherever they went they viewed Americans
in the best light possible, though they were well aware that there was
a lack of the kind of deference to which they were accustomed at
home; this they attributed to an egalitarianism that justly distanced
the population from its European antecedents. Fanny held on to her
initial belief that, over and above any egalitarian rough edges, here was
a land where people enjoyed political liberty and governed themselves.
It was her observation – to be totally contradicted by the indomitable
Frances Trollope, as well as the Scottish traveler Basil Hall ten years
hence – that in no other country were women held in higher estimation
or more appreciated than they were in America. She further insisted
that courtesy was paid to women at all times and in all places, and not
only to women of the prosperous classes but to those of the farming
and laboring sectors as well.

The first major destination to the south in the travels of the two
sisters was the city of Washington, whose broad architectural plan,
still to be released, had been designed by Pierre Charles L'Enfant, a
young French engineer drawing inspiration from Versailles. L'Enfant,
who had served in America's Revolutionary War, had been appointed
architect by George Washington during his presidency. The city had
been severely damaged by fire not many years prior to the visit of the
Wright sisters, during the War of 1812 with Britain, and now offered
to the visitors an uninspiring terrain of muddy streets and scattered

buildings. Fanny was happy to make the visit to the Capitol's future location on the borders of the Potomac River, for she was curious to observe the proceedings of a government in a country where an intense spirit of individualism reigned. It was of little consequence to her that the capital city of the New World should offer so uninspiring an appearance, for in such a want of grandeur the eager visitor perceived welcome democratic underpinnings. She attended sessions of the Senate as well as the House of Representatives, this at a time when President James Monroe was in the early years of his second term. He had been re-elected almost unanimously, and his administration has long been judged by historians as one that was particularly benign. Under his guidance, the United States stretched in size with the acquisition from Spain of the territories of East and West Florida, significantly expanding America's access to the sea. Further, the Missouri Compromise was enacted under Monroe's presidency – this in the very year that the Wright sisters were visiting. The Compromise involved the regulation of slavery in the free (Western) territories and was notable for having passed between the pro-slavery and anti-slavery factions in the Congress. Here was a fundamental issue in the nation's profile that would one day draw Fanny into passionate engagement. That like herself Monroe was of Scottish descent certainly did not go unnoticed by the visitor, nor would the fact that this fifth president had not only fought in the war against Britain but had witnessed the signing of the Declaration of Independence. Following the termination of his presidency, his name would forever be known chiefly by the enactment of the Monroe Doctrine in 1823, which established the independence of the new American nation against foreign encroachment. Such clearly momentous events in political history were thrilling to the British traveler.

As the House of Representatives under President Monroe was then debating the tariff measure of 1820, Fanny was witness to the eloquence of Congressman Henry Clay. She had met the congressman at the home of the French Baron Jean Guillaume Hyde de Neuville, who was then serving as his country's ambassador and, as noted above, had traveled to America after being banished by Napoleon. At the time of Fanny's visit to Washington, Congressman Clay was the Speaker of the House of Representatives and well known for his impassioned speeches. While thoroughly opposed from the onset of his career to the institution of slavery, he had little sympathy for the campaigns of the abolitionists, for he felt that some of their uncompromising demands seriously obstructed the path to a solution. Fanny was now all ears as Clay stepped up to defend the tariff measure:

> He seems, indeed, to unite all the qualifications essential to an orator, animation, energy, high moral feeling, ardent patriotism, a sublime love of liberty, a rapid flow of ideas and of language, a voice full, sonorous, distinct, and flexible, without exception the most masterly voice that I ever remember to have heard.[3]

Because the sisters had the good fortune to move about in the upscale social circles of Washington during their stay, Fanny was able to report that Henry Clay was no less eloquent in private conversation than he was in public debate. It is not known whether she ever broached the subject of slavery with him, but it was during this sojourn in Washington that Fanny developed an awareness of the horrors of black enslavement. Still, she evinced no sense of how strongly she would eventually feel, nor of any inclination to take an active part in its eradication. For the moment, Fanny was generous in her praise of American conduct, being utterly convinced that the exercise of political rights enjoyed by all Americans endowed them with a character quite peculiar to themselves, a judgment she based on the fact that she esteemed each American to be an active partner in the grand concern of the state: 'The constant exercise of the reasoning powers gives to their character and manners a mildness, plainness and unchanging suavity, such as are often remarked in Europe in men devoted to the abstract sciences.'[4] It is a thrilling assessment, if somewhat overblown.

After two years, the time came for the sisters to return to England. Soon after her arrival on home territory in June of 1820, Fanny devoted her energies to preparing her travel notes for publication. The book that emerged, entitled *View of Society and Manners in America*, was well received by the English liberal press, though not so by the influential *Quarterly Review*, a Tory organ, which denounced it as 'a most ridiculous panegyric on the government and people of the United States'. Not unexpectedly, it was favorably viewed by the press in

America, which recognized it as a flattering portrayal. More importantly, her enthusiastic views garnered for her two important friendships upon her return home: that of the philosopher Jeremy Bentham and, more impressively, that of the imposing French statesman the Marquis de Lafayette. She was to bask at length in the warmth of their friendships and to benefit from the wisdom of their political acumen. Quite fluent in French at this time, Fanny visited Lafayette frequently at his French country estate of La Grange, where she met any number of prominent French intellectuals, including the beguiling Benjamin Constant. They in turn enlarged her circle of French friends in Paris, a city where the social salons constituted lively arenas of wit and elegance; she set up a small salon of her own and indulged her eagerness to follow the course of French politics, which were fairly tumultuous at the time. The friendship with the Marquis so intensified that when the latter was extended an official invitation by President Monroe and the United States Congress to visit America in 1824, young Frances Wright crossed the Atlantic once again to make certain that she would be on hand (along with her sister) to greet the 67-year-old Frenchman on his arrival in the New World. Indeed, their growing attachment did not go unnoticed by the press, which began in time to make allusions to a possible romance – but although Lafayette had Fanny's portrait painted and hung in his study, continued curiosity on this level was never to be satisfied. Fanny would forever hold the Marquis as a political role model, particularly because of his selfless aid to the struggling American nation and his admiration of a number of Americans at the forefront of their country's history. (He named his son George Washington Motier de Lafayette, and in 1789 presented a Declaration of Rights to the French National Assembly based on the Declaration of Independence drafted by Thomas Jefferson.)

On their arrival in the capital, any number of dinners, balls and fetes awaited the popular Marquis, and Fanny and her sister were also invited. Lodgings had been secured for the two girls by a member of their ever-expanding social circle. While in Washington, Lafayette and his friends received an invitation from ex-president Thomas Jefferson, inviting them all farther south to Monticello for a first-hand look at the unique architecture of the university he was in the throes of building. And indeed its uniqueness attracted wide attention, for the author of

America's Declaration of Independence had now turned his acclaimed genius from politics to scholastics, evincing a passionate involvement in the architectural design of the new university. That he should undertake anything so daring, involving the design not of a single building but of an entire complex, was deemed admirable in a man of seventy-five. Here was an enthusiasm for the theory and practice of architecture that was very much in the English tradition of the gentleman amateur. Jefferson was to derive both his inspiration and much-needed instruction in planning the Virginia university mostly from British sources. His library, filled with the books of Andrea Palladio, William Kent, James Gibbs and Robert Morris, now included the works of William Chambers and Robert Adam, the leading architects of the time. Such an architectural venture in his advanced years, Jefferson declared, was to be based 'on the illimitable freedom of the human mind to explore and to expose every subject susceptible of its contemplation'.[5] It would be completed and open its doors in 1825. As the invitation by Jefferson himself to visit the University of Virginia while it was still under construction included the Wright sisters, it was without doubt that young Fanny, on the verge of launching a bold political experiment, felt she had secured a solid place for herself in the New World.

And most assuredly did Fanny need a firm toehold on American soil, for she had been for some time intensely preoccupied by a truly extraordinary endeavor: finding a solution to America's problem of slavery. This she boldly, if naively, planned to accomplish on her own initiative, for she sought neither the cooperation of an existing group, church or society, nor the foundation of a supporting organization dedicated to social reform. For most people with her sympathetic views toward the black population, legal abolition of slavery seemed the logical solution, and therefore most people with a sincere desire to promote emancipation joined the abolitionists' cause. But this was not a solution in Fanny's view. Where would the thousands of slaves and their families go without homes and without promised employment, she reasoned, when they were set loose from their bondage? And how would Southern planters react to the enormous loss in revenue upon the freeing of slaves? Fanny Wright studied these issues seriously, turning to every authority in her circle for advice and desperately seeking any possible models for what she hoped to do. She was aware that her dear friend Lafayette had himself attempted a scheme not dissimilar to her own ideals for the gradual emancipation of the black populace on his property in French Guiana; his attempt had been thwarted, however, by the onslaught of the French Revolution. That major tumult had sent the Marquis hurrying back home to France. She was also aware of similar schemes for a cooperative community that had been conceived by Robert Dale Owen, son of the famous socialist Robert Owen, who had arrived in the US from his native Scotland in that very year of 1824, to address the House of Representatives in the capital on this important matter.

Fanny resolved to take the plunge on her own initiative. All in all, it had been many months – indeed, over a year – that the young visionary had been wrestling with the problem of the role she could play in the great scheme of emancipation, be it small or otherwise. Now, in the summer of 1825, she was ready to present her plan to the Marquis, anxious to have his advice and approval. She also knew that he would soon return to France and it was likely she would not see him again for some time. Lafayette did not fail her, for he presented the bold proposal to several of his friends, all individuals of imposing power (among them were erstwhile president James Madison, reigning president James Monroe and Chief Justice John Marshall); he was subsequently happy to report their approbation to his young and zealous friend. Fanny also sought the advice of Thomas Jefferson – indeed, she hoped for his actual participation in carrying out her plan – but while he gave his approval, he was too engaged with the building of his university in Virginia to divert his attention elsewhere.

And what was the plan? It was surprisingly simple in concept, the outlines of which she laid bare to the world in a prospectus published in Baltimore in September of 1825.[6] The fundament of the plan was the gradual emancipation of a small group of slaves who would be selected (i.e. purchased from their holders) for labor that would eventually be reimbursed on property holdings leased for the purpose. Upon the lease of the land, from fifty to one hundred slaves would be brought to the area with their families and a system of cooperative labor introduced. The incentive for the workers would be their eventual freedom, as well as the liberty and education of their children. It was estimated that five years' service would be required for a laborer to return his purchase money with interest; Fanny was certain that the slaves would be induced to work harder under these newly established conditions, particularly with freedom in sight.

Of course, the *sine qua non* of this visionary scheme was the sizeable capital necessary to lease the land for the experiment and to pay for the various expenses of its operation. Not surprisingly, its author was willing to risk a good part of her inheritance on the project while seeking additional outside support. The initial cost of the experiment, involving about one hundred slaves, was estimated at about $41,000, added to which there would, of course, be further unseen costs at every turn of the operation. But as she had such a fierce determination to advance the cause of emancipation, Fanny busied herself with selecting an appropriate site and with the transfer of slaves to their new quarters. Two thousand acres of land were accordingly purchased in the state of Tennessee bordering on the Wolf River; this wide stretch of territory was located not far from the city of Memphis, with access to the mighty Mississippi. Fanny called her new property Nashoba, a Native American name for a wolf. A site in Tennessee had been chosen for it appeared to be a state noticeably enlightened in its views of the black population: there were at the time over twenty anti-slavery societies in existence. By the spring of 1826, the young Scottish visionary had recruited several friends to join her in the operation of Nashoba. Chief among them was Robert Dale Owen, whose enthusiasm in looking to the success of the operation was high. Fanny herself was meanwhile concerned, not surprisingly, that so bold a plan as this first tentative step toward the eventual emancipation of slaves would perhaps earn her a charge of presumptuousness and vanity. (Was there not a touch of both, as well as naivety, involved?) Meanwhile, there was much work to be done in setting up the idealized community of Nashoba, most of it physical labor in clearing the land, building cabins, buying provisions, transporting the laborers and adapting them to their new environment. Fanny, her sister Camilla and friends all participated. President Andrew Jackson was sympathetic to her efforts while Thomas Jefferson thought that her bold experiment was not without some promise.

Among the friends who offered keen participation was a fellow Briton named George Flower, whose support proved vital in the initial stages of the Nashoba experiment. A native of Hertfordshire, Flower had crossed the Atlantic to the New World some ten years earlier and was a member of a group of English farmers who had settled in Albion, Illinois. More than a member, he was no less than the leader of the Albion settlement and proved to harbor a vital fund of information with regard to the attractions as well as the many vicissitudes of frontier life in America. He was to inform Fanny that while Illinois was a non-slave state, politicians there did not look kindly on abolitionists, and that the blacks who worked on the English settlement were often menaced. Fully aware that the black population of Haiti enjoyed conditions that were far more endurable, Flower had eventually contacted the president of that formerly French-held territory with a view toward liberating the slaves on the settlement in Albion. President Jean Pierre Boyer, who then ruled the whole island (discovered by Christopher Columbus on his historic trip across the Atlantic) proved eminently agreeable to accepting the transfer of about thirty slaves; they were then assisted in making the long trek from the central United States to Haiti, located in the northern reaches of the Caribbean Sea. Flower eventually had word from Haiti that they were well received and happy with their new lot. Information of this nature was carefully tucked away in the mind of Fanny, who would one day find it, unexpectedly, of great use.

Meanwhile, George Flower made himself an eminent part of the preparations for the success of Nashoba. Both he and Fanny were well aware of the difficulties of establishing a new community that would be held together by ideals rather than by a strong central covenant such as religion. On American soil, there were thus far at least two utopian communities of English origin: the Shakers and the New Harmony settlement in the state of Indiana. The religious community of Shakers (formally known as the United Society of Believers in Christ's Second Appearing) had made its way to the New World in 1774, led by the charismatic preacher Ann Lee, while the New Harmony settlement was originated half a century later in November of 1824, when Robert Dale Owen came to the United States for the purpose of putting into practice his utopian ideals. Fanny and her sister had traveled to Indiana to witness the operation of this fledgling community and were impressed by what they saw. Yet ultimately it would not endure as the community of Shakers did, for unlike the latter it had no unifying religion. (Interestingly, on his first trip to the New World in 1842, Charles Dickens was curious to visit a Shaker community in upstate New York; while he found the community flourishing, he considered the religious aspect of their withdrawn lives to be unappealingly grim.)

Owen himself was an atheist who believed strongly in social regeneration based not on religious belief but on a rational philosophy of life. Eventually, his ideal community lasted only three years, though he held on tenaciously to his socialist principles; he and Fanny would remain good friends. Owen was to be named, as was George Flower, one of the ten trustees of the Nashoba settlement. Like Flower, he proved of enormous help in the manifold requirements of setting up the physical as well as the legal conditions that would make Fanny's slave-free colony viable. Owen, of course, had enormous experience in the vicissitudes of establishing a settlement of any kind that was based on social principles; undoubtedly he sensed difficulties early on.

By the spring of 1826, the idealized community of Nashoba was inaugurated; by the summer of 1827, all signs pointed to failure. This disastrous outcome was surely predictable. Already on arrival in Tennessee, Owen had been none too sanguine that the experiment would hold. He found that the land selected was not ideal, with scarcely 100 acres of it cleared; he observed 'slaves released from the fear of the lash working indolently' under the management of someone 'not at all fitted for the post of plantation overseer'.[7] There were also rumors, unfounded, of sexual license: they probably sprang from public knowledge of Fanny's positive views about the compatibility of the black and white populations at a time when miscegenation was an inflammatory word that invoked scornful disapprobation. James Madison (the fourth American president, then retired) who had sometime earlier been shown the Nashoba plan by Lafayette, now wrote to the latter underscoring some of the problems inherent in its failure. While he admired Fanny Wright's talents and the nobility of her purpose, he feared that she had

> created insuperable obstacles to the good fruits of which they might
> be productive by her disregard or rather open defiance of the most

established opinion & vivid feelings. Besides her views of amal-gamating the white & black populations so universally obnoxious, she gives an éclat to her notions on the subject of Religion & of marriage, the effect of which our knowledge of this Country can readily estimate.[8]

Madison, who had served as Secretary of State under the presidency of Thomas Jefferson, with whom he became great friends, was known for his espousal of emancipation as well as for his astute scholarship. Yet it was clear that while these two eminent politicians favored eman-cipation, neither one supported miscegenation. Jefferson, the record shows, had actually done little of significance to advance the cause of emancipation while he was the country's third president; as far as the notion of miscegenation was concerned, he had earlier written to a correspondent that the nation had to confront the true separation of the races inasmuch as this had been ordained not by law but by nature itself:

> Deep-rooted prejudices entertained by the whites; ten thousand recollections by the blacks, of the injuries they have sustained; new provocations, the real distinctions which nature has made; and many other circumstances will divide into parties, and produce convul-sions, which will never end but in the extermination of the one or the other race.[9]

Jefferson's letter (dated 25 August 1812) had been written long before the Nashoba experiment was conceived. Now the new colony was a reality and soon began to flourish. A first-hand look at the goings on in Tennessee was recorded by the English visitor Fanny Trollope, an established friend of Fanny Wright's who was witness *in situ* to the inauguration of the utopian experiment. Her reaction was to turn from it in horror. She had arrived in America with her family in the company of Fanny Wright herself, having been persuaded by the latter to find her fortunes in the New World, beginning with a life in the new Tennessee colony. Mrs. Trollope had gone in good faith to Nashoba but immediately fled from what she considered 'the savage aspect of the scene'. The settlement, located deep in the primeval forests of America's West, could offer none 'of those minor comforts which ordinary minds class among the necessaries of life', declared Fanny Trollope.[10] In her view, only something akin to religious fanaticism could have impelled a fellow Briton to waste her fortune on so bleak an undertaking. (Though Mrs. Trollope settled further north in bustling Cincinnati for a period of two years, she was none too content there either, as the world came to know from her oft-quoted *Domestic Manners of the Americans*, published in 1832.)

An unforeseen outcome of the doomed Nashoba experiment was the illness of its leader. Fanny Wright developed malarial fever from the conditions and climate in western Tennessee and was persuaded to return home to England for her recovery (which took place before too long). She booked passage for the journey east with Robert Dale Owen, with whom she had developed an abiding friendship, for they continued to share many similar views on social and political topics. By this time Fanny had garnered a measure of fame abroad for her bold enterprise, and she had more than a few admirers at home. She continued to feel that had she attracted significant English support, her Nashoba experiment would have had a better chance of survival. One person she had so hoped to attract as a follower was the widow of the poet Percy Bysshe Shelley, whom she did not know but whose parents – William Godwin and Mary Wollstonecraft – loomed large on her horizon as pioneering heroes in the quest for social justice. Though she was to meet Mary Shelley and spend a week with her, Fanny was not able to convince the author of *Frankenstein* to take up a pioneering life in America. Shelley's widow insisted that because she was made of 'frailer clay', she could not match Fanny's heroic spirit. She had been not at all sure why a young and wealthy woman would want to abandon a civilized life in England for what was clearly a life of hardship in the wilds of America.

On Fanny's eventual return to the New World (for she did return), she found an occupation that appealed to her on many levels and which would allow her to forget her recent failure. For Fanny was astute enough to acknowledge that the experiment of Nashoba was now well behind her and she needed to move on. Not that it was easy to accept its total collapse, for she had put her heart and soul into the project, as well as her money. Nashoba had been a failure, she reflected, for a variety of political, social and practical reasons, beginning with the choice of location in the harsh woodlands of western Tennessee. Beyond her naivety and a lack of managerial skills (which perhaps she was loath to admit), Nashoba had been too small and too isolated an experiment to attract the very crucial national attention and support it needed if it were to survive and to expand further. Indeed, it failed in every way to capture the imagination of the American public. Such lack of attention (and encouragement) had been registered early on by Fanny herself, who knew that a favorable focus on her experiment was absolutely vital to its success. She had also failed to convince open-minded friends in Britain to join her in what she was certain would prove an idealistic community; chief among the latter were Mary Shelley and Leigh Hunt. There was a serious financial loss, too, that did not go unnoticed by her English friends, for Fanny was obliged to accept with grace the disappearance of nearly half her fortune while turning her attention to the plight of the remaining thirty slaves who had been part of her humanitarian experiment. During her sojourn in England when she was ill she had left Nashoba's inhabitants in the care of an overseer by the name of John Gilliam, but she was ever conscious of their existence under tenuous circumstances. Eventually she made plans for them to be settled on the French island of Haiti. When she returned to the New World from England in late 1829, she followed through on these plans herself by arranging ship transportation for the slaves, traveling with them to Port-au-Prince, and arranging for their future as free citizens under the protection of the Haitian president, Jean Pierre Boyer. His willingness to accommodate American slaves had earlier been made known to her by George Flower.

Once re-established on American soil, Fanny teamed up with her friend Robert Dale Owen as publisher and joint editor of a periodical named the *New Harmony Gazette*, which would lead in turn to a program of lectures. Here were activities that would once more engage her wholeheartedly. The ever zealous and indefatigable Fanny would henceforth give all her attention to her role as co-editor with Owen of the new publication, and, in tandem with the gazette, would engage in an even more demanding role as a public lecturer. Clearly, she had not abandoned any of her intense humanitarian zeal. America continued to loom in her mind as a nation set apart that deserved to be supported

in every way; she was ready to lend some of this support in defense
of its basic egalitarian principles, which she feared would be eroded
without constant vigilance. She was convinced, as was Owen, that the
way to the enlightenment of the masses and to reform was through
education whereby the public, particularly the youth among them,
could be alerted to a wide range of influences that were corrupting
in effect. Chief among these influences were proselytizing religions,
capitalism and inadequate education. Once again her reforming zeal
was ignited and she was willing, at the age of thirty-three, to assume
another demanding self-assignment as a public advocate. The new
project with Owen appealed to her, indeed excited her imagination, for
she felt that much could be achieved through lectures and the press.
Clearly, the failure of Nashoba had in no way diminished her passion
for reform. To her own satisfaction and certainly to that of those in
the audiences she eventually attracted, Fanny emerged in her new
public role – unpredictably from all accounts – as nothing less than a
mesmerizing speaker.

The lectures by the committed Scottish orator, devoted to the
'progressive march of the world from error and suffering toward
wisdom and enjoyment' were held in as many as 150 major centers
of the Union at that time, ranging from Boston to New Orleans. For
the lectures that were given on three consecutive Sundays in July
of 1829 to crowded audiences in Cincinnati, we have the first-hand
account once again of none other than her friend Frances Trollope,
then residing in that city:

> That a lady of fortune, family, and education, whose youth had been
> passed in the most refined circles of private life, should present her-
> self to the people as a public lecturer, would naturally excite surprise
> anywhere, and the nil admirari of the old world itself would hardly be
> sustained before such a spectacle; but in America where women are
> guarded by a seven-fold shield of habitual insignificance, it has caused
> an effect which can scarcely be described […] all my expectations fell
> far short of the splendor, the brilliance, the overwhelming eloquence
> of this extraordinary orator […] It is impossible to imagine anything
> more striking than her appearance. Her tall and majestic figure, the
> deep and almost solemn expression of her eyes, the simple contour

of her finely formed head, unadorned, excepting by its own natural ringlets; her garment of plain white muslin, which hung about her in folds that recalled the drapery of a Grecian statue, all contributed to produce an effect, unlike anything I had ever seen before, or ever expect to see again.[11]

Fanny traveled tirelessly to deliver her lectures, taking passage on vessels along the Mississippi to destinations in Missouri, and then covering a wide stretch of the new nation by horseback, wagon and stage as she lectured in Indiana, Illinois, Kentucky, West Virginia, Maryland, Pennsylvania and New York. But she was not well received everywhere: if audiences increased as she moved east so, indeed, did the vitriolic comment.

For those unable to hear the eloquent speaker, Fanny had the lectures published, and while she very often held her audiences in thrall, as described by Mrs. Trollope – because of both the extent of her learning and her eloquence – the reaction of the press to what she had to say was in many instances less than flattering. They did not like her attacks on what she considered the mesmerizing effect of organized religions (she believed that religion and priestcraft together kindled discord rather than promoting love and tolerance), nor did they condone her tirades against the vicissitudes of capitalism, particularly the power of large banks. Again, her advanced views on the equal rights of women, birth control, and the emancipation of slaves were seen as unacceptable coming from a reformer who was both a woman and a foreigner. Her lectures in New York, while generally well attended, engendered hostility from the major papers. The *New York American* of 8 January 1829, claiming that she had shamefully obtruded herself upon the public, waiving alike modesty, gentleness and every amiable attribute of her sex, felt that it should take the liberty of calling her a female monster. Two days later, the *Evening Post* of 10 January 1829 declared that women ought not to engage in such pursuits and further clarified its position by stating that 'female expounders of any kind of doctrine are not to our taste.' Indeed, the editor of the *Post* urged her to return to England and start reforming her own country first:

> *Fair priestess of the fragrant rite*
> *That mingles 'spirits black and white',*
> *Then lady turn thee, yet again,*
> *To thy own land beyond the main*
> *Weeping and stretching o'er the sea*
> *Her fond imploring arms to thee.*
> *Yes, go, as is a patron's duty,*
> *Reform thy native country first.*[12]

Though decidedly negative, these denouncements naturally focused more attention on the public appearances of Fanny and made her name widely known. Was this not a good moment, then, the managers of the Park Theatre asked themselves, to mount her play again? Indeed it was. *Altdorf* was subsequently staged for two nights (22 and 24 January 1829) and attracted large audiences. Meanwhile, Fanny did not desist in giving her proselytizing lectures for the reform of American society, and was determined to remain undaunted by the continuing attacks of the press. Even leading intellectuals such as Philip Hone, erstwhile mayor of New York, who condemned her efforts 'to break down the moral and religious ties which bind mankind together', found her 'eloquent, bold, and singular in her opinions; the novelty of her doctrines has given her a degree of celebrity.'[13] She also continued her association with Robert Dale Owen in what they characterized as their Free Inquiry Movement. Her efforts were gallant; still, with increasing denunciations by the press, it was inevitable that her reform endeavors would eventually come to an end: she announced her departure for Europe in June of 1830, with Philip Hone declaring, 'Let her go home, or go to the Devil, so that she never visits us again.'[14] Since the press was by now following her every move the announcement of her return home did not go unheeded, and once more poetry was invoked to mark her leave-taking. The *New York Courier and Inquirer* published a witty, six-stanza poem to mark the return to Europe of the reformer whom they dubbed a 'petticoated politician'. The newspaper encouraged Robert Dale Owen to sing the poem 'in the most melancholy strain imaginable'. The first stanza immediately sets the tone of light-hearted derision:

Oh Fanny Wright – sweet Fanny Wright
We ne'er shall hear her more:
She's gone to take another freight
To Hayti's happy shore.
She used to speak so parrot-like,
With gesture small and staid;
So pretty in her vehemence –
Alas! Departed maid.
Tho' we are men of age mature
How can we rule ourselves?
Unless we all wear petticoats,
We're laid upon the shelves![15]

Thus ended the more than two years of Fanny Wright's tireless efforts in the United States to promote the causes of free inquiry and educational reform. But it was not the end of her association with the New World. Fanny had meanwhile married a Frenchman with the imposing name of Guillaume Sylvan Casimir Phiquepal d'Arusmont; the ceremony had been held in Paris and attended by her cherished friend the Marquis de Lafayette. The couple in time returned to America, spending a fair number of years on the west side of the Atlantic, but the marriage did not last. The Scottish reformer was to cross the ocean several times but spent her final years in America. It was in 1852 that Fanny the humanitarian, Fanny the visionary, and Fanny the reformer breathed her last in Cincinnati, Ohio. So passionate had she been in her abiding altruism that her tomb there was inscribed, according to her wishes, 'I have wedded the cause of human improvement, staked on it my fortune, my reputation and my life.'

CHAPTER 3

The American Peregrinations of Captain Basil Hall

D ISEMBARKING from the good ship *Florida* in May of 1827, Captain Basil Hall of the British Royal Navy was to traverse the imposing distance of 8,800 miles across the expanse of America, a country that he would find not yet fully formed geographically nor, in his estimation, fully informed politically. Indeed, the United States represented, in his view, not a new and audacious experiment in equality but one of Britain's 'occasional failures'. The Captain would gather copious notes on all he experienced, bringing to his observations a penetrating astuteness, as well as a self-assurance that was unshakable. With many years of travel on the high seas behind him, the 39-year-old officer of aristocratic Scottish descent had made his way across the Atlantic thoroughly prepared to render an account of all he would witness. As an experienced author, he was resolved to 'use [his] best endeavours to represent to [his] countrymen what was good, in colours which might incline them to think the American more worthy of regard and confidence, than they generally were esteemed in England.'[1] He well knew that the detailed account of his voyage, which would be published in no less than three volumes and entitled *Travels in North America*, would scarcely be popular on the western side of the Atlantic, yet he held that 'natives themselves ought, I think, to be rather amused than otherwise, by seeing themselves reflected from the mirror of a stranger's mind.'[2] While the much-traveled officer surely made some astute observations, the natives were not amused.

Captain Hall made the transatlantic voyage in the company of his young wife and daughter (the latter then a mere toddler), bringing with him letters of introduction to well-placed persons in all areas of his travels, starting with New York City where he had disembarked. There he was warmly received by Governor DeWitt Clinton, who gave him further letters of introduction; while he enjoyed the hospitality subsequently offered him in New York homes, Captain Hall regretted that his abstemious habits did little justice to the local repasts, typically piled high with oysters, lobsters, ham, salads and champagne. The brief stay in Manhattan was punctuated by the excitement of witnessing the outbreak of a fire, which was apparently not infrequent in the city during this time. Watching the volunteer firemen go about the business of extinguishing the blaze led the Captain, the next day, to give a well-received talk to the Fire Department. There he explained a new device invented in Edinburgh geared toward the safety of firemen in the handling of water hoses. A visit to City Hall included attending a session of the State Supreme Court, where the British visitor was immediately taken aback by the informality of dress: in his view, the absence of wigs and gowns in the attire of the legal profession diminished the dignity of the proceedings more than he would have imagined. It was the first of many departures from British custom that he was to feel were surely being made in an uninspired direction, and which led him to doubt the wisdom of the Americans stripping away so much of what had been held sacred for so long in Britain. Leaving the court, the Scottish visitor spent some time visiting City Hall, which he deemed a building of imposing size and beauty. That commanding structure had been completed just fifteen years earlier – designed with a marble exterior, a dome, a rotunda and a cupola – and was high on the list as a tourist stop thanks to the sweeping view of Manhattan from its roof. Captain Hall duly made his way to the top of the building and was impressed by the surrounding panorama. Less impressed was he with the showing of art that greeted him when next he visited a neighborhood gallery, leading him to make a sweeping pronounce-ment of what could be expected of any future American role in the world of aesthetics:

> Most of the pictures were flat, cold, and woodeny. In another gallery were placed, some excellent casts, and several exotic works of art, very few of which were worth looking at. I certainly do not except two by [Benjamin] West, that most formal of all painters. The same taste, or rather want of taste, which leads Americans to tolerate foreign rubbish, must circumscribe the efforts of that native genius which unquestionably exists, and would be called to the surface if by any means the standard of excellence could be elevated, and when so raised, could be maintained by the influence of wealth regulated by genuine feeling, by vanity, or by knowledge, or by mere fashion, or by all combined. How far this is probable, or even possible, as matters stand in that country, is very questionable.[3]

A trip up the Hudson afforded a visit to Sing Sing prison, where he approved of the orderly handling of prisoners and the imposition of absolute silence at all times. Indeed, he found the stricture of silence one of the most efficacious forms of 'moral machinery' that was ever put in action (while Charles Dickens, twenty years later, would find it inhumanly cruel, as would many others). The subject of prison discipline was of uncommon interest for the Captain, who discourses on it at some length and provides statistics comparing the United States and England with regard to the 'productiveness of the labour of convicts'. In his judgment, nowhere in the world was there a prison better managed than Sing Sing. What was to be admired in particular was the air of confident authority that permeated the administration of the secluded establishment: this allowed a visitor a feeling of perfect security despite the fact that he was walking about unarmed 'amongst cut-throats and villains of all sorts'.

As he sailed past notable properties flanking the Hudson, Captain Hall became acutely aware of America's abolition of entails and repeal of the law of primogeniture in the break-up of once-large estates. Was this not an unwise abandonment of British tradition? It certainly did not augur well, in his view, for the upkeep of valued property; indeed, there was already apparent an air of premature and hopeless decay in the area. A visit to West Point Military Academy occasioned high marks, though he observed that the cadets were remarkably lacking in erectness of carriage, a trait he came to notice in Americans everywhere he traveled, along with the American tone of voice. Moreover, at this early stage in the journey, Captain Hall could point out another deficiency high on the list:

> the most striking circumstance in the American character, which had come under our notice, was the constant habit of praising themselves, their institutions, and their country, either in downright terms, or by some would-be indirect allusions, which were still more tormenting [...] It is considered, I believe, all over the world, as bad manners for a man to praise himself or his family. Now, to praise one's country appears, to say the least of it, in the next degree of bad taste. It was curious to see with what vigilant adroitness the Americans availed themselves of every little circumstance to give effect to this self-laudation.[4]

The issue of laudation led the Captain to bemoan the fact that no national honors existed to reward the outstanding services of Thomas Jefferson, James Monroe, DeWitt Clinton and others whose lives had been devoted to their country. Nor did he feel that the elaborate receptions given to the Marquis de Lafayette (in the year 1784 and again in 1824) could be claimed to offset in any way the neglect accorded to other truly outstanding citizens of the United States. Visits to the New York State towns of Schenectady, Trenton Falls, Canandaigua and Rochester occasioned a stop of three days with an English friend in Canandaigua. There he felt very much at home; elsewhere it was always with a sigh that he exchanged the refinements to which he had been accustomed for the inevitable discomforts of a society that was developing so differently. Rochester, bordering on Lake Ontario, was a rapidly expanding town, and the Captain paused in his account to give a table showing its population increase since the year 1815 and a second table listing the principal occupations in which its inhabitants were engaged. He rightly attributed the prosperity of Rochester and neighboring New York State towns to their proximity to the Erie Canal, which immensely facilitated commerce in the area. The workings of the Erie Canal greatly intrigued the visitor, as would all systems of canals, locks and rivers (leading to the Hudson or Mississippi Rivers) that facilitated commercial transport. Before taking leave of Rochester, he noted that not one resident of the more than eight thousand was native born: most came from states in New England or from abroad. Two other significant observations were made at this time that would surface throughout Captain Hall's peregrinations: his bewilderment at the absence of a national Church and the deplorable state of male attire. That Americans had not adopted the Church of England in forming a nation did not redound to the happiness of its citizens, he steadfastly maintained, for does not the Church represent one of the strongest bonds of union among its followers? He was to discourse on this issue at great length, maintaining among other factors that the established Church in England, by its members, its wealth and its discipline, had acquired great power. Furthermore,

> It is infinitely useful […] in preserving the purity of religious doctrine, which ought to be the first consideration in every country; – and it is useful in alliance with the state, in maintaining the purity of political practice: – while in private life it is no less efficacious in giving confidence and uniformity to virtue, and true dignity to members.[5]

As to the second issue, regarding the state of male attire in America, he rightly asked: Why was not dress in this country considered to be an important branch of manners? (For Oscar Wilde, who would visit the States near the turn of the century, dress would also be of major concern, but from an exalted standpoint that would go beyond manners: Wilde considered the presentation of one's person a matter of art itself.)

The sight of Niagara Falls, next on Captain Hall's journey, proved not unexpectedly breathtaking. Not only does the Scottish visitor describe it as one of the most splendid sights on earth, but his anticipation had been so keen that he could not refrain from comparing it to a similar excitement he had felt some time ago – not in the presence of nature at its most awesome, but in anticipation of a meeting with the banished Napoleon. (That extraordinary encounter between the two Europeans occurred on the far-flung Atlantic island of St. Helena and was instigated by Hall's father, who had studied alongside the Emperor in France.) And now the Scottish visitor felt that he could not do justice to a description of Niagara, so overwhelmed was he by the sight of the falls; he spent a good part of his time there 'sketching' with his camera lucida. Then, because of his interest in engineering, he does not fail to report on the bridge that connects the main American shore with Goat Island. He found it to be one of the most singular pieces of engineering in the world, evincing not only the skill and ingenuity that went into its conception but the remarkable boldness of thought on the part of the engineer. Also in his description of his visit to Niagara we have one of the rare times that the Captain mentions his little daughter, who was brought to tears by the roar of the thundering falls. Her cries made him sensible, he recalled wistfully, of how much the sound of her little voice, properly pitched, was a match even for the thunders of the roaring cataract. Before leaving the area, the Scottish visitor noted that the scenery in the neighborhood of the falls was uninteresting and was rendered more so by the erection of hotels, paper factories, saw mills and numerous other raw, wooden edifices. Perhaps it was just as well, he mused, for the falls could then loom as the single, stark attraction.

After six weeks in the United States the visitor turned north to Canada, where the very air he breathed seemed at once different now that he was again 'in his Majesty's dominions', and where the transition from one country to another was in every way remarkable. He was to report that he found the inhabitants there speaking, acting and even looking like Englishmen, not betraying any discernible difference. The Canadian nation, he deemed, was not so unfortunate as to be independent of Britain, as the United States was: Canada was clearly not one of Britain's occasional failures.

It was curious, indeed, to observe how great a change in many of the most essential particulars of national character, and customs, and appearance, a short half-mile – a mere imaginary geographical division – could make. The air we breathed seemed different, the sky, the land, the whole scenery, appeared to be altered; and I must say, that of all the changes I have ever made in a life of ceaseless locomotion, I have seldom been conscious of any transition from one country to another more striking than this.[6]

On returning to America, the Hall family visited several towns en route to Albany, first making what was considered a delightful voyage along Lake George. Here – at last – remarks the Captain, they had come to some beautiful scenery in the United States, 'beautiful in every respect and leaving nothing to wish for'. On arrival in the New York State capital, the Scottish visitor was anxious to see the government in action. There he attended sessions of the Senate and the House of Assembly, describing them as being spun out to a most unconscionable length with a wasteful contempt for time. He attributed this to the fact that many members of the government were wanting in education and had come directly from 'the plow'; he could detect the mortification of the more sophisticated members until the sessions were finally concluded. The Captain reports that in Albany he was introduced with much kindness to very many people, but was often at a loss to satisfy those who sought praise of their country from the visitor. This was not only true of his experience in Albany, but throughout the states that he visited, with questions tending to put him in an awkward position. He was often asked in one form or another: Had you any idea of finding us so far advanced? The Scottish visitor was convinced that the praise of one's country, including praise of its manner and customs, was akin to praising oneself and moved away from such conversation as quickly as he could politely do so. Even so, while in Albany the visitor shared many a meal with state officials and did have long, informative conversations with them concerning government operations; he left the city feeling that he had made many good friends.

Continued pleasure was ahead as he proceeded in the direction of Boston, where the colors of fall (of early October 1827) lent an extra dimension of charm to the appealing towns of New England. He was particularly drawn to the setting of Northampton – often cited by other travelers – with its surrounding waterfalls and scenic mountain views. Located southwest within the state of Massachusetts, it was, in Hall's view, one of those beautiful New England towns on which it was impossible to lavish an excess of praise. Somewhat farther north, Boston was to offer few if any disappointments: he arrived in the city bearing more than twenty letters of introduction and admiring the elegance of many of its streets. Good conversations were ahead in visits to Harvard University, the General Hospital and the famed Lowell factory, all of which were viewed with a rare approbation. He was surprised to find that the doctrine of Unitarianism had made great advances in the New England area, and accepted an invitation to listen to a sermon in one of the churches of this denomination. While impressed with the speaker, he registered little accord with Unitarian principles; we find, rather, a stern note of disapproval as to the direction in which such a liberal doctrine would likely lead the American people. It was much to the detriment of the United States, Captain Hall staunchly believed, that Church and State had been separated; it was a view shared by many of his compatriots. By his own admission, he was led to dwell longer on this topic than would be expected, with an intent to emphasize this point.

> The difference between America and England in the important point of church government, appears to be simply this: – With them religion, like every thing in the country, is left to take its own course; we on the other hand, have chosen to collect together the experience which has resulted from long ages of trial and discussion, and to fix this condensed knowledge in one solid fabric. By means of the powerful [Church] Establishment so constructed, any violent or radical alterations in doctrine or discipline, are rendered well-nigh impossible [...] the Church of England has the good fortune of being diametrically opposed, in every circumstance to the religious institutions of America.[7]

A brief sojourn in the nearby town of Brighton became the unexpected occasion for a discourse by the Captain on the stature of women in

America. Invited to see a cattle show in Brighton, he was surprised to find in the large social gathering there a conspicuous absence of women – only nine in a crowd of several thousand. (Most observers would hardly be surprised – a cattle show would not be high on a lady's list of social engagements.) Nonetheless, Captain Hall found this Brighton stop an occasion for remarking on the male–female standing in America's social arena. He discerned a strong line of demarcation between the sexes in America in every part of the country through which his family passed, finding at least one reason why this was so: women were occupied with increased household duties imposed upon them because of a total want of good servants in America. It was not that he witnessed any case of incivility toward a female, but it was clear to him that women did not enjoy that station in society that was allotted to them in European countries. And here was an occasion to extol the role of women in his own country while harking back to the days of chivalry:

> In England no fair, no place of public amusement, no election, no court of justice, no place, in short, public or private, is ever thought complete without a certain, and most influential proportion of female interest being mixed with its duties or its pleasures. No farmer, any more than a nobleman, is satisfied to enjoy what is to be seen, without the anticipation of his family. No pleasure is ever thought worth enjoying except in female company. Such is the universal fashion, or long-established custom, call it what you will, which has transmitted to modern manners much of the grace and dignity of chivalry, without its extravagance.[8]

The Captain went further in asserting that the judgment of English women as a body was rarely – if ever – wrong; moreover, this steadfast capacity on the part of women applied also to their feelings and principles, which could not be said of English men.

A visit to several schools in Boston left the Captain unimpressed with an educational system of which Bostonians claimed to be proud. Why was it that young men could not be kept at their studies long enough before going out into the world and exercising their individual talents? In England a fixed amount of classical knowledge had been considered from time immemorial the indispensable mark of a gentleman. But while this was true, one might ask about the other classes in England, as the conversation did not seem to extend to the education of the lower classes. Captain Hall did hold that everyone discovers in the long run that an individual's best chance of success consists in conforming as nearly as possible to the established habits of that branch of society in which he or she happens to be born. But such a belief, he surely learned, was not one on which the American educational system was founded.

As he proceeded farther south in his journey, the visitor continued his habit of engaging in robust conversations with Americans en route, on a whole range of topics. This was particularly true of meetings with those to whom he had been given letters of introduction: they increased his circle of acquaintances and all received him with a warm welcome. It was at this point in his journey that the Captain was led to acknowledge that he had rarely met a more good-natured people than those he encountered on the American continent. He admitted that though he often put forth a provocative point of view, he never met an American 'out of temper'. More than that, he could not recall a single instance in which anything captious or uncivil was ever said to him. Farther south in Connecticut, an inspection of three public institutions near Hartford – the state prison, the asylum for the deaf and dumb and the institution for the insane – left the Scottish traveler impressed with the conduct of affairs in each of them. Yale College in New Haven also proved a worthwhile visit, for there

> it was extremely agreeable to see so many good old usages and ortho-dox notions kept up as rigorously, all things considered, as possible. How long the able and zealous professors of this celebrated establish-ment will be able to stem effectually that deluge of innovation and would-be improvements in doctrine, discipline and pursuits, which is sweeping over the rest of the country, and obliterating so many of the landmarks of experience, I cannot pretend to say.[9]

In the evening of his visit to Yale, Captain Hall was introduced to the eminent lexicographer Noah Webster, with whom he had a lively conversation. An ardent Yankee and revolutionary in every aspect of his thinking, Webster was a graduate of Yale whose spelling books would teach generations of Americans to read and write. At the time of meeting the Scottish Captain, the lexicographer was sixty-nine years old and had spent more than forty years of his life preparing a dictionary of the English language. He had, during the course of that work, acquired knowledge of as many as twenty-eight languages, and he included in his dictionary the technical expressions connected with the arts and sciences. In all that he accomplished Webster deliberately sought a departure from any cultural thralldom to Britain, and so it was that many English words in his lexicon subsequently acquired an American spelling. It is surprising, then, that the two men could have an agreeable discussion on the uses of so-called Americanisms, given the Captain's allegiance to all things British. Though the lexicographer agreed that an English expression ought to be adopted in preference to any new one, he insisted that stopping the progress of language with its constant innovations would be akin to halting the course of the Mississippi. The visitor was

> at first surprised when Mr. Webster assured me there were not fifty words in all which were used in America and not in England, but I have certainly not been able to collect nearly that number. He told me too, what I did not quite agree to at the time, but which subsequent enquiry has confirmed as far as it has gone, that, with very few exceptions, all those apparent novelties are merely old English words, brought over to America by the early settlers, being current at home when they set out on their pilgrimage, and here they have remained in good use ever since.[10]

Not long after this meeting with Noah Webster, the energetic Captain left New Haven with his family in a steamboat and proceeded along the Long Island Sound to New York Harbor. There, it amused him to watch the bustle of ships, from a point on the public promenade in Manhattan known as the Battery, taking off for various ports – Le Havre, London and Liverpool across the Atlantic, Charleston and New Orleans to the south – and he subsequently provided a colorful description of early-nineteenth-century sea travel. Every set of passengers, he writes, was accompanied by a huge mountain of chests, portmanteaus, bags, writing-desks, bird-cages, bandboxes, cradles, and the whole family of greatcoats, boat-cloaks, umbrellas, and parasols. The captains of the several packets were of course on board the steamer, in charge of their monstrous letter bags; while close under their lee came the watch maker, with a regiment of chronometers, which he guarded and coddled with as much care as if they had been his children. The several stewards of the packets formed a material portion of our motley crew, each being surrounded, like the tenants of the ark, with every living thing, hens, ducks, turkeys, to say nothing of beef and mutton in joints, bags of greens, baskets of eggs, bread, and all the et ceteras of sea luxury.[11]

At the time of his return to New York in November of 1827, the city could be felt pulsating with the excitement of an upcoming popular election, and during the ensuing month that the Hall family resided there, the ever-curious Captain resolved to learn what he could of the dynamics of America's governing system. In that very year, there were twenty-four states making up the Union, with a total population of 9.6 million. It was the visitor's strong belief that the government then in operation in the capital city of Washington, though forty years in existence, would never hold because it had no solid foundation – this despite the fact that Americans were convinced it was the most advanced form of government the world had ever known. While the formation of the two Houses of Congress was unique, declared the Scottish observer, the system was definitely not to be seen as a foolproof exercise in governance as it was, from top to bottom, one of avowed distrust of public men. Indeed, every art was employed, in his view, to complicate the machinery of politics in such a way that every man would act more or less as a check on his neighbor. Surely it was evident that a universal lack of confidence existed in all who participated in government, and this underlying tension, Captain Hall believed, was the mainspring of American political movements. The subject so fascinated him that no fewer than four chapters of one volume are devoted to it, in which he declares that his facts were assuredly not hastily assembled: he had the constant and friendly assistance of well-qualified authorities. And, indeed, he most certainly brought solid facts to his reasoning, though it is clear that he was, from the outset, not to be convinced that the American notion of democracy could be shared with the world at large as an enlightened model of government:

> A perfectly pure democracy, according to the usual definition, cannot, of course, exist in a large community, spread over a wide country; for by no conceivable means could such multitudes be brought together for the purpose of discussing public affairs. The Americans, however, by several ingenious devices, have arrived, it must be owned, as near the point aimed at as the nature of things will admit of. In booksellers' phrase, their work might be called 'The Science of Government reduced to the lowest capacity, or every man his own Legislator.'[12]

It was nonetheless with the greatest delight, the traveler resoundingly claimed, that he would now turn from the 'ungenial and irritating' topic of politics to the pursuits of science and literature. His interest in these matters was given a lively turn when he was invited to join a circle of distinguished New Yorkers who had established a society called the Lyceum of Natural History. They met once a week, and though the number of attendees was small, both the proceedings of the group and the information communicated were worthy of the highest praise. Inasmuch as Captain Hall had not expected to find many men of science in America at the time of his visit, he was quite taken with the avid pursuits of this group and, on being admitted to several meetings, was delighted to make a contribution regarding a significant series of rock and river formations witnessed on his travels from Canada to the States. His remarks on the topic of *Reliquiae Diluvianae* (to use his Latin term) in the vicinity of New York proved detailed as well as impressive. Perhaps most interesting to the members of the society was Captain Hall's disquisition on the formation of Long Island, which he held was composed from end to end of a mass of primordial matter – clay, sand, gravel and myriads of water-worn boulders of every description of stone, cast together in the most 'admired disorder', as a result of an immense torrent having swept over the Canadas and the Northern and Eastern states of the United States. It was clear from his report that the Scottish visitor derived great pleasure from his participation in the proceedings of the Lyceum and greatly regretted that his contribution was not more extensive.

En route to Philadelphia, the Hall family made a stop (by invitation) near Bordentown, New Jersey to visit the residence of Count de Survilliers, who was familiarly known as Joseph Napoleon Bonaparte, elder brother of the late Emperor, and who had resided in America for some years. Though not at liberty to divulge the details of the visit, the British traveler was happy to report that the Count, who had been made King Joseph of Spain by his brother,

> has gained the confidence and esteem, not only of all his neighbours, but of everyone in America who has the honour of his acquaintance – a distinction which he owes partly to the discretion with which he has uniformly avoided all interference with the exciting topics that distract the country of his adoption, and partly to the suavity of his personal address, and the generous hospitality of his princely establishment.[13]

It is unlikely that many in America at that time were at all aware of the presence of Napoleon's brother in their midst, though he lived in the States from 1817 to 1832; nor has history been as kind to the Count as was his visiting Scottish friend.

The subsequent stop in Philadelphia proved very satisfactory, particularly as the British traveler was invited to join a group of intellectuals who met weekly at the home of each member in turn, and with some of whose writings he was already acquainted. Extended visits were made to the city's new penitentiary, a building of distinctive architecture which led the Captain to describe it at length and to dwell once more – as he did on his visit to Sing Sing in New York – on the relative merits of the American systems of confinement. Inevitably, the city of Philadelphia with its several publishing houses and many libraries (there were no fewer than sixteen public libraries in the year 1824) led to an extensive discourse by the Captain on the subject of books as well as copyright, the latter being an issue that some years later would stoke the ire of the visiting Charles Dickens. An American publisher who succeeds in obtaining a copy of a book written in Europe, Hall learned, may reprint it and put the book into circulation without sharing the profits with the author, or having any connection with him at all. It was clear to the Captain from the many conversations he held with those in the publishing business (particularly at the noted firm of Carey and Lea in Philadelphia) that no copyright law would be in the making for some time. Indeed why would there be, he mused, since America up to then had very little good literature, in his view, to protect. Still, it was irksome to the Scottish traveler that America was found wanting in more than one respect as compared with the English attitude toward the enjoyment and circulation of literature. For one thing, the grand object aimed at by the American publishing houses was mere extent of sale; of this he was convinced. As cheapness would accordingly be the criterion here, it afforded an explanation, opined the visitor, for the miserable paper, print and binding by which almost all reprinted books in the country were disfigured. This in turn explained why few people prized or held on to their books, the traveler believed, inasmuch as he encountered few private libraries in his travels. Of course the rich maintained libraries, since they could afford to do so. What was to be deplored, in the visitor's view, was the fact that 'no system of mutual concert and assistance' existed among book publishers in America, nor was there any combined system of subscription and circulating books as there was in England.

The next leg of the visitor's journey led him to Washington, DC, where every day he could be found attending proceedings in the Senate, the House of Representatives or the Supreme Court. He reports on the conduct of the American government at length, finding it pertinent to make the familiar remark that while in Britain the king can do no wrong, it would appear that here the president could do no right. As he watched sessions held in the House of Representatives he sensed a great want of order in the proceedings of that body, inasmuch as House members presented resolutions of a great variety – touching on everything and anything – without reference to their relative importance or to any prior submission:

> I have before observed, that there is neither discipline nor organiza-
> tion in this body, as to the conduct of business. Consequently, any
> member brings forward the subject which is uppermost in his own
> thoughts [...] This indiscriminate and desultory mode of proceeding,

without concert amongst themselves, leads to the repetition of innumerable proposals already before the House, or which have been discussed over and over again in preceding Congresses. Such topics, it might be thought, should have been put to rest long ago. But, alas! nothing is allowed to settle in that busy and much agitated country.[14]

It was at this time that the Scottish visitor witnessed the sale of a slave, and saw the first notice of the formation of a Society for the Abolition of Slavery. He found it difficult to be drawn into this issue, being aware that Americans perpetually blamed Britain for having initially entailed slavery upon their country. Yet this argument could no longer hold in his view, for the extent and character of slavery had been completely altered with the recent acquisition of Florida and Louisiana, both of which coastal regions entered the Union as strategic slaveholding territories. As to the slow groundswell of abolitionism, it was his considered judgment that if interference with the slave system were ever to be seriously contemplated, either by a powerful executive or by a majority of the members of Congress from the non-slaveholding states, the inevitable consequence would be a division of the Union. In this particular instance, he was proved right.

The Scottish visitor subsequently made an extensive tour of the Southern states, witnessing the condition of slaves and coming to the astute judgment that precisely in proportion as the black man has a fair chance given him, so he proves equal in capacity to the white man. He traveled across the states of Georgia and Alabama en route to New Orleans, where it pleased him in that developing city to hear French, Spanish and English all spoken. He particularly looked forward to a trip up the Mississippi River on his way north, for he had an uncommonly keen interest in all the navigational aspects of his trip across the new continent. The Mississippi was of particular fascination, not only because of the size of this great artery but because of its depth, which, he held, gave this mighty stream its 'sublimity'. So keen was his interest that he included a drawing of the Mississippi in his three-volume account of his American visit, showing the wide arc of its serpentine curves and the track of steamboats as they headed either north or south. It was subsequently by steamboat along the Ohio River (a tributary of the Mississippi) that the Hall family reached Louisville in Kentucky, followed by a brief stay in Cincinnati. That Ohio town was to acquire a negative fame in the account of Frances Trollope, who had visited earlier that year. Though it was Captain Hall who urged her to publish her devastating memoirs, he himself reports that it was not without reason that Cincinnati had been touted as one of the 'much-cried-up wonders of the West'. The Captain found the town 'very pretty' as well as advantageously situated on the right bank of the Ohio River, where it appeared to have more the air of business and energy of purpose than any other locale since he left New Orleans. He attributed this vitality in part to its location in a non-slave-holding state, which endowed it with a spirited, pleasant character. Indeed, he was quite reluctant to leave this Western city with its agreeable and 'very kind society', but the health of their child dictated a return north. There was a stop in Philadelphia where, the visitor reported, everyone was so kind, as if to recompense the Hall family for the hardships they endured while traveling. The final destination was New York: there the Hall family members boarded the packet ship *Corinthian* in July of 1828 and, after an absence of fifteen months in America, were once again happily at home in England.

CHAPTER 4

The New World Enterprise
of Frances Trollope

'THOUGH I DO NOT quite sympathise with those who consider
Cincinnati as one of the wonders of the earth,' declared the
indomitable Frances Trollope, 'I certainly think it a city of
extraordinary size and importance.'[1] With that, the energetic traveler
and mother of five settled into the bustling American locality bordering
on the Ohio River for a period of two years. She had come to Cincinnati
in February of 1828 to establish a business, having been assured that
it was in all respects the 'finest situation west of the Alleghenies', but
she was to find fault with almost everything there.[2] She complained

of the lack of domes, towers and steeples that would give the rising city some architectural distinction; the lack of accommodation for tea-drinking in one's lodgings; the lack of pumps or drains of any kind; the lack of a dustman's cart; the presence of pigs in the street; the lack of science and other branches of learning that could seduce Americans from their pursuit of money; the lack of feeling shown for art; and, above all, the lack of manners. While there was certainly justification for many of her complaints, her opinion of the still-raw city was not shared by every European visitor.

The ever-perspicacious Alexis de Tocqueville, visiting just two years later, wrote:

> We are very satisfied with our recent sojourn in Cincinnati; it was terribly interesting. This city represents a completely novel scene; everything in it expresses hectic growth: lovely houses and cottages; freshly paved, imperfectly aligned streets encumbered with building materials; unnamed squares; unnumbered houses; in short, the sketch of a city rather than a city. But in the midst of these imperfect structures, there is the hum of life, a feverishly active population: that is Cincinnati today. It may not be thus tomorrow.[3]

Some twelve years later, Charles Dickens visited Cincinnati; he, too, responded to the bustle of the riverside location, characterizing the city as one of charm and animation. He liked the broad, paved wharf bordering the Ohio River, the clean red-and-white houses, the extremely good shops, the footways of bright tiles, and the large cluster of steamboats approaching the quay. Of course, the famed novelist (like de Tocqueville) had no intention of settling in Cincinnati, nor indeed anywhere else in the United States.

For the impoverished Fanny Trollope, a good deal was at stake in crossing the Atlantic to the promises of a New World. Cincinnati was to be the salvation of her family from bankruptcy in England, for high on Fanny's list of unrealistic aims in coming to these shores was to amass a sizeable fortune. Though neither she nor any member of the Trollope family had ever been in business, nor evinced any sort of commercial know-how, expectations were high. When she eventually left the Ohio city more destitute than ever, her account of her extended stay in America reflected her bitterness. The narrative proved to be a mesmerizing chronicle published in two volumes and entitled *Domestic Manners of the Americans*. No one could have predicted the sensation it would cause following its appearance in 1832.

A woman of decidedly Tory views, the 47-year-old Frances Trollope felt threatened during her time in America by the steadfast belief in equality that confronted her on that side of the Atlantic, and by the agitation for a reform bill to extend suffrage that had been raging for some time on the other. (That reform bill was ultimately passed in England in the year 1832, significantly expanding the size of the voting population, and introducing notable changes to the electoral system of England and Wales.) Was democratic America – with its lack of manners, art and refinement – a rehearsal for what she would witness at home? It was impossible for the voluble visitor to suppress the notion that she was of superior stuff, with a rightfully reserved place in a hierarchical society. Equality, for Fanny Trollope, was a synonym for an abysmal level of art, literature, education and speech, as well as for coarseness, arrogance and a want of all the refinements that she considered part of the 'chivalry of life'. She felt passionately about these judgments, which permeate her account with a ring of authority. As she wrote in her brief preface, democracy represents 'the jarring tumult and universal degradation which invariably follow the wild scheme of placing all the power of the state in the hands of the populace'. This she feared would happen to her cherished England. At issue for most Europeans in surveying the New World was always the question of whether the American nation represented a decided advance on European inequalities, or whether it had taken a giant step backwards. When *Domestic Manners of the Americans* burst on the scene in the United States in 1832, the young republic, then struggling to build institutions of lasting moral value, was outraged. Mrs. Trollope's book was excoriated in the press, and the author herself lampooned and vilified. Today, at the calm remove of some 180 years, the two-volume account is considered an invaluable (if highly prejudiced) record of Jacksonian America, marked by astute, first-hand observations. One also recognizes at this distance that there was much that Frances Trollope admired in the United States: its far-flung regions of untamed beauty; its amazing web of harbors, rivers, and canals that made for easy travel in so vast a territory; and 'the boldness and energy with which public works are undertaken and carried through'. Rather than provoking hostility today, her saucy opinions make for sprightly and amusing reading. Indeed, she was often right.

The Trollope family had been encouraged to look to the promise of America by their English friend Frances Wright, a close friend of Lafayette and, as we have seen, a wealthy, young progressive with ambitious ideas who had already traveled across the Atlantic. She had published glowing accounts of the new nation and was certain that the Trollopes could solve their problem of insolvency there. Her American base of operations in the cause of social reform was then the small, would-be utopian village named Nashoba in the wilderness of Tennessee, and it was to this far-flung and crude settlement that she invited the Trollopes to pay a visit. It appears that the two Fannys had felt themselves compatible enough, when the visit was agreed upon, to book transatlantic passage together. They set sail from England on 4 November 1827 and arrived at what was then called La Balize, the entrance to the Mississippi River, seven weeks later. For Frances Trollope and her family it did not prove to be an auspicious arrival, despite all the encouragement of Frances Wright and the happy prospect of finding solvency in the new nation.

The doleful sight of the muddy La Balize so imprinted itself on her memory that she laid the picture bare in the opening pages of her book:

> I never beheld a scene so utterly desolate as this entrance of the Mississippi. Had Dante seen it, he might have drawn images of another Bolgia from its horrors [...] By degrees, bulrushes of enormous growth become visible, and a few more miles of mud brought us within sight of a cluster of huts called the Balize, by far the most miserable station that I ever saw made the dwelling of man [...] For several miles above its mouth, the Mississippi presents no objects more interesting than mud banks, monstrous bulrushes, and now and then a huge crocodile luxuriating in the slime. Another circumstance that gives to this dreary scene an aspect of desolation, is the incessant appearance of vast quantities of drift wood, which is ever finding its way to the different mouths of the Mississippi.[4]

In tow with Fanny were three of her five children (Henry, aged sixteen; Cecilia, twelve; and Emily, ten), a manservant, and a struggling French artist named Auguste Hervieu who was her protégé. Left behind were two sons – Thomas Adolphus and the future novelist Anthony – and her husband Thomas Anthony Trollope, an impoverished and querulous lawyer bereft of any business acumen. The latter had fed the family's extravagances (they had no money but kept a liveried servant) by nursing the illusory hope that he would come into a great inheritance from a rich uncle. He never did. Instead, he instructed his spouse to set in motion the plans they had discussed for erecting an 'emporium' in Cincinnati, elaborate in size and style, where European fancy goods could be sold to a receptive Western clientele. As neither of the Trollopes had any instinct for business, it is not surprising that they concurred in what was surely an outlandish scheme. Thomas Trollope eventually joined his wife with their eldest son for a brief stay in America to oversee the plans for the 'emporium', and then left for England to plan the consignment of goods that would be stocked on its shelves and sold to waiting customers.

Unlike most visitors to the new nation, Mrs. Trollope had not initially entered the country by way of New York, armed with impressive letters of introduction and accordingly received in a manner that she believed was due her rank. Following the depressing spectacle of La Balize and its surroundings, New Orleans was the first city of major size on her Mississippi riverboat itinerary. It did not make a favorable impression, for there appeared on first sight very little that could gratify 'the eye of taste'. Still, its French and Spanish heritage appealed to the Trollope family, for there was certainly much of novelty and interest in the rising metropolis to attract newly arrived Europeans. Fanny Trollope duly noted the presence of an 'elite society', glimpses of architectural majesty, and the primeval glories of the surrounding forest in which she and her children took long walks. She regretted that her stay of a few days did not permit her 'entering into society', but observed that its two main components, Creoles and 'quadroons', were both known for their elegant modes of entertainment. In this Southern city the English traveler had her first encounter with slavery, to which she was strongly opposed, albeit, it would appear, with some reservations. She admired the 'grace and beauty of the elegant Quadroons' and railed against the inferior position assigned to them because of their mixed blood. During the earlier two-day journey on the Mississippi, she had been 'much pleased by the chant with which Negro boatmen regulate and beguile their labour on the river; it consists but of very few notes, but they are sweetly harmonious, and the Negro voice is almost always rich and powerful'. Later she made the provocative remark that:

> At the sight of every Negro man, woman, and child that passed, my fancy wove some little romance of misery, as belonging to each of them; since I have known more on the subject, and become better acquainted with their real situation in America, I have often smiled at recalling what I then felt.[5]

A high point of the Trollopes' winter visit to New Orleans was the sight of oranges, green peas and red peppers growing in the open air at Christmas time. Another delight was the luxuriant undergrowth of palmettos in the forest. Yet, so negative was the balance of her feelings toward the city that she was able to write off her visit with those stinging words, 'New-Orleans presents very little that can gratify the eye of taste.' On New Year's Day of 1828, the family moved further upriver. The Mississippi steamboat that carried the Trollopes to Memphis for the inland journey to Nashoba gave rise to a vehemently expressed judgment:

> We found the room [a lounge on the riverboat] destined for the use of the ladies dismal enough, as its only windows were below the stern-gallery; but both this and the gentlemen's cabin were handsomely fitted up, and the former well carpeted; but oh! that carpet! I will not, I may not describe its condition; indeed it requires the pen of a Swift to do it justice. Let no one […] commence their [American] travels in a Mississippi steamboat; for myself, it is with all sincerity I declare, that I would infinitely prefer sharing the apartment of a party of well conditioned pigs to […] being confined to its cabin. I hardly know of any annoyance so deeply repugnant to English feelings, as the incessant, remorseless spitting of Americans. I feel that I owe my readers an apology for the repeated use of this and several other odious words; but I cannot avoid them, without suffering the fidelity of description to escape me.[6]

The visit to Frances Wright's Nashoba was, predictably, not a success: by the time this brief encounter was over, the two Fannys had
grown far apart. They were an odd pair, anyway. Fanny Wright, who
according to the older Fanny was the 'advocate of opinions that make
millions shudder', was strongly committed to the democratic cause of
educating black people in America, willing to suffer discomforts for
her principles, and generous of mind and purse. She was a mesmerizing speaker and apparently also beautiful. Fanny Trollope – despite
Hervieu's adoring portrait of her – was a dowdy and vituperative elitist
who tended, by her own account, to look older than her years. The
senior Fanny tried hard to imagine how someone accustomed to the
civilized prosperity of Europe could bring herself to live in the wilds
of America. Did she not understand that any English friend would feel
distraught at the spectacle? The crude buildings in Nashoba had not
yet been furnished with any of those minor comforts that ordinary
minds class among the necessaries of life and the lack of which were
shocking to Fanny Trollope. But the latter at least judged approvingly
that the younger Fanny's whole heart and mind were occupied by the
hope of 'raising the African to the level of European intellect'. Of her
impression of Nashoba, Fanny Trollope wrote:

> Desolation was the only feeling – the only word that presented itself;
> but it was not spoken [...] It must have been some feeling equally
> powerful [such as religious fanaticism] which enabled Miss Wright,
> accustomed to all the comfort and refinement of Europe, to imagine
> not only that she herself could exist in this wilderness, but that her
> European friends could enter there, and not feel dismayed at the
> savage aspect of the scene.[7]

Because the scene in Nashoba was too savage for the older Fanny,
she cut her stay short and returned to Memphis in late January for
the onward journey to Cincinnati. It was there that she was joined
by her husband and eldest son, Thomas Adolphus, and plans were
drawn up for the erection of the 'emporium', though father and son
did not remain long, soon leaving for England to plan the consignment
of products that would be shipped overseas to America. They would
then be stocked on the shelves of the planned building and sold to

what surely would be eager crowds of local customers. Mrs. Trollope was left alone with her three children to look after things despite her utter lack of commercial talents. From the start, the ambitions of both husband and wife were out of all proportion to the local situation in Cincinnati, to the investment they could make for a business out of their own pockets and, most assuredly, to their combined business acumen, which was thoroughly lacking. When in time the 'Bazaar' was duly erected, no one in Cincinnati (or elsewhere) had ever seen the likes of such an edifice.

Rising three stories high, and crowned by an ornate entablature, it was built in a bizarre mingling of Gothic, Greek and Moorish architectural motifs. On entering, the visitor (and, hopefully, he would prove to be a customer as well) faced a grand, circular staircase and rows of Doric columns. There were also galleries for music and art, as well as a grand ballroom, with paintings and mosaics; the latter were to be seen everywhere and were supplied by young Hervieu.

Though the Bazaar was stocked with what were presented as the latest offerings from London and Paris, it was a total failure. The several thousand dollars' worth of goods ordered abroad by Mr. Trollope on borrowed money were eventually seized by the local Cincinnati sheriff to help pay the construction costs of the extravagant building; subsequently, the owners' household goods were impounded as well. Harriet Martineau, the astute English traveler who visited Cincinnati after Mrs. Trollope had left, characterized the Bazaar as a 'deformity'. Captain Frederick Marryat described it as a conglomeration of styles that ought to be labeled 'preposterous'. Meanwhile, with Mr. Trollope long since departed, taking his eldest son with him, Fanny Trollope was left to struggle along as best she could. Fortunately, there was the faithful Auguste Hervieu to offer comfort, and sometimes to provide financial rescue through earnings he was able to make from his art.

Fanny's eventual record of her two years in Cincinnati, while studiously avoiding any mention of the Bazaar, is charged with details about most aspects of the scene there, and is invaluable on that account. She writes of the schools, religion, entertainment, the 'peasantry', the market, the museum, the architecture, the pattern of marriages and the influence of the clergy. To a fair extent, the unfavorable is balanced by the favorable. She comments that the most advantageous feature of Cincinnati was its market, 'which, for excellence, abundance, and cheapness can hardly, I should think, be surpassed in any part of the world, if I except the luxury of fruits, which are very inferior to any I have seen in Europe.' Yet while all 'animal wants', as she termed them, were satisfied profusely, the simple manner of living in Western America was more distasteful to her because of its leveling effects on the manners of the people than because of the personal privations that such a manner of life rendered necessary:

> Till I was without them, I was in no degree aware of the many pleasurable sensations derived from the little elegancies and refinements enjoyed by the middle classes in Europe. It requires an abler pen than mine to trace the connexion I am persuaded exists between these deficiencies and the minds and manners of the people. The total and universal want of manners, both in males and females, is so remarkable, that I was constantly endeavouring to account for it.[8]

When Fanny Trollope took her leave of the city in March 1830, her feelings were unequivocal: 'We left nought to regret at Cincinnati. The only regret was, that we had ever entered it; for we had wasted health, time, and money there.'

From Cincinnati, Mrs. Trollope set out to tour the Eastern United States before eventually embarking for England. Wheeling, Virginia (now in West Virginia), was her first stop. It was dismissed, however, with not much more than the remark that it 'has little of beauty to distinguish it, except the ever lovely Ohio [River].' Nonetheless, it was in Wheeling that she felt comfortably served, 'with all that sedulous attention which in this country distinguishes a slave state'. She compared the pernicious effects of slavery with those of equality, and opted for the former. By this statement, she was very far from intending to advocate the system of slavery, she claimed, but so far as her observation permitted, she believed its influence was far less injurious to the manners and morals of the people than the fallacious ideas of equality.

Mrs. Trollope subsequently journeyed by stagecoach toward Baltimore, passing through the Allegheny Mountains, which she particularly enjoyed for the wealth of flora displayed at every turn.

There were many aspects of the northeast environment that were to her liking:

> As we advanced toward Baltimore the look of cultivation increased, the fences wore an air of greater neatness, the houses began to look like the abodes of competence and comfort, and we were consoled for the loss of the beautiful mountains by knowing that we were approaching the Atlantic [...] Baltimore is, I think, one of the handsomest cities to approach in the Union. The noble column erected to the memory of Washington, and the Catholic Cathedral, with its beautiful dome being built on a commanding eminence, are seen at a great distance. As you draw nearer, many other domes and towers become visible, and as you enter Baltimore-street, you feel that you are arrived in a handsome and populous city.[9]

A fortnight's stay sustained her favorable impression of the city, eliciting her frequent use of such words as 'handsome', 'agreeable', 'pretty', and 'delighted'. She did find fault with a Sunday sermon ('I am very attentive to sermons,' she wrote), and she was disgruntled that the theater was closed during her stay. Told that the opposition of the clergy was to blame for it, she wrote:

> The cause, I think, is in the character of the people. I never saw a population so totally divested of gaiety; there is no trace of this feeling from one end of the Union to the other. They have no fetes, no fairs, no merrimakings, no music in the streets, no Punch, no puppet-shows. If they see a comedy or a farce, they may laugh at it; but they can do very well without it [...] A distinguished publisher of Philadelphia told me that no comic publication had ever yet been found to answer in America.[10]

As to religion and how it was practiced in America, the observant visitor had views very much in line with those of her countrymen who derided the separation of Church and State. The populace everywhere appeared to her to be divided into an almost endless variety of religious factions and – because of the absence of a national religion – was exonerated from all obligation of supporting the clergy. She believed herself witness to the fact, during the course of her travels, that religious tyranny was nonetheless exerted very effectually without the aid of the government in a way much more oppressive than the 'paying of tithe'. It was her considered opinion that the object of all religious observances is better obtained when the government of the Church is entrusted to the wisdom and experience of the most venerated among the people. In America, it appeared to be placed in the hands of 'every tinker and tailor' who chooses to direct any variety of religious ceremony. Mrs. Trollope found that, in the smaller cities and towns, prayer meetings took the place of almost all other amusement. There was, to be sure, a distinct problem with this in her view. As the thinly scattered populations of most villages could pay no priests, they were forced to marry, christen and bury their kin without the benefit of clergy. Inevitably, Fanny tied this lack of a church–government connection to social behavior, which was ever her chief concern. Where there is such a connection so constituted as to deserve human respect, she stoutly believed, it produces a decorum in manners and language often found wanting where no such relationship exists.

A steamboat, traveling through the Chesapeake Bay to the Potomac River, brought the Trollope family from Baltimore to the capital. Mrs. Trollope was 'delighted with the whole aspect of Washington; light, cheerful, and airy, it reminded me of our fashionable watering places.' It had been laid out in a grandiose manner on the drawing board by Pierre Charles L'Enfant, the French architect–engineer appointed by George Washington, but at the time of the Trollopes' visit in 1830 many thoroughfares were still muddy and cows roamed some of the streets. Much of L'Enfant's grand plan had yet to be executed, as Mrs. Trollope acknowledged, prompting many foreigners to scoff at it. However, she herself saw 'nothing in the least degree ridiculous about it', though Harriet Martineau – for whom the capital city was an important visit in gaining political insight into the country – found little, to the contrary, that gained her approval some seven years later. Fanny admired the Capitol and its commanding position on a hill; the magnificent width of Pennsylvania Avenue; the imposing presidential mansion; the 'various public offices, all handsome, simple and commodious', and the 'very noble town-hall'. She was particularly struck with 'admiration and surprise' on viewing the Capitol, for she had not expected to see so imposing a structure on the western side of the Atlantic. That it stood so high and alone gave it a beauty and majesty that defied her pen to do it justice. She wrote that some might scorn Washington when it was compared with Philadelphia and New York, but she considered it 'as the growing metropolis of the growing population of the Union, and it already possesses features noble enough to sustain its dignity as such.' She was aware that Washington, as the capital city of the developing nation, had been laughed at by foreigners because it did not yet live up to the imposing scale planned for it. She had faith, nonetheless, that it would eventually do justice to the original design conceived by the French architect.

During her three-week stay, Mrs. Trollope visited whatever public buildings she could, commenting that there was much to see notwithstanding the 'diminutive' size of the city. She found that the residences of the foreign legations and their families contributed a tone to the society of the capital that distinguished it markedly from all other American cities. Then, too, Washington was the residence for a great part of the year of the senators and congressmen who 'must be presumed' to be the elite of the population with respect to both talent and education. Not to go unmentioned was the total and welcome absence of all sights, sounds, or smells of commerce: instead of drays, there were handsome carriages, and instead of salesmen of every description offensively plying their trade, there were 'very well-dressed personages lounging leisurely up and down Pennsylvania Avenue'. All of this could not fail, in her view, to make Washington a more agreeable abode than any other city in the Union.

As she continued to make the rounds of the capital, Mrs. Trollope took a particular interest in the Bureau of Indian Affairs where, she noted, the walls were entirely covered with original portraits of all the chiefs who had come to negotiate terms of settlement with the government. The visitor found that the portraits exhibited both a noble, warlike daring and a gentle simplicity. Fanny happened to be in Washington at a time when a vote was being taken in the Congress relating to 'Indian' affairs, specifically to the settlement rights of Native American tribes in Georgia and Alabama. As the vote taken in that year of 1830 was counter to Native American interests, she waxed indignant, insisting that if the American character was to be judged by American conduct in this matter, it should be declared lamentably deficient in 'every feeling of honour and integrity'. It was impossible, in her view, not to be revolted by the contradictions manifest in American principles and practice. On the one hand, she held, Americans inveighed against the governments of Europe, claiming that the latter favored the powerful while they oppressed the weak. While making such declarations, Americans could be observed hoisting the cap of liberty with one hand and flogging their slaves with the other. Moreover, Americans could be heard lecturing the populace on the indefeasible rights of man while at the same time driving from their homes 'the children of the soil', by which she meant the dislocation of the Native American populations.

Despite her indignation at the vote taken against the native tribes in Georgia and Alabama (particularly the Cherokees in the former state), Mrs. Trollope was anxious to witness for herself the legislative process as it transpired in a democratic country. She had been told, meanwhile, that when Fanny Wright was in Washington with the Marquis de Lafayette, the two Europeans had frequently attended the sessions of Congress and that the most distinguished members 'were always crowding round them':

Attending the debates in Congress was, of course, one of our great objects; and, as an English woman, I was perhaps the more eager to avail myself of the privilege allowed. It was repeatedly observed to me that, at least in this instance, I must acknowledge the superior gallantry of the Americans, and that they herein give a decided proof of surpassing the English in a wish to honor the ladies, as they have a gallery in the House of Representatives erected expressly for them, while in England they are rigorously excluded from every part of the House of Commons [...] The privilege of attending these debates [in the United States] would be more valuable could the speakers be better heard [...] but the extreme beauty of the chamber was itself a reason for going again and again. It was, however, really mortifying to see this splendid hall, fitted up in so stately and sumptuous a manner, filled with men, sitting in the most unseemly attitudes, a large majority with their hats on, and nearly all, spitting to an excess that decency forbids me to describe.[11]

With her notebook ever at the ready to record her observations, Fanny moved energetically about the capital and its environs. She visited the Senate as well as the House, finding that the senators, generally speaking, 'look like gentlemen'. She decreed the Senate chamber most elegantly furnished, while noting that it was of much smaller dimensions than the House of Representatives. What particularly caught her eye was a handsome room in the Senate building that was 'fitted up as a library for members'. She was pleased to note that the collection of books was similar to that typically amassed by English gentlemen but with 'less Latin, Greek, and Italian'. Her sightseeing trips took her to the Custis mansion in Arlington (it 'forms a beautiful object in the landscape'), and to many a sermon ('the churches at Washington are not superb'), and she was ever on the alert as to how American men and women dressed and behaved. 'The Episcopalian and Catholic [Churches] were filled with elegantly dressed women,' she briefly noted with approval, for she could never disassociate good attire from breeding and manners. As to the conduct of males, Fanny took the occasion to discourse at length on the American male's habit of chewing tobacco:

> I am inclined to think this most vile and universal habit of chewing tobacco is the cause of a remarkable peculiarity in the male physiognomy of Americans; their lips are almost uniformly thin and compressed. At first I accounted for this upon Lavater's theory, and attributed it to the arid temperament of the people; but it is too universal to be so explained; whereas the habit above mentioned, which pervades all classes (except the literary) well accounts for it, as the act of expressing the juices of this loathsome herb, enforces exactly that position of the lips, which gives this remarkable peculiarity to the American countenance.[12]

In August 1830, the Trollope party paid a two-week visit to Philadelphia. On the way there from Washington, the falls of the Potomac provided momentary rapture, prompting Fanny to adopt a dramatic literary tone reminiscent of Father Louis Hennepin's description following his discovery of the great Niagara cataract in 1678. 'The falls of the Potomac are awfully sublime,' Mrs. Trollope reflected, 'the dark deep gulf which yawns before you, the foaming, roaring cataract, the eddy-ing whirlpool, and the giddy precipice, all seem to threaten life, and to appal [sic] the senses. Yet it was a great delight to sit upon a high and jutting crag, and look and listen.'[13]

Philadelphia itself was pronounced a beautiful city, although Fanny found its rigid geometric street plan, ordered by William Penn, of 'wearisome regularity'. Just as Dickens would later, she longed for a crooked street. She acknowledged that the city was known for its handsome buildings, but to her, none could be termed truly splendid. In her view the famed State House (now called Independence Hall) had 'nothing externally to recommend it', nor was she impressed by her visit to the Pennsylvania Academy of the Fine Arts, where the works of two leading American painters – Washington Allston and Charles Ingham – were on view. Visits to performances in the Chestnut Street Theater and the Walnut Street Theater proved to be of no particular interest, although the Chestnut Street Theater, where she saw Edwin Booth perform in *King Lear* ('Very bad'), was 'prettily decorated'. There were the usual visits to churches, an attendance at a Quaker meeting, and an excursion to the Philadelphia Fairmount Water Works. The last left her duly impressed with its beauteous outlook on the Schuylkill River.

As to Philadelphia's women, Mrs. Trollope deemed them elegantly neat, although somewhat impoverished as to social life. The men came off less well:

> It is said that this city has many gentlemen distinguished by their scientific pursuits; I conversed with several well-informed and intel-ligent men, but there is a cold dryness of manner and an apparent want of interest in the subjects they discuss, that, to my mind, robs conversation of all its charm.
>
> The want of warmth, of interest, of feeling, upon all subjects which do not immediately touch their own concerns, is universal, and has a most paralysing effect upon conversation.[14]

Whether in or out of Philadelphia, she held that she 'never saw an American man walk or stand well; not withstanding their frequent mili-tia drillings; they are nearly all hollow-chested and round-shouldered.'

American women, too, never appeared to advantage when 'in movement'.

The Trollopes spent the winter in Alexandria, Virginia, where unusually severe temperatures caused the Potomac River to freeze over for the first time in thirty years. In the early spring of 1831 it was time to leave for New York City, to which she looked forward with great anticipation. 'I have never seen the bay of Naples, I can therefore make no comparison,' wrote Mrs. Trollope, 'but my imagination is incapable of conceiving anything of the kind more beautiful than the harbour of New York,' and she settled down with her family in Manhattan for seven weeks. She discovered much to her liking in the city: Broadway, with its attractive shops, neat awnings, excellent sidewalks and well-dressed pedestrians; City Hall and its surrounding park; houses with richly furnished interiors, although 'the great defect in the houses is their extreme uniformity – when you have seen one, you have seen all'; the handsome Merchants' Exchange; the plain, but very neat, churches; the several possibilities for theater-going; and the 'matchless' Hudson River. In addition, she seems to have enjoyed the company of friends in New York and by this time, too, she had abandoned any schemes to make money. Indeed, she liked New York well enough to compare it favorably with a European city: 'If it were not for the peculiar manner of walking which distinguishes all American women, Broadway might be taken for a French street,' she declared.

From New York the Trollope clan set off at the end of May 1831 for the falls of Niagara, with great expectations. On the way up the Hudson there were the New Jersey Palisades to admire; Revolutionary sites to visit ('It was not without a pang that I looked on the spot where poor [Major John] André was taken' – in reference to the British patriot who had spied for his country); the capricious masses of the Hudson Highlands to marvel at; the charm of West Point to delight the eye; and a continual succession of estates bordering the Hudson to lend more than a touch of sophistication to the trip. The journey from Albany to Schenectady was undertaken by stage, and thence they went by canal boat to Utica:

> I can hardly imagine any motive of convenience powerful enough to induce me again to imprison myself in a canal boat under ordinary circumstances [...] In such trying moments as that of fixing themselves

on board a packet-boat, the men are prompt, determined, and will compromise any body's convenience, except their own. The women are doggedly stedfast [sic] in their will, and till matters are settled, look like hedgehogs, with every quill raised and firmly set.[15]

Still, the Trollopes admired the magnificent cliffs through which the Erie Canal boat passed, particularly the lovely scene formed by the little falls of the Mohawk. From Utica they set off in a carriage for Trenton Falls, an awesome sight that caused Fanny to falter in descending a fearful footpath, 'But the whole effect was so exceedingly grand, that I had no longer leisure to think of fear,' she wrote. Rochester was:

One of the most famous of the cities built on the Jack and the Bean-stalk principle. There are many splendid edifices in wood; and certainly more houses, warehouses, factories, and steam-engines than ever were collected together in the same space of time; but I was told […] that the stumps of the forest are still to be found firmly rooted in the cellars.[16]

Determined to see the wonders of Niagara from British ground, Mrs. Trollope and her children crossed to Canada in a ferry:

I was delighted to see British oaks, and British roofs, and British boys and girls. These latter, as if to impress upon us that they were not citizens, made bows and courtesies as we passed, and this little touch of long unknown civility produced great effect.

Then, at long last, there were the roaring falls of Niagara. Like scores of visitors before and after her, Mrs. Trollope found it hard to describe with any originality her response to the world-renowned sight. 'I trembled like a fool,' she wrote, 'and my girls clung to me, trembling too, I believe, but with faces beaming with delight.' They spent four days of 'excitement and fatigue' around the falls before taking a last look on 10 June 1831. They then recrossed to the American side to head back to New York City. The Eagle Hotel, where they stayed in Buffalo, was:

An immense wooden fabric, [which] has all the pretension of a splendid establishment, but its monstrous corridors, low ceilings, and
intricate chambers, gave me the feeling of a catacomb rather than a
house. We arrived after the table d'hote tea-drinking was over, and
supped comfortably enough with a gentleman, who accompanied us
from the Falls; but the next morning we breakfasted in a long, low,
narrow room, with a hundred persons, and any thing less like comfort
can hardly be imagined [...] How greatly should I prefer eating my
daily meals with my family in a wig-wam, to boarding at a table d'hote
in these capacious hotels; the custom, however, seems universal
through the country at least, we have met it, without a shadow of
variation as to its general features, from New Orleans to Buffalo.[17]

The return journey to New York City took the Trollope party through
Avon ('a straggling, ugly little place'), the towns of Canandaigua,
Geneva, Auburn, and Utica, then back to Albany, where they boarded
a steamboat for the trip down the Hudson. Finally, in July 1831, the
Trollopes embarked for England. Before the end of her United States
tour, Fanny Trollope reviewed the notes she had accumulated, weigh-
ing them for relevance and accuracy and, she claimed, removing much
that was negative. Lest anyone should misunderstand her feelings
toward Americans, however, she penned a clear and ringing declaration for publication: 'I do not like them. I do not like their principles, I
do not like their manners, I do not like their opinions.' Still, America
ultimately gave Mrs. Trollope what she came for: financial salvation.
That reprieve did not come immediately, however, for the Trollope
family faced another bout of hardship with eviction by a British sheriff
in March 1834: they were dispossessed of Julian Hill, their house in
Harrow. Eventually, financial security was assured from the sale of
Mrs. Trollope's work when she set her pen to paper. Following the
publication of *Domestic Manners of the Americans* in 1832, the often-
impoverished daughter of a parson went on to fame and fortune as a
prolific author of travel accounts and novels. She continued to write
until she was seventy-six years old, and when she died seven years
later she had more than fifty volumes to her credit.

CHAPTER 5

The Political Mission of Thomas Hamilton

T HE SCOPE of a traveler's observations, we are informed by Captain Thomas Hamilton, can only be contained within the peculiarities that float on the surface of the society that is visited: whatever sunken treasures lie beneath remain unknown to him. True enough perhaps, but Captain Hamilton was no ordinary wayfarer; he had traveled extensively during his forty-one years and had come to the New World not only with a distinct style of viewing but with a quill artfully sharpened to reflect those views faithfully. On arriving in the New World in the winter of 1830, the Scottish visitor was surprised to learn that a novel he had earlier written was not only widely read by American audiences but was in its fourth edition. To his delight, he found himself treated like a 'lion', in addition to which he had arrived from England armed with the requisite letters of introduction that would gain a gentleman of his stature entry wherever he wished. While the novel has long since been forgotten, the two volumes recording this former British Army officer's account of his New World stay, entitled *Men and Manners in America*, have found an audience ever since their publication.[1]

Hamilton was well aware, as he boarded the packet ship *New York* in Liverpool on 16 October 1830, that the political scene he was leaving behind in England demanded as much of his attention as any adventures about to unfold on the opposite side of the Atlantic. Reform was in the air in the British Isles, of a kind disturbing to any of that country's elite and eventually leading to the Reform Bill of 1832. Being a confirmed Tory (though professing Whig tendencies), Hamilton was determined to discover for himself whether democracy was in effect nothing short of mob rule and, if so, what he could do to discourage its exportation from the New World to Britain. He declared:

> When I found the institutions and experiences of the United States deliberately quoted in the reformed Parliament as affording safe precedents for British legislation, and learned that the drivellers who uttered such nonsense were listened to with approbation by men as ignorant as themselves, I certainly did feel that another work on America was wanted, and at once determined to undertake a task which inferior considerations would probably have induced me to decline.[2]

Interestingly, his political fears recall the era when eighteenth-century Russian nobility worried that France's new constitutional republic might be viewed as an example to follow.

Hamilton did not shy away from producing another work on America and, addressing his two volumes to British readers, rendered an account that has significantly enriched the store of nineteenth-century impressions of the New World. In it he vividly depicts the cultural and political details of the new society emerging across the

Atlantic, viewed by an outsider during the heady decade of Jacksonian democracy.

Hamilton arrived in this new society with a personal manservant. It was not long before he was planning an extensive itinerary that would take him as far west across the continent as transportation allowed. The letters of introduction he brought with him opened many important doors, as did his fame as a novelist; there were also those who knew him as a writer for *Blackwood's Magazine*. New York City was the first port of call. He judged the bustling seaport to be quite pleasing, though he was aware that a British traveler, in visiting foreign shores, usually expects to find some 'tincture of the barbaric'. While there was surely something of this in America's liveliest city, he did not find 'a great deal' of it, nor did he find that the city offered anything spectacular to the visitor beyond the hurly-burly of the trade along its shores. He did come upon a bit of the barbaric in his early exposures to American speech: it had a peculiar modulation as it reached his ears, partaking of a snivel and a drawl; the sound of it, he confessed, was in no way euphonious. What he did admire were the young ladies who sauntered along Broadway turned out in their finest; he found them uncommonly pretty and made the further disclosure that he esteemed American females to be a decidedly charming addition to any social function that he attended. Indeed, he went so far in praise of their female pulchritude as to say that 'I do not remember to have seen more beauty than I have met in New York.'[3] As for the American males to whom he was introduced in Manhattan's circles, the first impression was distinctly pleasing, there being a simplicity in their composure that he contrasted with the certain 'farce of ceremony' practiced by European society. American republican plainness, he avowed, is more welcoming to a stranger.

Hamilton found little to say with regard to the city's architecture. For him New York's chief attraction, it seemed, was not one of its conspicuous buildings but Broadway itself, running as it did through the whole extent of the city and forming the dominant line from which the other streets diverged to the quays on the Hudson and the East River. He did not find City Hall worthy of notice, but made it a point to visit there while the courts of law were holding their sittings. To his amazement, he found in one of the courts that three-quarters of the jurymen were eating bread and cheese while the court was in session, and the foreman actually announced the verdict with his mouth full. It was clearly not a sight to convince a visitor that legislation in America had been inaugurated on very solid or enlightened principles. Subsequently, in conversation with a lawyer friend, Hamilton found himself passionately defending the British court predilection for robes, wigs, and maces. He carefully explained that inasmuch as law is the principal bond by which society is held together, homage was paid not to the presiding judge but to the law itself, in the person of its minister. It was exactly to avoid such conduct of the law as was practiced in American courts, Hamilton insisted, that the solemnities of British justice were rigidly maintained.

Nor did he find a level of performance in any of New York's three theaters (which he visited several times) that came up to his standards. Then on everyone's lips was the name of the actor Edwin Forrest, touted to be a leading tragedian, *primus sine secundo*. Despite this glowing halo, and despite holding his audiences in raptures, Forrest was deemed by the visiting playgoer to be a coarse and vulgar performer, utterly commonplace in his conceptions of character. The laudations bestowed on their leading actor by New York audiences (which would continue for several decades) appeared to him gratuitous. Outside the theater, somewhat more praise was held out for the heroic performance of the young men who manned the city's fire department. The British visitor witnessed no fewer than five conflagrations and joined in the admiration bestowed on the firefighters for their bravery and skill. Why there were proportionately so many fires in New York appeared to be a conundrum; Hamilton was convinced that in that city alone there were annually more fires than occur on the whole island of Great Britain.

Other attractions in New York included attendance at the weekly Literary Club, where Hamilton met some of the city's leading intellectuals including Edward Livingston, Albert Gallatin, John Jay and several other personages 'of high accomplishment'. He did not find it to be true, as was often said, that Americans had a strong prejudice against those coming from Britain. What he did find in his social excursions was a certain bluntness in American manners; this proved somewhat startling at first, particularly to a sophisticated European reared under a social regime more accustomed to the exercise of tact and a certain social distance. Then, too, Hamilton judged conversation in America to be generally pitched at a lower key: this he ascribed to the fact that Americans were inferior to the British in the extent and refinement of their learning. On the other hand he could state that in no other country that he had visited were the amenities of life so readily and so profusely opened to a stranger as in the United States.

Before long, the visitor broached with his acquaintances the question of slavery, declaring it a mistake in his view for anyone to suppose that slavery had been abolished in the Northern states of the Union by this date. While it was true that members of the black population were no longer bought and sold in the North, they were still so bereft of privileges and any sense of equality that it was an abuse of language to consider them free. Can they enroll in the militia? Are they admissible on a jury? These are the questions that Hamilton posed without expecting an answer, at the same time declaring that prejudices against the black population in America prevailed beyond a Briton's conception. He was aware that the legislature of New York had recently (in 1829) extended a limited right of suffrage to men of color, but he was adamant in stating his conviction that discrimination against black people would ultimately be erased not by law but by public feeling and opinion.

Leaving New York City, the visitor made his way via steamboat to the city of Providence in Rhode Island; there he noted a great absence of taste in the architecture but did not tarry long. From Providence he took a stagecoach traveling north, and though his destination was Boston – a distance of some forty miles – it took eight hours to reach the New England city in that year; this phase of his travel was, as a matter of fact, Hamilton's introduction to an American stagecoach. It was an unhappy one, in which he was pitched with inordinate violence against the roof of the wagon while traveling over roads that were in atrocious condition.

> [The stagecoach] was of ponderous proportions, built with timbers,
> I should think about the size of those of an ordinary wagon, and was
> attached by enormous straps to certain massive irons, which nothing
> in the motion of the carriage could induce the traveler to mistake for

springs. The horses, though not handsome, were strong, and apparently well adapted for their work, yet I could not help smiling, as I thought of the impression the whole set-out would be likely to produce on an English road. The flight of an air balloon would create far less sensation. If exhibited as a specimen of a fossil carriage, buried since the Deluge, it might pass without question as the family-coach in which Noah conveyed his establishment to the ark.[4]

Boston, on arrival, proved to have less of that rawness of outline and inconsistency of architecture that had struck the visitor on arriving in New York. He found nothing gay or flashy in the appearance of the streets or in the crowds, commenting that there, as in most other parts of New England, social conventions are more strictly drawn so that even the lower classes are distinguished by a restraint in behavior not observable in New York vicinities. Of great interest to the visitor in the region of New England were conditions in the state prison, located in Charleston, Vermont, where he had heard that silence was enforced among the prisoners with a surveillance that was strict and unceasing. Hamilton's report of this visit is surprisingly extensive (as though he were filing an official brief); he found nothing 'squalid or offensive' in the prison conditions, yet he was inclined to feel that the severity of the discipline was being carried too far. (Charles Dickens was later to view the imposition of silence in American prisons with genuine horror.) Religion in the area was also of great interest to Captain Hamilton, for he gained the impression that the New England states maintained something akin to the religious establishment found in England. The towns of at least four states – Massachusetts, New Hampshire, Vermont and Connecticut – were required by law to provide by taxation for the support of the Protestant religion, leaving the choice of the sect to the individual. If Christianity were thus considered a public benefit in this wide area, tending to the reduction of crime and encouraging the virtues essential to the prosperity of a community, why, Hamilton wondered, was there not an established Church throughout all of the American states as in England? This was, of course, a question pondered by many English observers, who felt that the lack of an official Church opened the way to varying sects of questionable, if not quack, beliefs. Education was another area that garnered this traveler's approval, and he found that the establishment of district schools for the education of all classes was to be applauded. He did not wish the fact to go unmentioned, however, that equality of education for all classes was not an American innovation: district schools existed in Scotland 'long before the pilgrim fathers ever knelt in worship beneath the shadows of the hoary forest trees'.[5]

And American habits of speech? The fruit of the American school-master's labors was, alas, not to be measured by the language of his pupils. Bad grammar was in circulation everywhere, Hamilton held, with the privilege of barbarizing the King's English assumed by all ranks and conditions of men. It was, he insisted, not only workers, whose massacre of their mother tongue would certainly excite no astonishment, who were guilty of poor usage:

> but I allude to the great body of lawyers and traders; the men who crowd the Exchange and the hotels; who are to be heard speaking in the courts, and are selected by their fellow-citizens to fill high and responsible offices. Even by this educated and respectable class, the commonest words are so often transmogrified as to be placed beyond the recognition of an Englishman [...] It were easy to accumulate instances, but I will not go on with this unpleasant subject; nor should I have alluded to it, but that I feel it something of a duty to express the natural feeling of an Englishman, at finding the language of Shakspeare and Milton thus gratuitously degraded.[6]

Hamilton did find some exceptions. He was quick to add that there existed in Boston a social circle almost entirely exempt from his critical remarks. Here were included merchants, lawyers, the clergy and others among the educated strata where the 'true delicacies' of social intercourse were scrupulously observed, and where more refinement of thought and knowledge of literature always enters the language. Within this group was fostered a taste for the fine arts and, here, Hamilton was led to comment briefly on painting and literature as they were then unfolding. He remarks on the work of Washington Allston, a leading Boston painter originally from South Carolina, who is today considered by critics the most important figure of the early Romantic generation in America. In particular, Hamilton noted that Allston had been engaged on the same painting for the last ten years, and wondered whether any painting was worth so much time; he commented that, had Raphael, Rubens, or Titian taken a decade for each of their masterpieces, many noble specimens of art would have been lost. The painting in question was *Belshazzar's Feast*, which Allston had begun painting during a visit to London and which was purchased while still unfinished by a group of Boston gentlemen. Hamilton was more impressed by the work of Chester Harding, with whom he became acquainted and whom he described as having artistic powers of the first order. Harding grew up on the Western frontier; his portraits are known today for a bluff, objective honesty.

As to literature, Hamilton was convinced that in this field of erudition – as in other aspects of higher learning – Americans had not earned high marks. And why? He was convinced it was because they could not discover for themselves any skills to be gained that would reward the time spent in these enlightened endeavors. Indeed, he claims to have heard the notion of scholarship bandied about in Congress as a reproachful pursuit:

> The sovereign people in America are given to be somewhat intolerant of acquirement, the immediate utility of which they cannot appreciate. This is particularly the case with regard to literary accomplishment. In regard to literature, [Americans] can discover no practical benefit of which it is productive. In their eyes it is a mere appanage of aristocracy, and whatever mental superiority it is felt to confer, is at the expense of the self-esteem of less educated men. If knowledge be confessedly power, and freedom from prejudice a nobler enfranchisement than mere physical liberty, then I fear that, in reference to this great and ultimate function, [the enlightened institutions] of the United States will be found wanting.[7]

He mentions two American authors of this period, Washington Irving and James Fenimore Cooper, but offers no literary criticism. Their names appear only with regard to the issue of copyright, their books having enjoyed greater privileges than ever accorded to British writers, Hamilton asserts. A duty of thirty cents was then being imposed on all imported publications; at the same time, books were not protected by copyright, so that foreign authors enjoyed no benefit from the popularity of their work abroad. (Dickens, of course, would have much to say about this during his visit in 1842, when the copyright issue would still be without resolution.) As he made his way to Philadelphia, Hamilton noted that here was one of the prominent publishing cities of the country, the other two being Boston and New York. Though there were some very respectable specimens of typography in the works these publishers issued, he held that reprints of British works were executed in the coarsest and more careless manner. At the same time, British editions of works of which the copyright had expired were quite as cheap as these American reprint editions.

During the sojourn in Philadelphia Hamilton frequently visited the courts of law, where he found much tacit respect paid to decisions rendered overseas in English courts. The fact that every published tome containing these deliberations was reprinted in the States imme- diately upon publication proved, he was convinced, a major boon to the cause of American legal justice. Without these guiding volumes, law in America would soon become a font of utter confusion, the British traveler insisted, inasmuch as little harmony of decision could be expected from twenty-four independent state tribunals. Without a constant influx of British legal rulings, he was convinced that the laws regarding property, for example, would be inundated by such a welter of contradictory precedents as to be utterly impracticable by any system. Such want of uniformity in the administration of justice could only be injurious, he was certain, to public morals and private security. As to the society of Philadelphia, there was no other American city in Hamilton's view in which the system of social exclusion was so rigidly maintained. The acceptance of a parvenu into the city's inner circle appeared to the visitor not without prolonged complica- tions, there being a sort of holy alliance maintained by its members to forbid all unsolicited approach. He had sensed the existence of an aristocratic feeling in New York but it appeared far less prevalent there than in Philadelphia, a city that could be termed the Bath of the United States.

Arrival in Baltimore rendered the traveler immediately conscious that he was in a slave state, inasmuch as all the domestics in his hotel who served the clientele were slaves. He confessed that there was a certain novelty of sensation, half pleasant and half painful, connected with their services, though he found all of them observant of the proprieties of demeanor and distinguishable from European servants by nothing but color. Hamilton was certain that the state of Maryland would not long continue to be disgraced by the existence of slavery within its boundaries, because this kind of labor was not required by the demands of land cultivation; in this he was correct, Maryland standing as a pro-Union state when Civil War erupted. His estimation of Baltimore society was that there were few pretensions of any sort, while he esteemed that the level of literary accomplishment was perhaps lower than in Philadelphia or Boston. A particular pleasure he had while sojourning in the city was meeting Charles Carroll (then in his ninety-fifth year), who was an original signatory of the Declaration of Independence and whose companions in younger days were John Jay, John Adams, Thomas Jefferson and Alexander Hamilton. Together Carroll and his visitor talked of America's extraordinary transition from a group of dependent colonies to a powerful confederation of free states, spreading a population of twelve million over continually expanding territory while possessing a commerce and a navy second only to Britain's.

The traveler's next stop was Washington, a city whose lack of architectural distinction at the time was readily acknowledged. During attendance at sessions in the House of Representatives, Hamilton deemed a sizeable proportion of the congressmen there vulgar and uncouth, although a moral sense of propriety was, admittedly, always entertained by the majority. While there was no deficiency of party spirit in either House of Congress, there was, in his view, an entire want both of discipline and of organization in the House of Representatives; he often found it impossible to grasp the very issue under discussion. Somewhat different was the scene in the Senate, where he was impressed with the measure of decorum that prevailed; this he attributed to the fact that senators are usually men of eminence and the tone of any debate is accordingly pitched higher; indeed, he asserted that the Senate contained men who would do honor to any legislative assembly in the world, and he was pleased to meet several of them. Edward Livingston was among those who left a vivid impression, as was Daniel Webster; the latter's powers as a debater and a lawyer were described as being unrivaled. There were a number of other Washington officials whose company he enjoyed socially; particularly outstanding in his view was Edmund Burke who, he esteemed, was so philosophically gifted that people of both America and Britain should read and digest some of his eloquent views. Eventually the British visitor was led to the office of President Andrew Jackson, with whom he enjoyed half an hour's spirited conversation. He found the features of the President strongly defined and the expression of his eye vivid, though there was nothing in his manner that could be described as courtly elegance. Their talk was related to European politics, principally the plight of Poland in her unequal contest with the vast power of Russia. Hamilton left the tête-à-tête with feelings of respect for both the moral and the intellectual qualities of America's leader. He had far less positive feeling, it proved, with regard to the structure and operation of the government:

> It is to be lamented that a government of greater vigour and efficiency was not originally adopted, since the very newness of political institutions is of itself a source of weakness. It is only by slow degrees that the intellect and habits of a people become accommodated to the operations of a government, that their prejudices are enlisted in its favour, and a sort of prescriptive respect is obtained which adds materially to the benefit it is capable of conferring. Had the federal government been so framed as to rest for support, not on the precarious favour of the multitude, but on the deliberate intelligence of the property and talent of the country, there could have been no assignable limit to the prosperity and intellectual advancement of this fortunate people.[8]

While in Washington, the traveler took time to visit the Capitol building and to inspect the historical paintings there by John Trumbull, an eminent artist who had spent a fair number of years training in England. Hamilton viewed all four of the famous canvases at great length, but could give them no superlative praise except to say that, in the figure drawn of George Washington there was a calm and unobtrusive grandeur that satisfied the imagination. Otherwise he felt that the paintings, commissioned by the government, all depicted historical panoramas so truly intractable that 'Titian himself' could not have managed their delineation.

By this time in his travels, Hamilton was convinced that the intellectual climate of the United States did not lend itself to fostering the growth of literature and philosophy, or indeed most aspects of higher learning. As for the inculcation of political and social ideas, it was his observation that this came primarily through the innumerable newspapers that circulated in all areas of the country, sparking the comment that the American press exerted an influence beyond anything known in Europe. While books circulated with difficulty, newspapers seemed to penetrate to every 'crevice' of the Union, and it was through this medium (however low-level it was likely to be) that the public was highly influenced. Hamilton felt, not approvingly, that the power exercised by newspaper journalists, who were shrewd but for the most part uneducated, probably reached nine-tenths of the country. That the minds of such a high proportion of the population were, for the most part, inaccessible by any other avenue gave rise to further disapprobation.

Hamilton left the Washington area for a trip to New Orleans that was undertaken by rail, and then by water on the Ohio and Mississippi rivers. An important stop as he journeyed south was the town of Cincinnati, situated on the banks of the Ohio and earlier made familiar to readers on both sides of the Atlantic through the vivid prose of the British traveler Frances Trollope. Hamilton found the streets and buildings of Cincinnati handsome, the quay a place of considerable trade, and throughout the area a thousand indications of activity and business. As he walked the streets, his attention was arrested by an extraordinary building that appeared so out of place as to give him the impression that it had been tossed on the earth by some 'volcano in the moon'. This was the so-called 'Bazaar' erected on the orders of Mrs. Trollope that was inevitably ridiculed by visitors as a monstrosity, and years later torn down. Hamilton claimed never to have heard of Fanny Trollope at the time of his visit to Cincinnati:

> but at New York I had afterwards the pleasure of becoming acquainted with her and can bear testimony to her conversation being imbued with all that grace, spirit, and vivacity, which have since delighted

the world in her writings. How far Mrs. Trollope's volumes present a just picture of American society it is not for me to decide, though I can offer willing testimony to the general fidelity of her descriptions. But her claims to the gratitude of the Cincinnatians are undoubtedly very great. Her architectural talent has beautified their city; her literary powers have given it celebrity. [Until then] ears polite had never heard of it. There was not the glimmering of a chance that it would be mentioned twice in a twelvemonth, even on the Liverpool Exchange.[9]

What Hamilton found inexcusable was that Cincinnati's town square had not yet been adorned with a statue of Frances Trollope, whom he deemed the city's great benefactress. He wondered, in this connection, whether gratitude had utterly departed from the earth.

The transatlantic visitor now looked forward, as he left Cincinnati sailing southward for a distance of about five hundred miles, to the moment when the Ohio River would meet the famous Mississippi, declaring that he could not remember any occasion of travel that had so excited his imagination. That mighty river had been so often a factor in descriptions of the young nation. While it turned out, to his great disappointment, that the prevailing character of the Mississippi is one of solemn gloom and that the scenery is wanting in grandeur, he could still appreciate its dramatic properties. To begin with, it can brook no rival with any other waterway and it finds none, he declared. 'No river in the world drains so large a portion of the earth's surface. It is the traveler of five thousand miles, more than two-thirds of the diameter of the globe. The imagination asks, whence come its waters, and whither tend they?'[10] Hamilton busied himself with these and other questions, at the same time that he provided some astute answers. On board ship, he found the usual gambling, drinking and swearing, together with an utter disregard for the 'decent courtesies' of society that he purposed to ignore, or to which he had gradually become accustomed.

Hamilton's initial reaction to New Orleans was that it would be absurd to call it a handsome city, though he did add that one could use the term picturesque. With the exception of the cathedral, he discerned no public buildings of any magnitude, and described the streets as generally narrow and filthy. Still, he was happy to discover that the city had a very well-bred and hospitable social circle in which a visitor encountered 'more easy politeness' than in most cities of the Union. He had heard a great deal about the beauty of the 'quadroon' women but rarely came across a fine countenance; the Creoles were ladies who struck him as handsome. What was definitely unappealing was the climate of the area. At no season of the year was New Orleans a healthy place of residence, he learned, because of the exhalations from the Mississippi as well as the vast swamps by which it is surrounded. To his further consternation, he became aware that slave auctions were held in the New Orleans Exchange nearly every day, a frequency he had not expected, though he had determined to see the procedure for himself. He pauses to describe an auction that he attended there, while subsequently allotting many pages to the evils of this practice. How long slaveholders could hold out against nature, religion and the common sympathies of mankind, Hamilton found it impossible to foresee. His own conviction (tinged with prophecy) was that total abolition was not likely to come about without a great and 'terrible convulsion'. That great convulsion was not to erupt until 1861 and lasted four destructive years.

From New Orleans Hamilton traveled along the Southern coast to Mobile, Alabama, which, he remarked, was a town of considerable importance and known to every Liverpool merchant. As it was the leading port of that state's cotton-growing industry, the quays were crowded with scenes of shipping, the number of exports from this port being inferior only to that of New Orleans. Except for huge warehouses and a crowded harbor, the traveler found scarcely any indications of wealth; there were no opulent residences to be seen. While wandering about in the neighboring forest Hamilton encountered many Native Americans with whom he attempted to converse, but he learned that their taciturnity was not to be overcome. The money he offered them was received with surprise rather than gratitude, as the donor reports briefly that they were not only without experience in returning thanks but were 'too manly' to make pretensions about something they did not feel. In Mobile, the Scottish traveler came upon one of his countrymen who had emigrated from the town of Hamilton; on leaving Scotland, he had made his way from New York to Mobile where his family had joined him and where he was currently enjoying success as a baker. At first their conversation centered on little other than the beauties of

Scotland, but then the Mobile settler was drawn into discussions of his place in the New World versus the Old:

> He dilated on his present comforts; told me he lived like a duke [...] had two slaves, could pay his debts any day in the week, and had lately been able, without inconvenience, to send a hundred dollars to his poor mother. In regard to emigration he expressed his opinions at great length. 'In Scotland, sir,' said this sagacious master of the rolls, 'there is so much competition in every trade that a great many must be unsuccessful [...] My story is that of thousands more; and surely these men had better come to this country, than continue struggling for a precarious subsistence at home. They may not get rich here, but they will be sure, if they are sober, industrious, and do not suffer from the climate, to escape from poverty. But it is not actual want of the necessaries of life, sir, which occasions the chief suffering of the poor tradesman in the old country. It is the cares and anxieties that continually press on him, that deprive his bread of its nourishment, and disturb his sleep by horrible dreams; it is these things that wear out both soul and body, and make him an old man before his time.'[11]

Still, there was another side to the emigrant baker's story: he confessed that he would never have left 'bonny Scotland' if he had been single, for the newcomer to America must mingle with a 'most profane and godless set'.

As he continued his travels north Hamilton was pleased to find himself in Charleston, which he deemed the only location – apart from New Orleans – that met the British idea of a city. He judged the public buildings to be very good, in addition to which there was a bustle and animation tending to redeem 'minor defects'. That a good number of the better residences were decorated by gardens stocked with orange trees was certainly to be admired; on the other hand there was the climate of the city to be deplored. The latter was more than a minor defect in the visitor's view inasmuch as a resident of the city was forced to be on the alert because of it: in certain seasons there was danger of fever. The sojourn in Charleston led Hamilton to the observation that a profound difference prevailed between those who lived in locations south of the Potomac and those who were residents of the New

England states. The Northerner he found to be shrewd, intelligent, persevering, phlegmatic in temperament, devoted to the pursuits of gain and envious of those who were more successful. Educated Southerners were distinguished by generosity, high-mindedness and hospitality, somewhat touchy and choleric but valuing money only for the enjoyments it could procure. As to the important issue of manners, Southern gentlemen were found to be decidedly superior to all others of the Union.

Hamilton's itinerary now led him back to New York, where, soon after his arrival, he took a boat traveling north on the Hudson, a river that he considered 'one of nature's felicities'. He spent a day visiting West Point, where has was conducted through the academy grounds by the commandant. He found the carriage of the cadets to be less soldierlike than was desirable, remarking that a detectable slouch in their posture was observable in the entire American population. Moving on to Albany, the visitor found none of the buildings to be distinguished yet noted a pleasing, antique appearance to the town, which he attributed to its Dutch background. He then found his way to a Quaker village in the area that he was curious to visit. On his arrival in the vast compound of that distinct community, public worship was in progress and Quaker members were engaged in singing, followed by a sermon. Hamilton found the music monotonous, the words that were sung nonsense and the sermon that followed very short of remarkable.

But he would soon have his experience of something quite remarkable not too far off: the sight of Niagara Falls. This wonder of nature gave the visitor untold pleasure, if not outright joy. Hamilton felt that in describing the sight (which runs to many pages in his account), it was not possible to escape the charge of exaggeration (and nor does he):

> The day – the hour – the minute when his eye first rested on the Great Horse-shoe Fall, is an epoch in the life of any man. He gazes on a scene of splendor and sublimity far greater than the unaided fancy of poet or painter ever pictured. He has received an impression which time cannot diminish, and death can only efface. The results of that single moment will extend through a lifetime, enlarge the sphere of thought, and influence the whole tissue of his moral being. I remained on the Table rock till drenched to the skin, and

still lingered in the hope that some flash of the lightning – which had become very vivid – might disclose the secrets of the cloudy and mysterious cauldron, into which the eye vainly endeavoured to penetrate. But I was disappointed. Far overhead the fearful revelry of the elements still continued; but the lightning seemed to shun all approach to an object of sublimity equal to its own.[12]

Hamilton mentions that during his stay of a week in the area it was impossible to enjoy anything that could be called sleep because the deep, hollow roar of the cataract was distinctly audible: whenever he closed his eyes there was a 'torrent foaming' before them. By day it gave him much pleasure to scramble along the lower level of the overhanging rocks and to approach within a short distance of the roaring waters. He admitted that while he was in the neighborhood of Niagara he could think of nothing else, yet, at length, he reports on the Canadian countryside to the north, which he found not only picturesque but more orderly in appearance than he had seen anywhere in the United States. When he departed from Niagara there would shortly be more of Canada on his itinerary, for the British visitor took this occasion to travel further northeast in order to visit Montreal and Quebec City. His stay in these Canadian sites was short; before long he found himself in the New York State town of Saratoga, where visitors from all areas of the United States were wont to make an annual pilgrimage. Hamilton dubbed Saratoga a village of hotels; they not only abounded in every street but, in his view, gave a character to the place. Though he only stayed a few days in this popular American watering place, he had strong views as to why it attracted so many visitors – views that all centered on the abominable climate that prevailed in most regions of the United States:

In the Northern and central States – for of the [unhealthy] climate of the Southern States it is unnecessary to speak – the annual range of the thermometer exceeds a hundred degrees. The heat in summer is that of Jamaica; the cold in winter that of Russia. Such enormous vicissitudes must necessarily impair the vigour of the human frame; and when we take into calculation the vast portion of the United States in which the atmosphere is contaminated by marsh exhalations, it will not be difficult, with the auxiliary influences of dram-drinking and tobacco-chewing, to account for the squalid and sickly aspect of the population. Among the peasantry, I never saw one florid and robust man, nor any one distinguished by that fullness and rotundity of muscle, which everywhere meets the eye in England.[13]

Hamilton moved on to another fashionable watering place not too far off named Ballston Springs; there he stayed for only two days, remarking that if he found Saratoga dull, he found Ballston 'stupid'. He soon departed for Albany and subsequently boarded a ship sailing south on the 'beautiful' Hudson in the direction of New York. It was now the month of July; Hamilton found that the gay and the wealthy had deserted the city, leaving only the 'busy' behind. Though there was little merriment to relish in the hot season, the British visitor still enjoyed the diversion of society as a fair number of his friends were in town. It was during these final New York days that he made the acquaintance of Robert Weir, a 37-year-old American artist who spent several years studying in Italy and was subsequently appointed professor of drawing at West Point. (There is mounted in the Capitol one of his monumental paintings, entitled *The Embarkation of the Pilgrims*.) The artist found a great admirer in his British friend, who predicted a great future for him in art and who was to leave the States in happy possession of a Weir drawing.

As he finalized the pages of his two-volume memoir, Hamilton turned to the subjects of the American press and American religion. Though as we have seen he had already expressed some views on these themes, he clearly felt that more commentary was due. Every Englishman, he contended, was surely struck by the poor quality of American newspapers as compared with those of his own country. He examined the papers circulating in all parts of the United States, and found them utterly contemptible in their pretense of talent; they concerned themselves with such base abuses as to bring on a feeling of indignation not only toward the journalists who penned them but toward the public who eagerly bought them and thus afforded them support. Political discussion in American papers seemed to be sparked, in the view of Hamilton, not by an appeal to enlightened argument and acknowledged principles but by an appeal to the vilest passions of the population. Because an editor is aware of the 'swallow' of his American readership, he offers nothing that would stick in the gullet of the reader. Hamilton's assault on the American press led him to acknowledge the lengths to which political hostility in Britain was often carried in the press:

> Our newspaper and periodical press is bad enough. Its sins against propriety cannot be justified, and ought not to be defended. But its violence is meekness, its liberty restraint, and even its atrocities are virtues, when compared with that system of brutal and ferocious outrage which distinguishes the press in America.[14]

And why was there this profound discrepancy? Hamilton felt that there was an easy explanation: newspapers were so cheap in the United States that they depended for support on the most ignorant class of the people and therefore were indifferent to refinement of both language and reasoning. In Britain, where papers were expensive, they catered for the most part to a class of comparative wealth and education. It was therefore the British visitor's fervent hope that the stamp duty levied on British papers would be maintained for years to come.

As he prepared to return home, the traveler reflected on his recorded impressions of the emerging American nation. He recognized, of course, that they were largely unfavorable, but he felt that it was to a country's benefit that errors and inconsistencies be unsparingly detected. The traveler thereupon urged 'enlightened' Americans who visited his own country to record their impressions of her institutions with the very same spirit of detachment.

CHAPTER 6

The American Debut of Fanny Kemble

'B Y MY TROTH, I am not nervous,'[1] avowed Fanny Kemble to visitors who called at her hotel some hours before she was to make her first appearance on a New York City stage. The English actress was under contract for an extended engagement in the city and, on that eighteenth day of September in 1832, she would mount the boards at the Park Theatre just opposite the public gardens fronting City Hall. New Yorkers, it seems, were in a fever of anticipation. 'There is no doubt that we shall be furnished with a theatrical treat of the highest order,' exulted the erstwhile mayor Philip Hone, then a leading social figure in the city.[2] He was right to be so expectant, for young Fanny Kemble had become the latest sensation in London acting circles and now, traveling with her father Charles Kemble – also a renowned actor – she had crossed the Atlantic to face the traditional uncertainties of show business, this time in the New World. Why was she not somewhat fearful? How could she claim that she was not nervous? 'Not because I feel sure of success,' she confided to her journal that afternoon,

> for I think it very probable the Yankees may like to show their critical judgment and independence by damning me; but because, thank God, I do not care whether they do or not; the whole thing is too loathsome to me, for either failure or success to affect me in the least, and therefore I feel neither nervous nor anxious about it.[3]

The Yankees assuredly did not damn her. True, they were still smarting from the assaults on American culture published just a few years earlier by Frances Trollope and her compatriot Basil Hall, but there was no sign of a lingering hostility that would be sensed by the young visitor. On the contrary, the 23-year-old actress could thrill to the roar of their resounding applause when the curtain came down on her sparkling performance as Bianca in Henry Hart Milman's *Fazio*. 'I have never witnessed an audience so moved, astonished, and delighted,' declared Philip Hone, for whom the theater had long been a great passion:

> Her display of the strong feelings which belong to the part was great beyond description, and the expression of her wonderful face would have been a rich treat if her tongue had uttered no sound. The fifth act was such an exhibition of female powers as we have never before witnessed, and the curtain fell amid the deafening shouts and plaudits of an astonished audience.[4]

It was an extraordinary Yankee response to her Gotham debut: How did Fanny Kemble herself react to the adulation? No doubt she was flushed with success but, as was her wont, she preferred to make light of it, remarking only that she 'got through very satisfactorily'. At the start of the play, tingles of apprehension had flooded her spirit for fear that her co-star William Keppel would muddle his part.[5] But she was able to overcome all fears, not only because of her uncommon self-discipline, but also in part because she placed great confidence in the support provided by her theatrical wardrobe. The gowns designed for her part as Bianca were very beautiful and would please the audience, she knew. Ever conscious of dress, Fanny had carefully seen to all of her stage costumes and had lugged them across the Atlantic in huge boxes. (The bodice she wore for her Covent Garden debut as Juliet, and again in her New York appearances, survives to this day as an American holding.) The Yankees, it would prove, were beguiled by both her appearance and her performances in the ensuing weeks whenever she appeared on stage. The actress's own account of her American experiences was to be daily logged in her journal, which she eventually published.

The first entries in that diary of the New World attest to a nostalgic leave-taking of England with the young actress tearfully clutching 'a bunch of dear English flowers'. Subsequently, as she traveled across the Atlantic, she learned what it was like to spend more than a month in cramped quarters at sea. Passengers shared ship space with 'cocks crowing, and the cow lowing, and geese and ducks gabbling as though we were in a farm-yard'. Often seasick during the course of the long thirty-five days, Fanny invariably overcame her misery to do a good bit of reading (Dante, Byron and Shelley are mentioned); sewing (she made two nightcaps); and translating (she rendered a fable and parts of the German Bible into English in order to improve her command of German). For the amusement of other travelers on board she sang and recited from the classics. We learn that sometimes in a calm a boat was lowered to let male passengers go rowing – 'I wanted to go but they would not let me go!' writes Fanny. On one occasion wild seas tossed her dinner into her lap; on another she comforted a passenger terrified by a raging tempest. While crossing the Atlantic, a good night's sleep was seldom to be had: she found her berth wanting and the word 'bed' a frightful misapplication of the term. 'Oh for a bed! a real bed! any manner of bed!' she yearned in the pages of her diary. Yet none of these setbacks overshadowed a poetic appreciation of ocean travel that Fanny often invoked. She rhapsodized: 'I have seen a universe of air and water. I have seen the glorious sun look down upon this rolling sapphire.'

On their arrival in Manhattan, the Kembles took rooms in the American Hotel on fashionable Broadway, across from the green that faced City Hall and not far from the theater. Everything that transpired in New York would prove to be of interest to the English newcomer who often viewed the city from a London perspective. Her irrepressible interest in the latest fashions led to people-watching out of her hotel window, where 'the park (as they entitle the green opposite our windows) is so very pretty and the streets so gay, with their throngs of smartly dressed people, that I find my window the most entertaining station in the world.' At the time of the Kembles' visit, Manhattan was still more a stretch of undulating meadows (with animals roaming in parts of the town) than a macadamized city. What constituted the town proper barely reached beyond Fourteenth Street, rendering it possible for town dwellers to make it on foot almost anywhere. As was her wont wherever she went, Fanny took to walking enthusiastically, observing with eager eyes everything in her stride – people, places, mores and amenities. Yet all the while she was committed to memorizing long passages for her star appearance on stage most nights.

During the next few weeks of the Kembles' residence in Manhattan, the actress was to appear in an astonishing variety of plays – often with her acclaimed father – all of which garnered flattering notices. Following *Fazio*, she charmed American audiences with Richard Brinsley Sheridan's *The School for Scandal* ('It's so English, how do they ever understand?' she wrote in her journal), Thomas Otway's *Venice Preserved* ('With Mr. Keppel who did not appear to me to know the words even'), George Farquhar's *The Inconstant* ('Played Bizarre for the first time. Acted so-so, looked very pretty'), James Sheridan Knowles's *The Hunchback* ('Wore my red satin and looked like a bonfire'), and Shakespeare's *King John*, *Romeo and Juliet* and *Much Ado about Nothing*.[6] These dramas represent kaleidoscopic changes in thespian tempo and a prodigious number of lines to commit to memory, yet Fanny appears never to have been fazed by the challenges, except for wishing that she could be equally sure of the others appearing on stage with her. We learn from her journal how indignant she became when a fellow actor faltered in his movements or stumbled over his lines; she was, more often than not, unhappy with William Keppel as a co-star. She went on stage thinking him highly unsuited for the role of

Fazio in Milman's play, terming him 'that washed out man' in her diary. During rehearsal he kept forgetting his lines, and when the curtain went up on that important evening, his uncertainty as to his positions and crossings on stage was so palpable as to nearly unsettle his leading lady. In the Otway play, her irritation reached fever pitch because not only had she been forced constantly to prompt the ill-favored Keppel (who 'stuck' to her skirts, she claimed), but once, 'after struggling in vain to free myself from him, was obliged in the middle of my part to exclaim "you hurt me dreadfully Mr. Keppel!" He clung to me, cramped me; crumpled me, – dreadful!'[7]

For all that, *Venice Preserved* delighted the audience (even Keppel was applauded, though Fanny determined not to go on the stage again with 'that gentleman' for a hero). Here was a strong-minded young lady with an intellectual grasp of the theater, and with sights set most perceptively on what constituted a good play, good acting, appropriate sets, striking costumes and inspired interpretation of the role. Only when these components of stagecraft were brought to their highest pitch were they worthy of applause, or worthy of the kind of giddy adulation that greeted actors: nothing less, in her view, warranted approbation. But show business, as was well known to Fanny, was notoriously fickle; no player, manager, or director could ultimately control the reception of a play or any ensuing histrionic incongruities. The very incontrovertibility of this fact led her to denounce what she called the 'worthless clapping of hands'. Applause that was undeserved, the voluble actress insisted, 'is what, by the nature of my craft, I am bound to care for; I spit at it [my craft] from the bottom of my soul!'[8]

Strong language. Theater-goers in New York would have been perplexed to learn that Fanny Kemble was a reluctant actress, even after several years of being at the top of her calling. She had overcome the doubts that she had entertained from the beginning as to the wisdom of contemplating a stage career, writing at the age of eighteen to a London friend:

> Nature has certainly not been as favourable to me as might have been wished, if I am to embrace a calling where personable beauty, if not indispensable is so great an advantage. But if the informing spirit be mine, it shall go hard if, with a face and voice as obedient

to my emotions as mine are, I do not in some measure make up for the want of good looks.[9]

How prescient were these remarks to prove! Though formally untrained for the stage, she had mastered the theater's demands and not for a moment was her lack of beauty called into question, for she brought to her roles an uncommon level of feeling. Yet the nature of the acting profession constantly prompted deep introspection. She would often ask herself: What do these appearances ultimately make of me? What have I become? 'I am an actress, a mimicker, a sham creature – me [...] how I do loathe my most impotent and unpoetical craft!' Particularly surprising are such thoughts for someone whose 1829 debut in Covent Garden had riveted the attention of all who were there. 'All of us were in love with you,' declared William Makepeace Thackeray, who figured among the throng of discerning admirers that October night in London.[10]

Fanny's disdain for her profession seems even more surprising in light of the fact that her father, Charles Kemble, was an eminent Shakespearean actor whose interpretations she admired wholeheartedly.[11] When she heard him in the role of Hamlet, she made the judgment that it was impossible 'to conceive Hamlet more truly, or execute it more exquisitely than he does. The refinement, the tenderness, the grace, dignity and princely courtesy with which he invests it from beginning to end enchanted me.' Moreover, her mother Maria Theresa de Camp and many other family members had also been on the stage. Her uncle John Philip Kemble was a distinguished thespian, and still more renowned was her father's sister, Sarah Kemble Siddons. Fanny too had an abiding passion for Shakespeare's plays, long passages of which she could recite at will; she was well versed in the literature of her country and she could boast fluency in French and Italian as well as a fair grasp of German that provided entry to foreign drama and classics. By the age of seventeen she had already written a play entitled *Francis the First*, which was later performed in Covent Garden and published in several editions.

In all of these ways Fanny was intimately tied to the theater, but her vaunted hope was to be a dramatist, not an actress. She was abruptly ushered onto the stage by her parents in order to save her father from bankruptcy: he owned a share of the then failing Covent Garden Theatre, and a new face was desperately needed to attract larger audiences. Urged on by her parents, the young Fanny (then twenty years old) filled the role splendidly and rescued her father from the financial morass in which he found himself. Still, she considered that she had been launched 'in an arduous profession, travelling from city to city in its exercise'.[12] She was also constantly troubled by a nagging feeling that being an actress robbed her of a certain nobility.

Well, acting had certainly not entered the ranks of what were considered exalted professions in either Britain or the United States by the 1830s, though the theater had no want of ticket buyers flocking to its doors for diversion. In the New World, the vices of the theater were denounced from the pulpit throughout many areas of the developing country; still, New York City's reputation as dynamic and daring was too well established for the Church to hold sway. Religion had scarcely been a consideration in settling Manhattan as it had elsewhere in the New World: rather it was the lure of trade and its profits that had beckoned colonists to its Atlantic shores. Had not Thomas Jefferson been moved to describe the fledgling seaport as 'a cloacina of all the depravities of human nature'?[13] Because the acting profession was seen as contributing to these 'depravities', many eighteenth- and nineteenth-century families (whether in New York or across the Atlantic) would not admit thespians of any rank or popularity into their homes. It was inevitable, then, that polemical argument about the immoral atmosphere emanating from playhouses would make its way into the New York drawing rooms where Fanny was invited. Now an acclaimed figure in theatrical life on both sides of the Atlantic, the vivacious performer was quick to defend the merits of the theater despite her personal misgivings about the acting profession:

> Were the morality that I constantly hear uttered a little more consistent […] I think it might be more deserving of attention and respect. But the mock delicacy, which exists to so great a degree with regard to theatrical exhibitions, can command neither the one nor the other. To those who forbid all dramatic representations, as exhibitions of an unhealthy tendency upon our intellectual and moral nature […] I have but one reply to offer to it: the human mind requires recreation;

is not a theatre, (always supposing it to be, not what theatres too often are, but what they ought to be,) is not a theatre a better, a higher, a more noble and useful place of recreation than a billiard-room, or the bar of a tavern? Perhaps in the course of the moral and intellectual improvement of mankind, all these will give way to yet purer and more refined sources of recreation, but in the mean time, I confess, with its manifold abuses, a play-house appears to me worthy of toleration, if not of approbation, as holding forth [...] a highly intellectual, rational, and refined amusement.[14]

In her extended disquisition on the subject, Fanny went on to refer to plays that were often cited as objectionable, such as Farquhar's *Inconstant*, in which she starred. She upheld the moral thrust of the play while admitting that some of the lines were indeed racy. 'But in spite of the licentiousness of the writing, in many parts, the construction, the motive, the action of the play is not licentious,' she held; 'the characters are far from being utterly debased in their conception, or depraved in the sentiments they utter.'[15]

New York's own defiant reply to the talk of playhouse immorality was to flaunt the presence of several theaters in its midst: they served an 1832 population totaling not quite 250,000. New Yorkers were diverted with plays, operas, recitals, circuses and melodramas that catered to varying levels of cultural taste. For her performances in the city, Fanny Kemble had been engaged to play in the most elegant of its playhouses. The Park Theatre was then under the management of Stephen Price and Edmund Shaw Simpson, whose commitment to attracting star players from abroad boosted the success of their enterprise, particularly among the *haut monde* of the city. Known as the New Theatre when it was built by a consortium of well-to-do New Yorkers in 1797, the Park took its name from its location on Park Row at what was then the northern end of town. After the original structure was destroyed by fire in 1821, the theater was rebuilt at this location, which had been rendered even more desirable a site by the erection there in 1812 of City Hall. The latter building, boasting a dome and rotunda, was one of the more remarkable of its time.

There was little that did not stimulate Fanny's restless intellect during her stay in Gotham – from notions of democracy in the New

World to the reasons for the peculiar stride of American ladies. She found that some democrats in New York were as 'title-sick as a banker's wife in England'.[16] Moreover, she was irked to discover that ill-breeding often passed for a sign of independence. As to the weird shuffle noticeable in the stride of Gotham ladies, she attributed this to an exaggerated imitation of the current French fashions. Fanny's reflections, penned in her journal, provide a lively memoir of Gotham in the early 1830s, a city to which she had come with some reluctance. The journal also proves Fanny to have been uncommonly cultivated, vivacious, and motivated by a strong sense of purpose stemming from her unusual, colorful background. She also proves to have been by turns assertive, willful and condescending. Arriving in New York, she was soon invited to some of the best homes, where one of her hosts reported:

> She appears to be perfectly self-possessed. She talks well, but will only talk when, and to whom she chooses [...] She has certainly an air of indifference and nonchalance not at all calculated to make her a favorite with the beaux [...] I am confirmed in my opinion that she has astonishing requisites for the stage.[17]

This is the voice of ex-mayor Philip Hone, who had attended her smashing debut at the Park Theatre and predicted before he went 'that it would be no half-way affair; she would make the most decided hit we have ever witnessed, or would fail entirely; and so it proved.' Hone was at the time a commanding social figure who entertained New York's most prominent visitors. He had assisted at the highly festive welcome for the Marquis de Lafayette in 1824 and would be at the head of the entertaining committee to honor Charles Dickens in 1842. Hone's mansion was on the same stretch of fashionable Broadway as the American Hotel where the Kemble guests were lodged. Few important happenings in New York escaped either his participation or mention in his diary; there is more than one mention of Fanny for he entertained the Kembles in his home on more than one occasion and eventually they became friends.

As the actress threw herself into New York life with gusto, she was always conscious that she had entered the precincts of a sometimes baffling new world; she identified herself as descended from

Europeans who had wantonly displaced the natives, and as now privy to a great experiment in democracy. The liberal side of her was enthusiastic about a political venture in equality, but her upbringing in a time-honored monarchy prompted strong skepticism. She sincerely believed that a republic was the highest form of government, yet the 'feeling of rank, of inequality, is inherent in us, a part of the veneration of our natures […] 'tis my conviction that America will be a monarchy before I am a skeleton.'[18] There was much she found to criticize in this upstart of a city, but she was occasionally willing to wax anti-British when it was due, stating that the roughness and want of refinement that were legitimately complained of in America were mitigated by instances of civility that would not be found commonly elsewhere, and in particular that the demeanour of men towards women was infinitely more courteous in the States than in her homeland. She was also conscious that she had arrived close on the heels of another English Fanny – the outspoken novelist Frances Trollope who, as has been noted, gave serious offense with her book *The Domestic Manners of the Americans*, published in the very year of the actress's arrival in America. 'I did not read it,' the younger Fanny avowed, and then made the perspicacious remark that 'she must have spoken the truth though, for lies do not rankle so.'[19]

Still, the bad press given to Frances Trollope did not intimidate the ever-confident Covent Garden star who was inclined to report the scene as she saw it. Her first taste of the daily comforts to be had living in Manhattan left much to be desired. The American Hotel had been recommended to the Kembles – there were three of them: Fanny, her father and her beloved aunt Dall – as the best Gotham had to offer; it was, by her sophisticated reckoning, miserable. (Though located in the best of neighborhoods, it would be considered uninhabitable by today's standards, for the hotel had no bath, private or shared.) Extended ablutions were made in a public facility such as the Arcade, the one Fanny frequented just behind City Hall. Because this seemed European enough to her, she had no complaints, although this was not the case with the hotel's rooms, which she described as 'a mixture of French finery and Irish disorder and dirt […] inferior accommodations and extravagant charges'. Whenever the hotel experienced a sudden influx of visitors, sitting rooms were converted into bedrooms containing four or five beds. The service was trying because the 'number of servants was totally inadequate to the work.' Worst of all was the inundation of mosquitoes and ants:

> The ants swarm on the floors, on the tables, in the beds, about one's clothes: the plagues of Egypt were a joke to them; horrible! it makes one's life absolutely burthensome, to have creatures creeping about one, and all over one, night and day [...] to say nothing of those cantankerous stinging things, the mosquitoes [...] I sit slapping my own face all day, and lie thumping my pillow at night.[20]

How was the fastidious visitor to endure the unendurable? One tried and true way for the cerebral Fanny was to resort to the panacea of conceiving poetry. Perhaps, she told herself, a mocking quatrain inspired by the beloved bard would do it:

> —*To bed — to sleep —*
> *To sleep!—perchance to be bitten! aye—*
> *there's the scratch:*
> *And in that sleep of ours what bugs may come,*
> *Must give us pause.*[21]

Before submitting to interrupted sleep, Fanny would sometimes walk to the Battery in the evening – a distance of two miles from her hotel. Just that year, a sea wall had been erected with a broad flagged walk in front and a row of seats extending the length of the promenade. Here the latest in men's and women's fashions could often be seen, paraded by those who had come to watch the colorful flotillas of incoming and outgoing ships. With its incomparable ocean view, the Battery was an oasis of peace from the noise of the two thousand carts that noisily conveyed merchandise hither and yon in the city's streets. Still, it was the saunter along busy Broadway by day that offered Fanny a glimpse of city life that she never tired of observing. With her passion for the latest in fine clothes, she scrutinized New York's female population, particularly those who were wealthy enough to afford the requisite change of attire several times a day (from walking dress to carriage dress to dinner dress to evening dress). As had other travelers, she found a good many of New York's women extravagantly turned out: 'They never walk in the streets but in the most showy and extreme toilette, and I have known twenty, forty and sixty dollars paid for a bonnet to wear in a morning saunter up Broadway.' Her own penchant for eye-catching headgear led her to give loving attention to a prized bonnet made for her in London and brought over in one of the twenty-one large boxes of props and costumes. Dismayed to find that the bonnet had been 'squeezed to a crush' en route, 'I pulled it out, rebowed, and reblonded [sic], and reflowered it, and now it looks good.'[22]

Outside of New York, the English visitor extended her observations of American life with excursions into the countryside. She particularly enjoyed turtle hunts across the Hudson, boat rides up the river, and, most of all, galloping astride a splendid horse. Fanny was, by all accounts, a fine equestrienne, smartly turned out as she sought every opportunity to ride. Ah, but what miserable steeds the New World had to offer!

> The horses here are none of them properly broken; their usual pace being a wrong-legged half canter, or a species of shambling trot denominated with infinite justice a rack. They are all broken with snaffles instead of curbs, carry their nose out, and pull horribly; I have not yet seen a decent rider, man or woman.[23]

On evenings when she was to appear on stage she could walk if she chose, rather than ride in a hackney stage or mount a horse: there was but a short distance from her hotel to the Park Theatre. On her first visit to the playhouse, Fanny had registered no disappointments: she found it handsome and well designed, with lots of gold carving and red silk about it 'looking rich and warm'.[24] Engraved views of the city in the 1830s invariably featured the exterior of the Park Theatre as one of the city's striking buildings; Fanny reckoned that it was about the size of the Haymarket in London. With a frontage of eighty feet on Park Row and seven doors opening into a good-sized vestibule, the Park was considered quite palatial in its day, for example in an early-nineteenth-century watercolor of the interior by John Searle showing a packed house. Three tiers of boxes were offset by three chandeliers, each bearing thirty-five oil lamps, while lighting in less grand playhouses about town relied on candles ringed around a hanging barrel hoop. Accommodation in the Park Theatre's pit, however, was still primitive, since it had not yet evolved into the parterre of later years that housed the best seats in a playhouse. Women of the 1830s were never seen in the pit, nor would-be gentlemen, for who would choose to sit on backless benches ranged on a floor that was dirty and riddled with holes? 'The place was pervaded with evils smells,' according to a Victorian observer, 'and, not uncommonly, in the midst of a performance, rats ran out of holes in the floor and across into the orchestra.'[25] Surely this deterioration transpired long after the Kembles had gone, for Fanny does not mention a population of rodents competing with her for the audience's attention; nor does she accord the ignominy of their presence a vituperative quatrain.

The theatrical season of 1832 to 1833 at the Park has gone on record as being the most brilliant in the playhouse's history. Following appearances there, the Kembles played in Philadelphia, Washington, DC, and Boston, before returning to New York for further performances. While in Philadelphia, the actress makes brief mention of the excitement that was palpable surrounding the coming election of the next American president. The streets were very full of men, she noted, hurrying to the 'town house to give their votes'. The political contest at the time was between the rugged Andrew Jackson and the eloquent Henry Clay; while Fanny believed that the 'aristocratic' party (i.e. the Whigs) was the stronger of the two political parties, this proved not to be the case. The ever-popular Jackson was elected for a second term and, to a certain extent, was able to shift the power of the Congress to the presidency. If Fanny entertained any notions that America would move toward the establishment of a monarchy, she was witness to the fact that the Jackson–Clay contest led most assuredly in the opposite direction. For Jackson was proud to identify himself with the common man, sharing his mistrust of special privileges and, indeed, of breeding; he was far removed from the ideals of Thomas Jefferson, who had aspired to a nation in which educated patricians governed for the good of the masses. Jackson's opponent Henry Clay ran for the presidency more than once and was each time defeated. Still, he would forever be known as one of America's most eloquent speakers, a talent he put to passionate use in the cause of the emancipation of slaves. Had they met, the actress would surely have enjoyed a friendship with him, for he was a highly skilled equestrian.

Fanny was to spend two years treading the American boards; she was a success wherever she went, attracting admirers young and old. Her stay in Philadelphia would become notable, however, for more than stage appearances. While she was in the Quaker City, one of the more distinguished among the gentlemen who became part of her social circle was the artist Thomas Sully. He limned several handsome likenesses of her and particularly enjoyed depicting her in some of the notable roles that she played. (Sully also painted a portrait of the young Queen Victoria that is admired to this day.) Fanny prized her portraits by Sully, and the two developed a warm friendship, but her most ardent admirer was a socialite from the Quaker City named Pierce Butler, who was to become her husband. He and Thomas Sully were cousins. The first mention of Butler in Fanny's journal, dated 13 October 1832, is a cryptic entry but does not fail to refer to his fortune: 'He was a pretty spoken, genteel youth enough; he drank tea with us and offered to ride with me. He has, it seems, a great fortune; consequently, I suppose, in spite of his inches, a great man.'

It was probably much to everyone's surprise that Fanny returned Butler's affection and married him in 1834. Indeed, she gave up her acting career for him, writing finis to her Park Theatre ovations. 'You know that in leaving the stage I left nothing that I regretted,'[26] she wrote to a friend with that consistent posture of detachment from her craft. But she was otherwise to regret the marriage: it gave her few years of happiness. Notwithstanding the fact that Pierce Butler had married a lady of the stage, he did not permit members of the acting profession into his home. Friction between the two heightened immeasurably on Butler's inheritance of a slave-holding plantation in Georgia, for much to the horror of her uncompromising spouse, the liberal, high-minded Fanny proved a staunch abolitionist. Two daughters born early in the marriage were to become the actress's lifelong pride and joy, though she lost custody of them in the acrimonious court proceedings leading to a divorce. 'One reason, and perhaps the fundamental one, for the ill success which attended my marriage,' declared Pierce Butler in a published statement, 'can readily be found in the peculiar views

which were entertained by Mrs. Butler on the subject of marriage [...]
She held that marriage should be companionship on equal terms.'[27]
It was a truly astonishing statement. Fanny proved too vibrant, too
assertive, and endowed with too strong a sense of self to be held in
the kind of marital bondage that the Philadelphia scion demanded.
And her strong feelings against the institution of slavery, which she
had witnessed first-hand on the Butler plantation in the South, led her
to write a scathing denunciation of that practice entitled *Journal of a
Residence on a Georgian Plantation in 1838–1839*. It became one of
her best-known publications.

Following the divorce in 1849, Fanny Kemble Butler divided her
time between England, the Continent and the United States, ever passionately discoursing on the intellectual issues of the day. She proved
her independence by establishing a new reputation as a public *diseuse*;
her readings of Shakespeare in the US and abroad were overwhelmingly popular in the ensuing decades. Philip Hone, who was an enduring friend and attended readings in the spring of 1849, reported fully
on the New York scene:

> Mrs. Butler, the veritable 'Fanny Kemble', has taken the city by storm.
> She reads Shakespeare's plays three evenings in the week, and at
> noon on Mondays, at the Stuyvesant Institution, in Broadway, a room
> which will hold six or seven hundred persons, and which is filled
> when she reads by the elite of the world of fashion: delicate women,
> grave gentlemen, belles, beaux, and critics, flock to the doors of the
> entrance, and rush into such places as they can find, two or three
> hours before the time of the lady's appearance. They are compensated
> for the tedious sitting on hard seats, squeezed by the crowd, by an
> hour's reading – very fine, certainly, for Fanny Kemble knows how
> to do it – of the favorite plays of the immortal bard. She makes $2,000
> or $3,000 a week, and never was money so easily earned. There is
> no expense except the room and the lights, and the performance is
> a 'labor of love'. Shakespeare was never paid for writing his plays as
> Mrs. Butler is for reading them.[28]

While Hone probably exaggerated the dollar figures, it is clear that
through the readings, Fanny became financially independent. Ten

years later she was again admired for her vocal resources when she gave readings of Shakespeare in New York. The notable Manhattan lawyer George Templeton Strong, writing in his diary for 15 January 1859, felt on hearing her recite *The Tempest* that she had 'half a dozen voices in her; drew a separate stop for each character; produced a deep, sullen, brute roar and snarl for Caliban that seem an impossibility from any feminine windpipe.'[29]

To the end of her days, Fanny Kemble was a vibrant force wherever she went, exercising a talent for conversation that attracted a host of admirers. The erstwhile actress's exuberance once led her to exclaim to a friend: 'How much delight there is in the exercise of our faculties. How full a thing, and admirable, and wonderful, is this nature of ours!'[30] Well past the age of sixty-five, Kemble learned to use the newfangled machine known as a typewriter for her literary pursuits. At the age of eighty, she ventured into a new exercise of her faculties by writing a novel. There was about Fanny Kemble, declared the novelist Henry James, an incomparable 'abundance of being'.[31]

CHAPTER 7

The American Odyssey of Harriet Martineau

T HE YOUNG ENGLISHWOMAN who took passage aboard the
sailing ship *United States* – alighting in the New World on 4
August 1834 – had been steadily accumulating fame on both
sides of the Atlantic. Of French Huguenot descent, Harriet Martineau
was an author of some distinction when she fixed on the notion of a
trip to America, planning an odyssey of two long years in a world that
shared her language but was otherwise unknown. Possessed of a
remarkable intelligence, as well as a proclivity for measured judgment,
she had put her talents to writing a series of so-called *Illustrations of
Political Economy*, which won her a number of prizes in England and
also charted paths in the incipient field of political science. In time

her output as writer would reach a count of well over fifty books, among them numerous novels and a translation of the works of the philosopher Auguste Comte, and would gain her a role as a leading editorialist for the *London Daily News*. Through the force of her personality and her writings, she had accumulated a wide circle of friends among the English intelligentsia. Erasmus Darwin courted her for a time, while his brother Charles, who found her decidedly homely, deemed her views compelling. Her decision to endure so long a trip away from England was made without any consideration of the fact that she was severely disabled: she was deaf, as well as afflicted with virtually no sense of taste or smell. Accompanying her to the far side of the Atlantic were three indispensable companions: a young lady by the name of Louisa Jeffrey and two ear trumpets. The daughter of William Makepeace Thackeray would make the pronouncement to her father that Miss Martineau was one of the most sensible women in all of England. Clearly, she was indomitable as well.

Martineau arrived in Jacksonian America at a time when the issue of slavery was moving into the forefront of political discussion and assuming a markedly passionate tone. Disembarking in New York and then making her way through locations in the northeast, the 32-year-old traveler found in this area of the country views that were compatible with her abolitionist stance, but did her best nonetheless to avoid prolonged discussions of the matter. She had charted for herself a definite itinerary throughout the country and was anxious to be found acceptable wherever she went. Her contacts on the western side of the Atlantic were impressive, numbering influential friends in political as well as social circles: throughout her journey she would make ample use of them, often enjoying accommodation in sumptuous homes that spared her the experience of uncomfortable boarding houses.

At the time of Martineau's visit, the United States was far from being fully formed: though it had recently acquired the territory of Florida from the Spanish, that important area with its open access to the sea would not achieve statehood until 1845. Further west, the country had been doubled in size as the result of the Louisiana Treaty concluded under the presidency of Thomas Jefferson just three decades earlier, while areas in a wide stretch of the land bordering the Pacific were still in Spanish or French hands. That the character of each region in this new world was influenced by its European origins was acutely observed by Martineau, who was also well aware that territories newly acquired gained their admission into the Union – following the Missouri Compromise of 1820 – as either slave or free states. This latter distinction would have significant bearing on how she was received as she went from one part of the country to another. Travelers espousing the cause of abolitionism were not only unwelcome in the South but, as she would discover, in various sectors of the North.

From the very start of her travels, the ever-alert Martineau made keen observations. She had looked forward to her transoceanic passage with great eagerness and dutifully recorded all that transpired aboard the packet ship *United States*. Much excitement was to be found, she reported, in watching a shoal of porpoises come to race with the ship, or being the first, as the days went by, to spot a sailboat that would come close in line with the packet. There were the hazards of sea travel, of course, and these are listed systematically by the traveler: a desperate want of room (remedy: keep everything in tight order), seasickness, the hardness of the beds, the constant burning out of candles, the stringent use of water, the low supply of cider that could be carried, the rattling overhead of the sails when they were shifted at night and the looming danger (in summer) of getting sunburned. There were, of course, other occasional problems, such as one of the sheep jumping overboard and thereby diminishing the supply of mutton for supper. Landfall was finally made in New York after forty-four days on the high seas. Though the moment of first setting foot in a foreign city, she comments, is commonly spoken of as a perfect realization of forlornness, her experience was to the contrary: 'New York always afterwards bore an air of gaiety to me from the association of the early pleasures of foreign travel.'[1] Initially, the English visitor did not spend much time in Manhattan after disembarking in the city, though she reports that she received 'trains of callers' at the boarding house in which lodgings had been procured. There were members of Congress, candidates for State offices, fellow passengers, and 'other friends of our friends', who came to visit, very few of whom she identifies by name. She found neither Broadway nor the city's architecture remarkable, nor was the boarding house a place in which she cared to linger. Nonetheless, after far more than a month of rolling seas, the fact that the furniture in the rented room stood solidly in place appeared quite worthy of her praise. And is it not also quite worthy of praise that the energetic traveler could manage, while on the uncertain rolling seas, to write the first draft of a major treatise? Entitled *How to Observe Morals and Manners*, the book, subsequently published in London, was to be deemed a major pioneering work in sociology.

During the course of her brief stay in Manhattan, the author met with several politicians of prominence, but declined in her written account to elaborate on her impressions because of 'the want of interest in the English about the great men of America'. This she attributed to the fact that most American papers were so in the habit of reviling anyone in political office that little interest was engendered abroad even in the activities of such powerful statesmen of the time as Henry Clay or John Calhoun; indeed, 'every man of feeling and taste recoils from wading through such a slough of rancor, folly and falsehood as the American newspapers present.' What gave Martineau pleasure during her limited Manhattan stay was attendance at a Unitarian Sunday meeting where the devotional service was delivered in a voice never equaled in all her experience for 'music and volume'. (This laudatory comment was made at a time when Martineau was a leading writer for the *Monthly Repository*, an important Unitarian periodical.) The astute traveler then closed the chapter of her visit to the busy city with a most surprising observation:

> One of the first impressions of a foreigner in New York is of the extreme insolence and vulgarity of certain young Englishmen, who thus make themselves very conspicuous. Well-mannered Englishmen are scarcely distinguishable from the natives, and thus escape observation; while every commercial traveler who sneers at republicanism all day long, and every impertinent boy, leaving home for the first time, with no understanding or sympathy for anything but what he has been accustomed to see at home, obtrudes himself upon the notice. I was annoyed this evening, on my return home, by a very complete specimen of the last-mentioned order of travelers.[2]

Martineau was soon off on a boat trip up the Hudson, where the high points of that excursion were a visit to West Point Academy (admirably conducted, she found) and, ultimately, after traveling overland to Buffalo, the thunder and majesty of Niagara Falls. Every foreign visitor was expected to wax ecstatic at the apparition of this natural wonder, but in the three volumes entitled *Retrospect of Western Travel* resulting from her New World trip, the English traveler made it a point to refrain from poetic exuberance on paper. 'To offer an idea of Niagara by writing of hues and dimensions,' she wrote, 'is much like representing the kingdom of Heaven by images of jasper and topazes.'[3] Still, never being at a loss for words, she devotes an entire chapter to the experience.

A topic that appeared to interest Martineau somewhat more than Niagara was the condition of prisons in the Unites States. She had been convinced that the system of solitary confinement pursued at the Eastern State Prison in Philadelphia was the best that had yet been adopted, and certainly this was the reputation it had in England. A visit to that very prison, however, lessened the admiration entertained for this mode of punishment. The visitor found the convicts, almost without exception, looking pale and haggard owing to the bad ventilation of their cells and to the circumstances in which they were held. What she deemed appalling was that the prisoners were denied the 'forgetfulness' of themselves and their miseries, a forgetfulness that would most certainly be likely to come about in the play of conversation now forbidden to them. A fundamental postulate in the management of the guilty, she proffered, was to treat them as men and women, for was not their humanity the principal thing about all of them? Their guilt, she held, was only a temporary state. The sympathetic English traveler was apparently allowed to make a fair number of visits to the prison, during the course of which she had personal conversations with an unusual number of inmates; she relates some of them with great feeling. She was aware, as a social reformer, that much remained to be done in terms of coming to an accord regarding what would be considered the most just treatment of prisoners. While the system of solitary confinement was deemed by many to constitute a work of mercy compared with harsher punishments, Martineau was convinced that milder and more just methods of treating moral turpitude should certainly be found. Until that time, she had nonetheless been persuaded that imposed silence was the best method of punishment that had yet been tried.

Following the visit to Philadelphia, Martineau spent a brief period in Maryland, where she was conscious that she had now set foot for the first time in a slave state. She had, of course, come across black people in the populations up north, but they were all free citizens. While she truly desired to see the workings of the slave system first-hand, she dreaded 'inexpressibly' the first sight of a slave and could not help speculating on the lot of every black person she initially saw. When she was told that the 'handsome mulatto' who had served her tea at a friend's house in Baltimore was a slave, she was surprised that she had encountered first-hand someone of his class but was 'glad it was over for once. I never lost the painful feeling caused to a stranger by intercourse with slaves. To see slaves is not to be reconciled to slavery.'[4]

Martineau looked forward to spending time in the Capitol, where she had all the proper contacts for gaining first-hand knowledge of government operations, politics being a subject in which she took a very informed interest. Here was the seat of the noble experiment known as democracy, which in its Declaration of Independence had abolished class distinctions and promised its citizens an egalitarianism previously unknown in Western societies. What, indeed, was the true nature of this egalitarianism? It was a question she pondered as she met politicians who had a direct bearing on the issue: President Andrew Jackson, Supreme Court judges, the aging Chief Justice John Marshall and distinguished members of Congress. She found her attendance at the sessions in the Senate particularly rewarding, judging that the Senate represented a most imposing assemblage of politicians:

No English person who has not travelled over half the world can form an idea of such differences among men forming one assembly for the same purposes, and speaking the same language. Some were descended from Dutch farmers, some from French Huguenots, some from Scotch Puritans, some from English cavaliers, some from Irish Chieftans. They were brought together out of law courts, sugar fields, merchants' stores, mountain farms, forests, and prairies. The stamp of originality was impressed upon every one, and inspired a deep, involuntary respect.[5]

During her five weeks' stay in Washington, she was entertained at the highest political and social levels, beginning with dinner in the home of President Jackson, with whom she had a prolonged conversation; she found that his slow manner of speaking betokened the fact that his time 'had not been passed reading books'. Indeed, Jackson was the very first of America's presidents to shed any signs of refinement, and though born an Anglo-Irish subject was exceedingly anti-British (in no small part because he was the last United States president to have been a veteran of the American Revolutionary War). While many in America considered him far too uncouth, it was his unabashed straightforwardness that won him his popularity and election as seventh president. Martineau was well aware of the contradictions in Jackson's personality: here was someone who relished his role as a so-called true man of the people, yet he counted among the country's rich slave-owners. Clearly, her abolitionist views would hold no weight here.

Like any other eager tourist, Martineau had looked forward to visiting the capital, yet she found Washington most unattractive. Arriving there in January of 1835, she found that:

> The city itself is unlike any other that ever was seen, – straggling out hither and thither, – with a small house or two, a quarter of a mile from any other; so that in making calls 'in the city,' we had to cross ditches and stiles, and walk alternately on grass and pavements, and strike across a field to reach a street. Then, there was the society, singularly compounded from the largest variety of elements – foreign ambassadors, the American Government, members of Congress, flippant young belles, 'pious' wives dutifully attending their husbands, and groaning over the frivolities of the place; grave judges, saucy travelers, pert newspaper reporters, melancholy Indian chiefs, and timid New England ladies.[6]

Little escaped her scrutiny as she made the rounds of the capital's interminable social gatherings. For one thing, the varieties in American manners were particularly conspicuous to her in this political atmosphere: Southerners, with their inherited social style and grace, appeared to the greatest advantage; New Englanders were apparently far too cautious and deferential to be at ease, while the 'odd mortals that wander in from the West cannot be described as a class; for no one is like anybody else.'[7] And there were profound differences in governmental views as well that Martineau's access to official corridors allowed her to witness. She was never certain as to what could be expected from members of either political party, nor from senators and congressmen who shared the same party allegiance. As for the President himself, she discovered, his views were never reliably predictable by anyone who followed the course of his tenure: he was to invoke the presidential veto more than twice as often as his predecessors. It was during this visit to Washington, with its rounds of receptions, formal dinners and social gatherings, that Martineau was able to attest to a rather small but surprising exercise in egalitarianism. Foreign ambassadors, it appeared, continually struggled with the question of hiring proper servants, above all in the function of high-level gatherings with heads of state. For the British ambassador, matters were always at crisis as tradition demanded livery for any solemn occasion. No American, she learned, could ever be found who would wear livery.

A particular honor was bestowed on the young traveler when she made her visit to the Supreme Court: she was offered the reporter's chair, enabling her to hear more comfortably a good segment of the pleading that went on that day; she was also pleased to witness the presence of some remarkable American politicians at court, among them Daniel Webster and Henry Clay. She found Webster a compelling presence and noted how the court filled up after he entered; Clay had meanwhile become a personal friend, for he was an ardent abolitionist. (Both Webster and Clay held views in opposition to Jackson.) There was no doubt in the mind of the British traveler that the two Houses of Congress, plus the Supreme Court, were peopled with men of marked passions and abilities. Because they would often exhibit such violently opposing views whether of the same party or not, it was a wonder to her that laws were eventually promulgated. Indeed, it was during the Jacksonian era that these strongly opposing views, noted by Martineau, had led to the polarization of national politics. Under Jackson, two parties emerged out of the old Democratic-Republican Party, the Democrats and the Whigs, with Jackson identified as a Democrat. (The two politicians admired by the visitor – Webster and Clay – had placed their allegiance with the Whigs.) Martineau was led to remark that it was probably only at state funerals (one of which she attended) that politicians could be seen sitting knee to knee, 'with sentiments shared for the occasion'. All of these small details were of great interest to her, for little in Washington escaped her attention. Her visits to the Supreme Court, to the Senate, to the House of Representatives, and to the Library of Congress not only filled her time in Washington, as did a round of social events; they also filled her notebooks with a wealth of detail. Much of what she recorded would appear in print and would constitute a reliable record of Jacksonian America. Every visitor to Washington, she advises her readers, should spend time visiting the two houses of Congress and the Supreme Court when they are in session, for here could be acquired an indelible impression of democracy at work. In her view, a first-hand impression of American politics, with all its inherent contradictions, could be gained in no other way.

While the political goings-on in Washington greatly absorbed the traveler's attention, she found after a stay of some weeks that the city itself continued to have little appeal, despite several diverting excursions. Indeed, she was thoroughly convinced it would not long hold out as the country's capital. On one of the milder winter days of her stay, she made her way to the dome of the Capitol where she and her party could gain a commanding view of the area and saw, plainly marked out, the basin in which Washington stands surrounded by hills that are interrupted by the waters of the Potomac. There were a few 'mean houses' scattered about, with the sheds of a navy yard on one bank of the Potomac and a few villas on the other. Clearly, there was very little to be admired, she continued to insist, particularly since the allotted space had been intended to be 'busy and magnificent'. Martineau thereupon came to a sweeping conclusion:

> The city is a grand mistake. Its only attraction is its being the seat of government; and it is thought that it will not long continue to be so. The far-western states begin to demand a more central seat for Congress; and the Cincinnati people are already speculating upon which of their hills or table-lands is to be the site of the new Capitol. Whenever this change takes place [and she was most certain it would], all will be over with Washington: 'thorns shall come up in her palaces And the owl and the raven shall dwell in it.'[8]

This would appear to be a bit of wishful thinking on the part of the distinguished traveler, while at the same time it reflects the total want of appeal of America's capital in the early years of the nineteenth century. While Martineau had spent a fair amount of her traveling time in the Potomac River city because of her intense interest in the operation of government, she was apparently glad when the visit ended. She admitted to the satisfaction of gaining political knowledge of the country first-hand but was still 'heartily' glad when it was time to leave. Indeed, the time spent there, she noted, was by far the least agreeable of all her experiences in the United States.

Embarking on a tour of the South, Martineau stopped in the town of Madison, located in the state of Virginia, where she had been invited by ex-president James Madison and his wife to visit for a few days. She found the aging politician with as keen a mind as ever, expressing views on many topics ranging from the theories of Malthus to the Corn Laws of Britain, but never was he more animated than when talking about slavery, when the erstwhile President ridiculed the idea that states with a slave population could ever maintain an uprising against the North. In this he proved clairvoyant. From Madison the traveler hurried on to Charlottesville, where she was anxious to visit the University of Virginia, declaring herself the first foreign traveler to do so. She was, of course, impressed by the lofty ambitions of the university, but though its physical setting and placement of buildings truly constitute the highpoint of Thomas Jefferson's architectural plans, she did not dwell on the uniqueness of this elaborate design. Yet it is without doubt that the aging ex-president had conceived of something extraordinary in planning the education of the nation's aspiring intellectuals. His vision for a prominent university in the South was of an 'academical village' rather than one large central building that would define the school's architectural profile. For this innovative scheme, he drew inspiration from Louis XIV's favorite chateau at Marly, which he had visited. Ten 'pavilions' were erected, five each in rectangular rows terminating in an impressive rotunda, with interlacing gardens and trees a vital part of the planning. When the university opened its doors in 1825, it was clear that Jefferson had been able to orchestrate the practical and aesthetic elements of conceiving a university into a learning unit of remarkable balance and beauty. Martineau was no doubt aware of the uniqueness of the place, for certainly she could compare it favorably with the remarkable universities of England, but she gave her attention at some length to the scope and efficacy of the nine professorships assigned to the university. It was a source of wonder to her why no provision had been made for a professor of Divinity.

At this point in her odyssey Martineau had done a good bit of travelling, yet there was much more time to be spent on the road ahead. There was no end to the cautions that had been given her against journeying through the Southern states, not only in view of her abolitionist stance but on practical grounds: she was warned of the poor condition of most roads and the poverty of wayside accommodations. For the most part, she had traveled by stagecoach; a fair amount was done by canal boat or small ships on the Hudson and Mississippi rivers. She also journeyed by rail when that was possible, and occasionally on horseback; her claim is that she was never upset but once in a coach during all her travels. Indeed, the worse the roads, 'the more I was amused at the variety of devices by which we would go on, through difficulties which appeared insurmountable, and the more I was edified at the gentleness with which our drivers treated female fears and fretfulness.'[9] It was via rail and stage that she journeyed further south to visit friends in South Carolina, Georgia and Alabama.

Charleston, she found, deserved its renown for hospitality. Carriages were provided at the hotel whenever needed and servants arrived to carry out any orders of the day. Additionally, there were always small touches of courtesy that never escaped her attention:

> There was scarcely a morning during our stay when some pretty present did not arrive before I rose: sometimes it was a bouquet of hyacinths, which were extremely rare that year [...] sometimes it was a dish of preserve or marmalade; sometimes a feather fan, when the day promised to be hot; sometimes a piece of Indian work [...] One morning, I found on my window seat a copy of the Southern Review, [...] a bouquet of hyacinths [...] a basket of wafers, [... and] a set of cambric handkerchiefs, inimitably marked with complimentary devices.[10]

Martineau deemed such gestures pleasant enough; nonetheless, the stops made throughout the Southern territories were all overshadowed for her by the presence of slavery. She held to her resolve that she would never broach this painful subject in any household where she was a guest; still, the issue of slavery was inevitably a topic of conversation in most places that she visited inasmuch as her abolitionist views were widely known. Not unexpectedly, various arguments were put forward in the defense of slavery as she went from one slaveholding household in the South to another. She found all of them untenable, including an argument grounded on the narrow premise that human rights were observed when sufficient subsistence was accorded to slaves in return for labor. For the most part, forthright discussions of the slavery issue were assiduously avoided by the British traveler. Then, too, she refrained from dwelling on the issue of her personal safety in the subsequent account of her travels. Because she was an ardent abolitionist, Martineau's life was often threatened during the course of her two-year odyssey. This she learned from friends who would find the occasion to give her proper warning. More of this aspect of her travels emerged when, many years later, her autobiography was published:

> Newspapers came to me from the South, daring me to enter the Slave States again, and offering mock invitations to me to come and see how they would treat foreign incendiaries. They would hang me: they would cut my tongue out, and cast it on a dunghill, and so forth. The calumnies were so outrageous and the appeals to the fears of the Slaveholders so vehement that I could feel no surprise if certain interested persons were moved to plot against my life. I was represented as a hired agent, and appeals were made to popular passions to stop my operations.[11]

Slavery, she firmly believed, diminished both slave and slaveholder.

Martineau was also convinced that almost all the instances of extreme violence perpetrated against abolitionists – floggings in the market place, tarrings and featherings of travelers under suspicion – could be traced to the chicanery of slave-traders and not to ordinary American citizens. The slave-traders on the great rivers were generally foreigners, she held, calling them desperate 'outcasts' from European countries, who would employ any means to silence their enemies and protect their profitable trade. Considering the threats to her life for her stance as an abolitionist, the 32-year-old traveler was brave indeed to continue her journey to slaveholding states; she did, though, have many friends in the South who were concerned for her safety and, happily, nothing ill transpired.

Continuing along the southern rim of the continent, the traveler's next major stop was New Orleans, which she found as unendurable as it was colorful in many aspects with its French and American Creole populations. For one thing, in the month of April the mosquitoes were a perpetual plague (the city stood in a virtual swamp) forcing Martineau and her friends to wear gloves and prunella boots all day long; for another, she found that she could never avoid the horrors of slavery, which she seemed to face here in every guise. Not surprisingly then, she looked forward to leaving the city for her trip on the Mississippi River aboard the *Henry Clay*. This would be a fairly long trip of nine days before she would disembark for her destination in the state of Ohio. As the ship made its way north, she found much to relate in terms of the 'great mixture' of passengers, the routines of dining or playing at chess, and the ever-interesting sights on both sides of the river. She noted that there were slaves on board serving Southern families as well as slaves who made their way to the ship at designated stops carrying trays of provisions on their heads to be deposited on board. Because they passed so many islands in various stages of growth, she compared the experience to 'being set back to the days of creation', and because she found herself in perpetual amazement at the grandeur of the river, she ends her chapter on this trip with the exclamation: 'If there be excess of mental luxury in this life, it is surely in a voyage up the Mississippi, in the bright and leafy month of May.'

Cincinnati was her next major stop – a city that had been tainted in the minds of European readers by the account published by Frances Trollope just three years earlier. Where Mrs. Trollope had painted an overwhelmingly negative account of the Ohio settlement, Martineau found much to praise. She expressed a high respect for the citizens of Cincinnati, not one of whom she felt was without the comforts of life; she noted the handsome private dwellings, the new church of St. Paul, two fine banking houses and the many schools. The one architectural deformity she found in the entire city was the Bazaar built under the direction of Mrs. Trollope. Nonetheless, it was now in a large room of this very building that the first concert ever offered in the city was to be held, featuring the music of Mozart, and Martineau attended with great satisfaction. The opposite Kentucky shore looked rich and beautiful to the visitor, who noted that the river was covered with every kind of craft – steamboats moored six or more abreast – giving a respectful notion of the commerce that distinguished the area. During the course of a drive through the city with a resident physician, all the buildings and schools newly built in 1835 were pointed out to Martineau; the physician also informed her that Cincinnati had one of the most salubrious climates in the area. All of this was most impressive in the eyes of the traveler, as was the view of the city from across the Ohio River. She crossed that river with a group of friends who, on arriving in Covington, were guided in climbing a hill for a better view of Cincinnati. There she perceived that instead of being shut in between two hills, that western Ohio city stands on a noble platform around which the Ohio River turns while the hills rise behind. These many experiences in the region now led Martineau to declare that she would prefer Cincinnati as a residence to any other large American city, not only because of its amenities, but because it was enthroned in a region of inexhaustible beauty.

If the area surrounding Cincinnati held much to admire, so did the entire region much further north of New England that now beckoned to Martineau in the remaining months of her visit. She found the Massachusetts town of Northampton (which was to become the seat of Smith College in 1871) to be among that area's most beautiful, waxing poetic as she pointed out that the 'celebrated Mount Holyoke and Mount Tom are just at hand, and the Sugarloaf [mountain] is in view; while the brimming Connecticut [river] winds about and about in the meadows, as if unwilling, like the traveler, to leave such a spot.'[12] In this area of the country, she had many friends among the intelligentsia. A visit to Amherst College gave much pleasure, for there she was invited to a lecture on geology attended by an uncommon number of girls. She learned that they were from the houses of the farmers and mechanics of the village and could attend if the topic held out any appeal. This was a gladdening sight in her view, for it testified to the eagerness for education among the local population as well as the simplicity of manners. She very much doubted whether such a spectacle was to be seen outside of New England. In the earlier phase of her American visit, Martineau had been invited as a guest to the Harvard University commencement of 1834. It intrigued her to dwell on the fact that the first Harvard commencement was held in 1642, only twenty-two years after the landing of the pilgrims, and that among the contributions toward the founding of this great university had been humble gifts from the surrounding community: these, it charmed her to note, included a peck of corn as well as a flock of sheep.

While traveling throughout the northeast, Martineau visited several institutions for the deaf and the blind. She learned that in 1830 the total number of deaf and mute of all ages in the United States was 6,106, and because the subject was of such personal interest to her devoted an entire chapter in her travel account to her sentiments and experiences. In one institution that she visited, she recounts that:

> I caused my trumpet to be tried on several [pupils] and found that some could hear, and some imitated the sounds conveyed through it. The teachers rather discouraged the trial, and put away all suggestions about the use of these means of getting at the minds of their pupils. They were quite sure that the manual methods of teaching were the only ones by which their charge can profit [...] My own belief is that there are, in these institutions and out of them, many who have been condemned to the condition of mutes who have hearing enough to furnish them with speech, imperfect to the listener, perhaps, but inestimable as an instrument of communication, and of accuracy and enlargement of thought.[13]

Martineau herself had become deaf around the age of twelve, but never dwelt on her handicap, declaring that her trumpet was an instrument of remarkable fidelity. She further felt that it often gained her a degree of intimacy in conversation that was not accorded to the hearing. No doubt this was true: the reader is in total ignorance of her disability when reading any of her remarkable volumes.

Among the noted intelligentsia of the New England area she held the greatest reverence for the mind of Ralph Waldo Emerson, who was a Unitarian (as she was herself) and just a year younger than her. She predicted that he would rise to great intellectual heights and marked him out as one of America's true thinkers, quoting him at length in a chapter entitled 'Originals'. She particularly admired his independence of spirit, which she believed he achieved only through discipline. 'It is an independence equally of thought, of speech, of demeanour, of occupation, and of objects in life: yet without a trace of contempt in its temper, or of encroachment in its action.'[14] Another individual whom the traveler singled out for praise was William Lloyd Garrison, who started life as a printer's boy and went on to become a leading abolitionist. She recounts how he withstood great ignominy for his views from a large part of the American population, as well as enduring a three-month term in prison. Garrison had only recently gone to England to further his cause and had been received with great cordiality by English abolitionists. While Martineau did not always approve of the tone of Garrison's printed censures, she admired the forcefulness of his character and held him in high esteem for the cause that he so spiritedly espoused. Many English persons, Martineau averred, were convinced that there was less originality of character on the far side of the Atlantic than could be found among the populations of Europe. But while American ingenuity was for the time largely expended in business and in the politics of creating a free society, the ever-observant traveler held, she was nonetheless convinced that in time Americans would put their imaginative powers into literature and the arts.

It was inevitable that the traveler would be asked to attend an abolitionists' meeting in the northeast region of the country, and to this she finally consented, although not without trepidation: there had been warnings of a possible mob protest. She had hitherto been fearful that her anti-slavery views would shut many social doors to her, but now she was nearing the end of her journey and was in the company of a like-minded group. The meeting went off with little incident, but in writing of it later she was anxious to convey to her European readers what she called the 'signs of the times in Massachusetts', to which she devoted many a page in her book. Her aim was to show how fearful political conditions would remain in America until the question of slavery was resolved. In the year of her visit, letters had been sent by governors of the Southern states to the new governor of Massachusetts demanding that laws be passed condemning abolitionism in all its forms. Though this did not take place, neither were the abolitionists assured of their right to meet in protest. Yet in the next Massachusetts elections, a set of representatives was returned to government who, by an overwhelming majority, passed a series of anti-slavery resolutions. This proved to the overseas visitor that the voting population – rather than the 'aristocracy' of elected officials – could be trusted to maintain the great principles on which their embryonic society of America was founded.

With the termination of her odyssey, Martineau promised that there would be no book on her American travels when she arrived home to England in August of 1836. But there were no less than three publications: *Society in America* (1837), *Retrospect of Western Travel* (1838), and *How to Observe* (also 1838). It was in the first of these that she offered a summation of her reaction to the New World across the Atlantic:

> I regard the American people as a great embryo poet; now moody, now wild, but bringing out results of absolute good sense: restless and wayward in action, but with deep peace at his heart: exulting that he had caught the true aspect of things past, and at the depth of futurity which lies before him wherein to create something so magnificent as the world has scarcely begun to think of.[15]

It is a summation that has the ring of poetry while carrying with it an expression of the author's abiding goodwill.

CHAPTER 8

The Daring Adventures
of Charles Augustus Murray

E XCITEMENT WAS TO BE HAD right from the start by young Charles Augustus Murray as he boarded ship for a stay of two years in the New World. During that time he would spend a summer with the Pawnee tribe of Native Americans out West and cover uncharted territory by horseback, foot and wagon. For so extended a stay, the 29-year-old Scotsman, a product of Eton and Oxford, had carefully tucked into his luggage an inexhaustible supply of goodwill, together with an erudition that would bring sparkle to the pages of an eventual two-volume memoir. Unexpectedly, the first of these qualities was to serve him exceedingly well during what proved to be a hair-raising crossing of the Atlantic aboard the packet *Waverley*. Sailing from Liverpool in April of 1834, the ship headed across the Atlantic, then almost foundered in mid-ocean thanks to a profound leak, terrifying every passenger and causing all men on board exhausting toil at the pumps. As anxious days passed, half the cargo was thrown overboard, a threatened mutiny was quelled, and prayers nervously offered. Finally, the sloping hills of the Azores came into view: here was a sight that was strikingly beautiful to all on board.

New York was young Murray's first view of the American shore. He found sailing up the Narrows an attractive welcome, and was struck by the graceful rigging of the multitudinous vessels crossing the seas in all directions. Though he was not to linger long in the city – a boat trip along the Hudson River with an English friend having been planned earlier – time was found for a saunter down Broadway. There the young traveler encountered along his path a steady parade of young ladies handsomely turned out; they unquestionably confirmed the encomiums he had so frequently read extolling the beauty of American females. The subsequent boat trip along the Hudson River proved a high point in Murray's travels on the east coast; on board, he was pleased to meet the novelist James Fenimore Cooper again, having already met him in London and been particularly interested in his most famous novel *The Last of the Mohicans*. During this trip stops were made via railroad and carriage at West Point, Albany, Schenectady, Ballston, Saratoga, Geneseo and Lockport, and although the newly constructed railroad proved to serve all the requirements of speed, safety and economy, its velocity was not to be compared, noted the Scotsman, with the Liverpool and Manchester line. The final destination on this portion of his journey in the east left the traveler truly awed:

> How can language convey impressions too tremendous and sublime even for the mind to bear? How can it presume to embody a scene [Niagara Falls] on which the eye could not gaze, to which the ear could not listen, and which the oppressed and overwhelmed power of reflection could not contemplate without feelings of awe, wonder, and delight, so intense as to amount almost to pain! [...] The clouds

of foam that rise from the boiling caldron spring upward in snowy wreaths of vapour, and the rocks and woods around are tinged with the ever-changing rays of the rainbow.[1]

Such was Murray's delight in viewing Niagara Falls that he calls on the poetry of Byron (*The Bride of Abydos*) to reflect his sense of wonder, insisting that at such a sight even the most haughty or daring are equally humbled. It was indeed proving, for those crossing the Atlantic westward, to be the high point in viewing the scenery of America's east, equivalent to a traveler's first glimpse of the Matterhorn.

A steamboat leaving from near the falls took Murray to Canada, where, after a brief stay, he retraced his steps south, spending time in often remote areas of Vermont, New Hampshire and western New York State, making his way by hired horse and wagon as well as on horseback. More often than not during the many weeks of travel in rural areas, he would find accommodation at odd hours that were decidedly makeshift, and hosts whose manners also left a lot to be desired. If he had been a 'true John Bull', he noted, his experiences would have led him to fret and sulk. Nonetheless, he could report that he was always accommodated at the most unseasonable hours with never a complaint to be made about 'cleanliness, good victuals, or civility. All that a traveler requires is a sufficient knowledge of the world, to prevent his mistaking manners for intention; and a sufficient fund of good temper in himself to keep him from being irritated by trifles.'[2] Proceeding further south into more industrialized areas, Murray stopped in the Massachusetts town of Lowell, noted as the first manufacturing village in the nation, where the cotton mills were turning out forty million yards of cotton per year. Though it could not vie with Manchester, Leeds or Glasgow in wealth or population, it far exceeded those towns, noted the visitor, in the neatness and cleanliness of the streets and buildings. Subsequent stops were made, with very little time spent, in Boston, New York, Philadelphia and the capital city of Washington, DC; the traveler was anxious to hurry on to a rural area of Virginia where he had business to enact and where there were welcome opportunities in the wide open spaces for his favorite exercise of walking from sunrise till evening. There, too, among friends, he could indulge in his love of the hunt, skillfully felling deer and other wild beasts to the amazement of accompanying huntsmen. Beyond the hunt, there proved the occasion for another kind of pleasure:

> In no other part of the world has my national pride been more grati-
> fied than in this country; which, abounding as it does in settlers from
> almost every nation in Europe, affords a fairer opportunity than can
> be found at home of comparing their respective characters under
> similar circumstances. I think I can confirm with equal truth and
> pleasure that the Scotchmen who have settled in the United States,
> have earned for them-selves a higher average character for honesty,
> perseverance, and enterprise, than their rival settlers from any other
> part of the old world.[3]

Leaving the rural pleasures of Virginia, Murray made his way back to Washington, where he was curious about the level of debate in the two houses of Congress. Luck was his in hearing two of America's most distinguished speakers of the time, Daniel Webster and Henry Clay, arguing a legislative measure concerning relations with France during the second term of the presidency of Andrew Jackson. Webster, he felt, would find few equals in oratory on either side of the Atlantic though it was his judgment that he would be outdone by Clay (a vehement opponent of the Jackson government) in exciting the passions of a popular assembly. After enjoying the social whirl of Washington for a short while, Murray made his way to the city of Richmond in Virginia by stagecoach on roads so poorly staked out that he felt himself fortunate that the coach was not overturned, as two earlier stages had been. Still, the constant jolting as well as the plunging in and out of mud holes was exhausting, and totally unexpected of a road that was the principal artery from Washington, DC, to the capital city of Virginia. Fortunately, Richmond held out some nice rewards in the congenial society he enjoyed, particularly that of the ladies; there, too, he had an educational glimpse into the growing practice of keeping slaves, which he found to be inhuman and unholy. Murray discerned a large difference between the respective conditions of the domestic and the farm-laboring slave. Domestic laborers, who lived under the same roof as their owners, rarely experienced the lash, he noted, a fact reflected in their relatively relaxed behavior, while the outdoor slave was entirely at the mercy of the overseer who spared neither threats nor lashes in the discharge of his office.

A stop at Jamestown stirred heightened feelings in the traveler, who was dismayed to find that this historical cradle where the first colonists landed in 1607 was now a rather desolate spot. Little remained to evoke that momentous era except for the ruins of the church that marked the place where Christianity was first introduced to the New World. Murray was more than slightly shocked at this parade of irreverence, particularly at the appearance of pigs and cattle roaming over America's earliest ancestral monument:

> Some may think this a light and trivial matter – I cannot agree with them: it appears to me an amiable, if not an instinctive feeling in our nature, to have a regard to all the concerns, the habits, the deeds, as well as the houses and more material relics of our forefathers; how much more so to venerate the spot of which the dust is kindred to our own animated clay, where sleep the men to whom we owe the land and the liberty we enjoy. I will defy any one who pretends to understand or appreciate a stanza of Gray's matchless Elegy to look upon this desecrated churchyard without mingled feelings of indignation and pain. If I were an American statesman, I would watch, and endeavour to correct this national defect.[4]

It is not difficult to sympathize with Murray's feelings of indignation and pain when one further learns that it was here in the British governor's palace that his own grandfather had once lived, surrounded by the pomp and pageantry of royalty as he served the Crown in the time of King James I. It was, accordingly, a very distracted Scotsman who went on to visit the College of William and Mary, also connected to British rule inasmuch as it was endowed by William III and Mary II. Before finally leaving the state of Virginia he visited Norfolk, where he admired what he called its 'noble harbor' and acknowledged the celebrated hospitality of the local merchants. After a few days during which he was cordially received by the British Consul, he made his way back to Washington, DC, and from there to Baltimore.

Murray's visit to the capital of Maryland had one indelibly memorable moment. This took place during a stroll in the city's museum where he paused to admire two figures based on the irrepressible writing of Robert Burns. These were the Scottish characters of Tam o'Shanter and Souter Johnnie now appearing before the visitor as life-size sculptures. To the utter delight of Murray, a scene enfolded that riveted his attention, and he tells us why:

> It was simply this. The merry cobbler was sitting in stone, with the broad smile upon his countenance, and the half-emptied can in his hand, when suddenly I observed a delicate arm passed round his neck, and a profusion of dark tresses mingled with his grey locks! It was a young girl, one of the most lovely creatures that ever I looked upon: her hair was dark and glossy; her eyes black and brilliant, beneath eyebrows most delicately pencilled, and shaded by lids the fringe of which threatened to tickle her rosy cheek; her nose was of that fine correct form so distinctive of American beauty, and round her sweet small mouth played two dimples that Psyche might have slept in; in delighted and unconscious beauty did she hang her arm round Johnny's neck of stone, her full cherry lips almost touching his rough cheek! I could not forbear gazing more intently perhaps than I ought; she blushed deeply, and changed her position.[5]

With this vision no doubt reluctantly left behind, Murray moved on to Philadelphia, Pittsburgh and Cincinnati, traveling chiefly by train. While he accepted the relaxed manners of the many Americans he encountered en route, he was certain that such freedom of conduct would undoubtedly be considered 'impertinent' elsewhere. Cincinnati appealed to him: he admired both the convenience and beauty of its location on the banks of the Ohio River and its amazing rise in industry, calling it 'that precocious daughter of the West'. He was well aware of the published memoirs of Frances Trollope excoriating her experiences there; he flatly denied that he had seen one single instance of rudeness, vulgarity or incivility. Indeed, he found Cincinnati amazing in terms of its rapid growth in wealth and population, declaring that he was 'filled with astonishment and admiration at the energy and industry of man, and [also filled] with pride at the self-suggested reflection, that this metamorphosed wilderness is the work of Britain's sons.'[6]

Louisville and Lexington in Kentucky were the next stops on the journey; he planned, in the latter city, to pay a visit to Senator Henry Clay, of whose eloquence he had already spoken. At the home of the Senator he was surprised to meet Harriet Martineau, and though many of his opinions differed from hers he had nothing but praise for what he called her strong and original mind. Days later, while visiting one of the educational institutions in Lexington, Murray fell into conversation with an English clergyman teaching there, who confided that he found the capacity for learning of the young men in America to be definitely high, there being fewer 'book-dunces' than he remembered in England. Still, he confirmed that they were badly grounded in the classics. The traveler himself felt that it was not easy to meet a young American college graduate who could or would read Pindar, Euripides, Horace or Juvenal for pleasure; it was his fervent hope that the situation would in time improve.

St. Louis in the state of Missouri was the next major stop on the Scotsman's itinerary; there he had the pleasure of meeting the aging William Clark, the Superintendent of Indian Affairs for the United States who had gained impressive laurels for his contests with the buffalo, the grizzly bear and the 'wild Indian'. William Clark is best known for his participation in the famed Lewis and Clark Expedition of 1803, the first American peregrination overland to the Pacific coast, commissioned by Thomas Jefferson, then president of the United States. Indeed, Clark was held in high respect by the many Native American tribes that then peopled the western stretches of the country. And it was into these Western stretches that Murray proposed to travel in order to gain a better understanding of 'Indian' culture – the term by which he knew it, and which shall be employed here for that reason – by living among a tribe of American natives for a while. His first important stop in this direction was Fort Leavenworth in Kansas, situated on a promontory formed by a sweeping bend of the Missouri River. Nearby was the village of Liberty, where Murray and a traveling companion stayed for several days making preparations for their highly anticipated trip into the wilderness. Here the two men made important purchases of foodstuffs and equipment, including six horses: two to be ridden for the trip ahead, three to be used as pack animals, and the sixth for the servant who was to accompany them. In this area of Kansas, the European traveler espied a tribe of Kickapoo Indians and soon after a larger tribe of Pawnees. An opportunity for a closer look arose when the chief warriors of the latter group were invited to dinner at the fort. The Scotsman found 'these genuine children of the wilderness' to be as wild and unsophisticated as he had been led to expect, yet astonishingly self-possessed. Their dress consisted of a belt of deerskin worn around the middle with a flap passing between the legs, and fastened again to the belt behind; their legs were covered with deerskin leggings and their feet by moccasins, while on their shoulders they wore a blanket or a buffalo skin.

> Most of them had earrings, bead-necklaces, and armlets; the two principal chiefs wore round their necks a large medal each, on which was engraved the head of the late President of the United States [presumably John Q. Adams]. The greater part of them were lusty, and a few even fat, giving no outward evidence of the privations to which their mode of life renders them so liable. Generally speaking, they were of middle height, with fine chests, arms well-proportioned but not muscular, with fine-shaped legs. I do not think there was a countenance among them that could be pronounced handsome, though several were pleasing and good-humoured; but the prevalent character of their expression was a haughty impenetrable reserve, easily distinguishable through the mask of frank conciliation, which their present object rendered it expedient for them to wear.[7]

He subsequently learned that the tribe of Pawnees lived some distance from Fort Leavenworth and that they came annually – about 150 of them with women and children – to collect annuities and a certain number of guns as part of the payment for the land ceded by them on the Kansas River. The Scottish visitor subsequently resolved to accompany the tribe on their return home and received an assent from the tribe to do so, traveling with a French–Pawnee interpreter who was their government agent and who always referred to the Indians as '*les sauvages*'. Murray was accordingly given several instructions to be followed on the trip, the most important being a warning not to tempt the Indians with liquor at mealtimes or at any other time. During the course of the trip, estimated at about a thousand miles, the Scottish traveler was happily able to exercise his outdoor skills with a shotgun, and often brought down the food for a meal. At the end of each day, he carefully recorded his adventures, many of which included innumerable mishaps caused by roughing it outdoors, matched by nature's wonders to be indelibly remembered along the way. He noted that the Pawnees, who had only lately become acquainted with firearms, soon destroyed the weapons by firing off powder, by overloading and by a number of 'other follies'. It transpired that sleep, so welcomed at the end of a tiring day – even in a rough tent – was not to be had undisturbed during the long trip for, among the Pawnees, 'silence was not among the goddesses of the night'; it also transpired that the loquacity of the Indian females knew no bounds, and that their children were given to much screaming. Then, too, there was the constant howling of a variety of animals. In addition, writes Murray, he made daily trips to the nearby streams since he had not learned to consider cleanliness as a useless and supererogatory luxury, but he was not always successful in finding a place free of 'biped and quadruped competitors in ablution'.

The Scottish traveler in time learned that one of the unholy occupations of the Indians was to send out horse-stealing parties whenever the opportunity presented itself. Although this was strictly forbidden by the United States government as a condition for receiving the annuities for ceded lands, it took place frequently. Meanwhile, when more distant tribes came in to hunt in the buffalo prairies, they in turn would steal the horses from the Pawnees, yet the latter were forbidden to make reprisals. As the Scottish traveler continued to observe the behavior patterns of the Native Americans for days and days on end, he came to realize that this venture of his into the wild was the only method of becoming truly acquainted with the domestic habits and undisguised character of America's natives:

> Had I judged [them] from what I had been able to observe at Fort Leavenworth, or other frontier places, where I met them I should have known about as much of them as the generality of scribblers and their readers, and might, like them, have deceived myself and others into a belief in their 'high sense of honour' – and their hospitality – their openness and love of truth, and many other qualities which they possess, if at all in a very moderate degree; and yet it is no wonder

if such impressions have gone abroad, because the Indian, among whites, or at a garrison, trading-post, or town, is as different a man from the same Indian at home as a Turkish Mollah is from a French barber. Among whites he is all dignity and repose; he is acting a part the whole time and acts it most admirably.[8]

With regard to Indian women, Murray declared that he never saw one instance of beauty in either face or figure, nor neatness of dress, cleanliness in appearance, or any other attractive attribute characteristic of females. He considered the life of Indian women one of perpetual degradation and slavery, while admiring the good humor with which they performed their labors. So carefully did the Scottish traveler observe and record the customs of the Indians during that summer of 1835 that he presents a virtual primer on North American Indian culture, covering every aspect of Native American life from childhood to adulthood. He enchants the reader with descriptions of the Indian's elaborate toilet, his effeminacy, his courage and his skills in the buffalo chase, as well as offering details regarding religious and tribal ceremonies, feuds, 'medicine feasts', war songs, the art of the bow and arrow, Indian superstition and Indian knavery. Meanwhile, the European adventurer had learned more than a few words and signs of the Pawnee language, all of which lend an intimacy to his exchanges with the Native Americans and heighten the immediacy of his stories.

A return to Fort Leavenworth was now planned. This would take several weeks, during the course of which Murray and his party experienced a fair share of unpleasant outdoor adventures, with sleep often interrupted by a pack of wolves in full cry after a deer, with damp sheets and no fire, with little indication of a river or stream for hours on end and with firewood very scarce. But nearly always there was the vision of a starry sky as night came, and the long-distance traveler would watch with uninterrupted pleasure the 'mystic dance' of the constellations and star clusters as they created the poetry of heaven with their silent, twinkling movements. Still, when it was finally reached, the fort was a welcome sight, and also very welcome were the hospitality that was offered and the sweet tranquility of a good night's sleep. Murray confessed that he had for so long sat cross-legged on the ground that he literally felt difficulty in sitting on a chair as well as in adjusting to the social (formal) climate of a drawing room. He had, moreover, difficulty in accepting the various delicacies that were offered without causing havoc to the tea table. Near the fort was a village of Kickapoo Indians, a branch of the great Northern nation of Indians that included the Potawatomies, the Chippeways, and other tribes. Murray took the time to attend a Kickapoo ceremony and observed that, living so near the white settlements, the Indians of this tribe had gradually lost many of the traits of their original character.

After selling his horses and bidding goodbye, the Scotsman headed east: this he did via a steamboat headed for the city of St. Louis, where he spent only a few days, pleased to enjoy the musical entertainment provided by a German family. Curiosity then led him to the town of Galena in Illinois, located not far from the Mississippi River, which was noted at the time as the seat of the extensive United States lead mines. Here the veins of lead in the surrounding hills proved both exceedingly numerous and rich, and, here in Galena, Murray found what he called the most wonderful mixture of humanity, coming from all parts of the world but chiefly from Derbyshire, Cornwall, Ireland and Germany. Any comer to Galena was entitled to stake off ten acres of unoccupied land, claim it as his, and become owner of all the minerals he could find in that territorial range. Some, he found, amassed a fortune within a short time. Not far from Galena, the traveler stopped at Prairie du Chien, an old French village located within a short distance of an American military post. To his great delight, he was welcomed to join a party of military officers about to embark on a hunting expedition. During the course of this venture, Murray encountered a tribe of Winnebago Indians who joined the expedition for a short stretch along with an interpreter. He naturally attempted to learn some key words, but their language proved to be so dreadfully harsh and guttural that a basic vocabulary was not easily mastered, as 'lips, tongue, and palate, seem to have resigned their office to the uvula in the throat, or to some yet more remote ministers of sound.'[9] An ever-eager huntsman, Murray was able to indulge himself in shooting ducks, pheasants and grouse, but he wanted most of all to fell a deer. This he did not manage at this time, despite careful stalking and planning. He did make frequent visits to the lodges of Indians scattered about the area, mostly Winnebagos and Menominees. He found that some of the girls of the latter tribe served as mistresses to the military and other personnel attached to the garrison – a connection they did not find disreputable and adhered to with customary patience and fidelity. During this time out west, the Scotsman found as many occasions as he could for walking miles on end – often in peril – as he hunted, admired the wild, unusual scenes and communed with nature through the voices of the many poets he was wont to recite. On these occasions, he admitted that he sometimes felt himself a poet:

> Indeed I have never known such excitement from any exercise, not even from the headlong gallop of a buffalo chase, as I have experienced from a solitary walk among mountains; thoughts crowd upon thoughts, which I can neither control, nor breathe in words; I almost feel that I am a poet, but (as Byron beautifully expresses it) I 'compress the god within me'. All the beloved dwellers in the secret cells of my memory walk by my side, – I people the height of the hill, and the shades of the forest, not only with those whom I have known, but with all my friends from fairy land; and, in these illusions of my waking dream, I forget time, fatigue, and distance, and sometimes lose my way![10]

The way was not lost, however, to the city of St. Louis, the Missouri state capital to which the traveler now returned for a second stay. Murray had friends there, and although he held that St. Louis was one of the least social and hospitable places he visited he enjoyed some musical soirees among the impressive variety of Europeans who had settled there, and was able to exercise his fluency in Italian, French and German. There, too, an occasional Scottish song was extracted from him, and he found it delightful, during his sojourn, to hear the compositions of Beethoven and other musical giants played with a taste, feeling, and execution that would not have been lightly esteemed on the banks of the Thames, the Seine, or the Rhine. Traveling south, mostly by steamboat on the winding Mississippi River, Murray stopped at his next major port of call, New Orleans. As he approached the city the river put him in mind of the Thames to the east of London, where the shores of Kent and Essex are low and flat. Society in this Southern American city was divided into two distinct segments – the American and the Creole – and the gayest and merriest part, he deemed, was to be found in the Creole neighborhoods. As luck would have it, he was invited to a Creole ball with music admirably performed by amateurs on the harp, piano, flute, violin and clarinet. Murray much admired the dress, looks and demeanor of the female society there, and found it thrilling to approach and to dance with any young lady present without going through the ceremonial ordeal of introduction. On the streets, and especially on the levee, the population proved to be a highly amusing and motley assemblage, with the prevailing language sounding to the Scotsman like that of Babel: Spanish, Portuguese, French and English, mixed with a few wretched remains of Choctaw and other Indian tribes; whatever tongue was used, all fell on his ears in the loudest, broadest and strangest dialects.

The traveler soon left his American moorings for a trip to Havana, where he attended a cock fight, a bullfight, an Italian opera and the annual spirited carnival. Murray noted that although a treaty had been enacted in 1817 for the abolition of slavery in Cuba, there was little evidence of it being enforced. Nor did he think that the slave trade would be suppressed until it was officially declared piracy by the great naval powers, because the profits in buying and selling slaves were so high that speculators in the trade laughed at the means employed for its prevention. Yet Murray knew that the situation boded ill and he often discussed solutions. He believed that a force of cruisers should be maintained on the African coast by the great sea powers, sufficient to destroy all the hopes and profits of those engaged in this inhuman traffic. But this was not to be. After attending two balls and a dinner with the Cuban governor, the traveler set sail northward for Charleston.

Murray was not able to award this South Carolina city, of which he had heard so much, the encomium of being beautiful – but he did admit that a gentleman who did not find the society there eminently agreeable should be characterized as difficult to please. He ventured to say that the Carolinian character is more akin to that found in England while that of New Englanders more redolent of the lowland Scots. Southern colonists were mostly Episcopalians, he observed, many of them descendants of the oldest and noblest families in Britain who had retained, until shortly before Murray's visit, a predilection for institutions that were little regarded by their North American brethren. Norfolk, farther north along the Atlantic, was the next port of call, followed by a stop in Baltimore still farther north on the coast. Merriment on board the steamboat taking him to Maryland was provided by a hundred or more seamen, fresh from an assignment on a man-o'-war; they danced, drank, shouted and frolicked with all the uncouth merriment peculiar to 'these Tritons' newly released from discipline. Murray felt in watching them that although American sailors could handle a ship and a thirty-two pounder as well as any seamen in the world, they did not dance as well as the British 'tars'. Immediately on leaving the ship, the traveler proceeded to Washington, DC, where he enjoyed the society of friends and was invited to a good number of diplomatic dinners offered by President Andrew Jackson and other statesmen in honor of the newly arrived British Ambassador. Attendance at several sessions of Congress confirmed the Scotsman in his belief that the general tone of manner, eloquence and debate was more gentlemanly and businesslike in the Senate than in the House of Representatives. He had some complimentary words for Vice President Martin Van Buren, whom he characterized as a shrewd and able statesman, deeming his conversation both constructive and amusing. Van Buren subsequently succeeded Jackson as president of the United States.

Of all American cities Philadelphia proved to be the favorite of Murray, and it was to this capital of the state of Pennsylvania that his travels now brought him. More quiet and more leisure, more symptoms of comfort were to be found there than elsewhere, averred Murray, who also noted that Philadelphia yielded to no place in the beauty of its women. Additionally, the traveler made the acquaintance there of several literary men whose conversation he found immensely rewarding, among them a scholar deeply versed in the dialects and structure of the various Native American languages. Indians were shortly to be again on the mind of the traveler for when he reached his next destination of New York, he was greeted with surprise by many of his friends in Manhattan: some thought he had long since gone back to Europe, others that he had been scalped by the Indians with whom he had had extended contact. It transpired that the Pawnees had joined forces with the Comanches, a numerous and warlike tribe;

together they had attacked a trading station and killed all of the sixty men garrisoned there. 'Had the Seminole war and the other causes of Indian excitement occurred while I was in the West,' writes Murray, 'it is probable that I and all other Whites, who were in their power at the time, would have been destroyed.'[11] Indian affairs were beginning to assume a very threatening aspect in the traveler's estimation because the war belt had been passed in secret from the prominent Seminoles to many Northern and Western tribes. Further, he judged that the American army was too small in number at the time to protect an entire quarter of the frontier and, though he understood that the government proposed to increase the number of soldiers, they would still prove quite insufficient unless the state militias were called on. But preoccupation with Indians was not to interfere with the traveler's stay in New York: he was happily received by friends he had already made there. He particularly enjoyed the entertainments staged by the St. George Society, a benevolent institution that was formed to assist destitute Englishmen finding themselves without money or friends in the city. One elaborate dinner, attended by roughly 200 people including some of the city's most respectable citizens, gave him truly untold pleasure:

> The dinner, wines, and music, were good; and the toasts were all thoroughly English, and given with English feeling; nor do I believe that King William's health was ever drunk at the Thatched House or London Tavern with such unbounded, uproarious, and long-continued cheers, as at this transatlantic meeting. My blood warmed and my spirit was stirred at hearing the names, the sentiments, the songs, associated with my youth and childhood, 'familiar in men's mouths' so many miles from home; and I felt pleasure in hearing from many sons of Britain present, that though their lot, with that of their wives, brethren, and children, is now cast in this Western continent, they look back with affection upon their Parent – with reverence upon her institutions, and upon her glories with pride. Long may the feeling be cherished – widely may it be spread – and never may any temporary causes of disagreement again make the nations forget their identity of language and blood![12]

Beyond stirring sentiments and good times with friends, Murray was busy while in New York completing the rough notes that he had systematically kept during the two years of his visit.

He had clearly come to the United States without prejudice or predisposition of any kind, and had formed an independent judgment that was reflected in the warmth of his prose. Although he had still a bit more traveling ahead, he wanted to take the time to review his notations and to make certain while in the United States that he had recorded the scene as accurately as he had witnessed it wherever he went. This led him to embark on an overall summary of American society in which it seemed natural to begin with views of America's working class. This ever-expanding layer of society was possessed, in his opinion, of privileges and power so great as to render it master both of the government and of the Constitution. Indeed, America's working class struck the traveler with the greatest surprise and admiration, he held, because of the lack of pauperism. That gaunt and hideous specter, he went on to explain, had extended its desolating march over the populations of Asia and Europe, destroying its victims by the thousands in the midst of luxury and wealth. That pauperism had never carried its ravages into the United States appeared to him a blessing of untold magnitude. Another blessing was in the realm of education: here, the advantages of schooling were enjoyed by the poorest classes in every part of the country. Alas, he could not claim this to be true of the class of slaves laboring in the South, a condition to be abhorred and desperately in need of remedy. Murray realized that the question of abolition was one that invoked immediate and volatile reactions. He himself highly endorsed a proposition put forward by Chief Justice Marshall that a government fund be created for the purchase and emancipation of slaves, anticipating their eventual removal to other regions. That this had not been acted upon was incomprehensible to Murray.

There was yet another issue in his review of American society that the Scotsman found somewhat baffling, though it was of an entirely different nature: this was the state of religion in America. He felt that Americans carried their dislike of England's alliance between Church and State to such a height that they hurried to the opposite extreme, creating endless sects to a nonsensical degree. Some of the sects he found to be among the most absurd, others the most extravagant in the civilized world; in particular he did not condone the dependence of the clergyman on the caprices of the congregation for his subsistence. There is no part of America, the visitor found, where sufficient provision is made for the religious instruction of the people or for the maintenance of a well-educated clergy. While some regions evinced much more stability in this regard than others, the religious scene appeared fearfully changeable and uncertain. Still, Murray readily acknowledged a consideration of religious practices was a subject too vast for his accurate assessment, while conceding that any view on his next subject – regarding American conduct – was still more difficult.

A Scotsman, he was well aware, was very apt to designate as 'vulgar' all that differed from polite circles in London, whereas it was his own observation that social conduct varied widely from region to region as he traveled throughout the settled states of the New World. Because social deportment was related to education, Murray had not failed to observe that a significant segment of the population (certainly among those he met) had had the benefit of higher education, yet most had emerged from college with merely a considerable quantity of superficial attainment. A minority entered the world well read, while the majority lacked the eloquence streaming from a truly classical education. Young men, he found, did not have an acquaintance with current literature or evince a pronounced taste for music and poetry; neither did they exhibit any skills in modern languages. Though these were attainments of secondary importance in Murray's view, he found them indispensable in lending a certain charm to the daily intercourse of society as well as rescuing drawing-room conversation from insipid gossip. A good many of these observations he found to be in evidence, too, among the members of Congress, most of whom were not conversant with the classics but were highly astute as to business interests. He was certain that this limited erudition was the cause of the dreadful declamatory style and interminable length of the orations to which listeners in Congress were subjected, though he happily made exceptions in citing the eloquence of Clay, Calhoun and Webster.

Also within his summary was a topic not without interest to the visiting Scotsman – that of the schooling of young ladies. He felt they were superficially educated in the major subjects and less advanced in the accomplishments considered in Britain to be particularly feminine:

dancing, drawing, music, needlework and modern languages. They entered society much too early, often being allowed to make their social rounds unaccompanied; it caused Murray some concern that too much independence was likely to diminish that 'coy submission' and 'sweet reluctance' that he always considered the most attractive and endearing attributes in a woman. Moving beyond the subject of women, the Scottish visitor turned to a discussion of the 'national vanity' with which Americans were consistently charged by British writers. He himself did not view this vanity as an egregious offense, for it existed everywhere he went, and he declared that it was never carried to a greater height than in Britain:

> There is not a popular poem, or ballad, or proverb, in which our unequalled superiority over every other people is not set forth; neither is there a sailor in our fleet who does not believe that one Englishman is equal to three Frenchmen, as certainly as that three and one make four. Look again, at the gallant nation just named, and see in their drama, in their ballads, in their proclamations, whether it is not assumed as an indisputable fact, that, of the habitable earth, France is the mistress – Paris the capital. No reader who is even slightly acquainted with the literature of Germany and Spain, or of ancient Greece can have failed to observe the prevalence of the same characteristic in all those countries, especially in that last mentioned. The philosophic Thucydides prefaces an eloquent speech, which he records of Brasidas, the Spartan commander, with this parenthesis: 'for he was not a bad speaker, so far as a Lacedemonian can speak.'[13]

For the last few weeks of his American tour, Murray left New York to undertake an excursion with a friend through parts of Pennsylvania, New Jersey and upper New York State. As he traveled north, he found that Albany had become a considerably larger town since his visit two years earlier, and he took pleasure in a visit with the Van Rensselaer family whose large holdings in the area he deemed to be in excellent hands. Another agreeable pause was an afternoon spent in Cooperstown with James Fenimore Cooper, whom he called 'the Walter Scott of the Ocean'. Much of this local visiting was conducted on horseback as the untiring traveler proceeded through Auburn, Syracuse, Geneva and other towns on the principal path between Buffalo and New York. In the town of Syracuse Murray saw a few Indians of the Oneida tribe, but found them to be squalid, diminutive and degraded, a condition in pronounced contrast to the members of the same tribe out West. Subsequently, he met a former resident of Wyoming who had grown up there in Indian territory, had become associated with the Seneca tribe and had learned several Native American dialects. He spoke of the Indians he had known with great affection; Murray had meanwhile learned following his return from the West that of all the great tribes uncontaminated by civilization (meaning whiskey), the most mischievous, treacherous, and savage were his old friends the Pawnees.

It was now time to prepare for the voyage home. The energetic traveler made his way back to New York, where he had booked passage on *The Oxford*, a magnificent packet (as he termed it), headed for Liverpool. His memoirs, subsequently published in two volumes and entitled *Travels in North America*, conclude with a message to both his British and his American readers. But far more important to the latter audience was a declaration he had made in earlier pages:

> If I were an American, I confess I should be proud of my country – proud of its commercial enterprise – of its gigantic resources – of its magnificent rivers, and forests, and scenery – still more proud should I be of its widely diffused education and independence, and of the imperishable memory of its heroic father and founder![14]

Clearly, Charles Augustus Murray was of a disposition to put the most balanced interpretation on everything he witnessed in the New World. He never returned to America but he did marry an American girl, and went on to a colorful diplomatic career.

CHAPTER 9

The Clairvoyance of Thomas Colley Grattan

THE UNITED STATES, declared Thomas Colley Grattan, 'is designed by God's destiny for the greatest well-being of the greatest number; but that well-being is to be found in a simple, economical existence, which makes the country a paradise of mediocrity, but of nothing more. Genuine Democracy can produce nothing more.'[1] It was into this 'paradise of mediocrity', then, that Thomas Grattan came in the year 1839, not as a tourist full of wide-eyed expectations but as an official visitor assigned the rank of British Consul to the State of Massachusetts. For nearly seven years he held this post, long enough for him to commentate at length on all aspects of American life, and far, far too long a period – so said he – to be absent from an elegant mode of existence in England to which he had long been accustomed. Indeed, a residence in the New World, he was convinced, must at best be felt by the man of European tastes and habits as a banishment. The British diplomat, of Irish heritage, was then forty-seven years old; he took up residence in the city of Boston with his wife and children, and kept his notebook ever at the ready. His observations were eventually published in a two-volume account entitled *Civilized America*.

It was as a thoroughly experienced traveler on the Continent that Grattan had journeyed to the New World, though this was his first post anywhere in the cloak of diplomat. He was pleased that his assignment placed him in Boston, which he considered the most civilized of New World cities; indeed he characterized it as the greenest spot in the comparative wasteland of America. He also found the majority of the New England population during his stay to be of English descent, and although there appeared to be a steady influx from among the Irish at the time, he noted with satisfaction that in the more elevated circles of Boston's society in which he mingled, there were no non-English elements. He was particularly impressed by the manners and charm of that city's ladies as he settled with his family into the routine of life there, but he was less than enthusiastic when it came to sizing up American men: he judged them to be rather dry and cold in manner, and mostly – alas – with no great breadth of mind. There were exceptions, to be sure, among the round of American males he would continually encounter, yet Grattan could confirm by experience what he always instinctively felt: that it is unfair and absurd to measure the gentlemen of America by a European standard:

> They have no resemblance but to Englishmen, yet their inferiority to those is undoubted. It strikes me at every turn, and on every possible occasion – in society in business, in literature, science, art. They can bear no comparison with the stock from which they sprang. They are of the same blood, but of a different breed. The Anglo-Saxon race deteriorates with transplantation. It requires the associations of Home to preserve its lofty attributes; and under Republican forms, it must

be content to exhibit a mediocrity, conducive to the general weal, but fatal to individual distinction.[2]

Fortunately for the Consul, he found Americans to be more acceptable when acting or socializing together in large groups, and this was the ambiance to which his work frequently led him. He also noted that there was less servility among Yankees toward one another, more self-respect, and a greater appreciation of the relative value of men and possessions; nonetheless, he discerned that there was at the same time little of what he would call heart. He observed that Yankees were afraid to go to any great length on the road of the affections, while declaring – with exclamation point – that no one ever died for love in New England! Such statements invite the question of whether the British Consul at one point lost, if ever so temporarily, his heart to a pretty American lass, as would Thackeray during his visit to New York. Alas, that will never be known. What we do know is that he found the women of America superior, beyond all comparison, to the majority of the men in appearance and manners, particularly in the principal cities. He deemed them to possess an ingenuous and easy air, nearly equivalent to the good breeding found in Europe.

In his position as consul, Grattan was often invited to dinners, parties and celebratory occasions of all varieties, to the extent that he was moved to devote an entire chapter to detailing his social experiences as a resident in America. He was led to make the sweeping statement that, in the conduct of most convivial affairs as he witnessed them in Boston, the preponderance of 'animal appetite over intellectual feasting' was flagrant. He could not imagine that Americans would derive very much pleasure from these events, particularly as he detected a capricious indifference toward close acquaintances and friends. Few of those he met could be said to be on a footing of real friendship; moreover, any close intimacy in his view was almost entirely confined to the circles of family relations. He believed he could point to the origin of such defects in the American social system, though it was so widespread and obstinate as to defy any very speedy remedy:

They arise from the extremely superficial nature of all the moral qualities among the people. No one feels very deeply on any subject.

Nothing profound can be cited as characteristic of the United States. The word passion in its best and most solemn sense has no application here. And even its commonest meaning is rarely exemplified. Intense emotion does not exist, and a fiery temper is seldom, if ever, met with. All the affections, so to call the sentiments of this people, are the result of habit or of a sense of duty. Not having their roots in the heart, they are plucked up as easily, and thrown aside as careless, as garden flowers, whenever they show the least failure in fragrance or bloom.[3]

That the diplomatically correct Consul should wax poetic on the subject of affection once again leads to the suspicion of a thwarted romance. But this is admittedly pure speculation.

The first politician of distinction with whom the British diplomat became acquainted was Edward Everett, then Governor of Massachusetts. Because his fairly frequent contact with the man who was the future Minister to London and future American Secretary of State was both social and professional, Grattan came to know Everett well and devoted lengthy pages to rendering his profile in terms of the play of national politics. He found the native Bostonian unassuming and urbane but his speeches and his writings (for which he became renowned) nothing more than finished specimens of artificial eloquence; he was further convinced that no man was ever less fitted for the work of public life than Everett. Part of this sweeping statement was based on the latter's vacillating position on the question of slavery and part on the fact that Everett was in Grattan's view, like all other Americans, guilty of subservience to a political party despite his own views. In the estimate of the Consul, loyalty of this kind was thoroughly inadmissible and constituted the general disgrace of American statesmen, scarcely one of whom took up for conscience's sake a position opposed to the party to which he had pledged himself. Indeed, here was a fact that Grattan repeatedly declared to constitute the general ignominy of American statesmen, noteworthy in the case of Everett, for the latter was opposed to slavery, then a volatile issue, but dared not express abolitionist views for some time. Ever the vigilant diplomat, Grattan recites the facts of the Governor's career that he felt were more or less typical of an American politician. He recounts that when

Everett gave up his professorship at Harvard University to become a member of the House of Representatives in 1826, he felt the necessity of conciliating the sentiment of the Southern states and went to the utmost extreme by vindicating the system of slavery there in order to avoid a civil war. Accordingly, when he was elected governor of Massachusetts ten years later, many of the abolitionists voted against him. It was only by degrees that he returned to an abolitionist stance and, in time, became an ardent Unionist.

A first trip to Washington, DC, gave Grattan the opportunity to meet a good number of politicians and to witness the exercise of American government first-hand during an era dominated by border considerations and the volatile issue of slavery. His impression of the capital city itself was very positive, although it had hardly then assumed any claim to the grandeur that was manifestly intended in the plans of Pierre Charles L'Enfant, its French architect. Still, the Consul admired some of the public buildings, which he found worthy of any location in Europe, and could not shake a feeling of shame upon recalling the heavy damages by fire and plunder inflicted on the nascent city by British forces during the War of 1812. 'Every English visitor to Washington,' he declared in a surprising outburst of sentiment, 'should bear those deplorable transactions in mind, and let the pride of superiority over the people he mixes with be tempered, by the thought of what many of them witnessed, and what all must feel.'[4] Society in Washington was on a very agreeable footing, the visitor found as he made the rounds of many diplomatic functions and attended a 'very handsome' dinner given by President Martin Van Buren. The latter had briefly served as American Minister to London and Grattan found him to be good-tempered, though he was neither one of the master spirits of the New World nor possessed of any brilliancy of talent. He was the first president to be born an American citizen, and though his term of office was beset by several crises, including the financial panic of 1837 and votes taken on several issues pertaining to slavery, Grattan mentions little of Van Buren's rocky four-year term. A 'more or less remarkable' person whom he met was John Ross, who was part Native American and at that time chief of the Cherokee tribe of Indians, whom he represented in Washington. There were at this time many important issues regarding the fate of Natives in America, yet we gain little insight from Grattan on these issues; he confessed that, despite the intelligence he received from Ross, he had scant interest in Native American affairs. Several centuries had made it evident, in his view, that Indians were an inferior race of beings, unable to work out a destiny or to stamp out a distinctive character, and an enigma in creation, as if born without a purpose and dying without a sign. Two of the most numerous and formidable tribes, the Comanches and the Apaches, were at the time struggling against the United States and Mexico, he paused to say, but having no history to look back upon, they had little hope to lead them onward. He was later to devote an entire chapter to the condition of Native Americans, which would reflect not only his lack of interest in the specific issues concerning their welfare but his feeling that the history of the seventeenth-century maiden Pocahontas had been wildly romanticized.

The political views of John Caldwell Calhoun, on the other hand, proved to have more than passing interest for the British Consul; here was a politician of Scottish–Irish descent who had been an advocate of the War of 1812 with Britain and was a passionate defender of states' rights (the latter indicating that he was a slaveholder). Grattan was aware that this member of the House of Representatives was held in uncommonly high esteem for the eloquence of his speeches and for the passion of his views. It was on the issue of slavery that the British Consul had some extraordinary conversations with the Southern Senator who, he reports, maintained that slavery constituted a necessity for the purposes of civilization, that both black and white races are bettered by this practice and, even more astonishing, that no people can become truly humanized or great who have not possessed slaves. Calhoun, widely admired for the depth of his intellect, held ideological opinions on other issues as well. For Grattan, the Senator was remarkable for the flexibility of his opinions rather than the depth or solidity of his understanding. Here was yet another characteristic, he pointed out, that was typical of American politicians: their political shiftings and changes were noteworthy – there was scarcely one among those he encountered who had not converted from one political creed into another directly opposed to it.

Despite holding these views with regard to the general run of American politicians, Grattan looked forward to hearing the speech of the renowned Daniel Webster in the House of Representatives. He had originally met Webster in London when the latter was on a visit there and had been rather impressed at the time, finding that his 'brilliant eyes, deep set, and overhung by large brows and a lofty forehead, shone like the signal lights of genius.' Ultimately, he found him to be a politician praised way beyond his merits. Then, too, much to the Consul's utter disappointment, Webster did not publicly acknowledge the princely treatment he had received in England during several months there. This was seen as unforgivable. Worse still, he did not take the opportunity of

> expressing his admiration and wonder at the great superiority of England over America, in those very points which to an ambitious, haughty, and 'aristocratical' parvenu must have appeared the most important. Wanting the candour to tell the truth, the tact to conceal it skillfully, and the courage to enter on a subject which was so difficult of management, he shirked it altogether. [American] speakers and writers have very rarely the manliness to call the attention of the people to the immense superiority in science, literature, and the arts, of the liberal countries in Europe over their own.[5]

Neither at this time, nor at any time after, did Grattan feel that Webster lived up to his reputation as a great politician, a great speaker or a great man. Indeed, in the view of his European listener he was 'like a great bird whose body was too big for its feathers'.[6] As to the notion that Webster (or any other renowned politician) should be thought of as an American aristocrat, Grattan fairly bridled at the idea.

It was, moreover, time to set the record straight. The most frequently misused words in the American vocabulary, according to the British visitor, were 'aristocracy' and 'gentleman' inasmuch as they were totally misunderstood on the western side of the Atlantic. The word 'aristocracy', he hastened to explain, derives from that form of government that places the supreme power in a privileged class – in the nobles of a country – and therefore it defines a political, not a social, grade. To call the wealthy citizens who live in better houses and give more elegant dinners the 'aristocracy of America' is to give them a mere sobriquet that carries no meaning. The trouble seemed to be that while the two words were associated with good manners, Grattan found no standard for acquiring social polish in the American system because of the want of an elevated class to provide models of refined behavior. Accordingly, to make the acquaintance of anyone coming up to English notions of a finished gentleman was not to be expected, for

> Everyone knows that it takes three generations to make a gentleman. And as that implies three generations of liberal education and all the appliances of gentility, ergo, it is very rare, if to be found at all among Americans; for such a thing as grandfather, father, and son in one family preserving their fortune and station is almost unheard of. The fluctuations of property are sure to reduce one generation out of three to a low level; and thus it is that we see so many persons of respectable manners just bordering on good-breeding, and so few that are thoroughly well-bred. […] The nobility of England, which is really the class to which those ambitious Americans would claim a similitude, forms a picture at once the most graceful and dazzling that civilization can present. The elegance of style and suavity of manner, the intellectual culture, the patronage of talent, the profuse expenditure, the self-confidence arising from security of social position, and the air of superiority in those who have great power as their inheritance, are but items in a combination nowhere to be paralleled. To be born an integral part of this [British] system is, perhaps, the most fortunate accident that could befall a man.[7]

Unfortunately for Americans, they had separated themselves from this 'superior' society and formed one peculiar to themselves. Still, they could not – in the view of the Consul – be considered a 'New People'. Under that appellation he feared that every step towards improvement tended to be over-lauded, every fault excused, and every crime palliated. Eighty years and upwards had passed, he noted, since the fiat of freedom was pronounced on the great expanse of territory now called the United States.

He thought rather that Americans should be judged by the same rules of right and wrong as those by which the Old World was governed, their merits and defects being those of the various nations from which they emanate. As a new country, he held, the United States could boast of the fact that its advantageous position across the Atlantic protected its vast territory from the wars that are the curse of other countries. He knew that conflicting claims, local jealousies and sectional rivalries all threatened to disrupt the newly formed Union, yet he was certain that the American people were well aware that the strength of the individual states consisted in the union of them all. At the time of his service as a consul, this was a question that raised itself over and over again with regard to the divisive issue of slavery, of course testing the mettle of many a politician. But Grattan was of the opinion that Americans were not a passionate or impulsive people, exhibiting no virulent animosity such as existed at the time between French and Prussians, Spaniards and Portuguese, Italians and Austrians, Turks and Greeks. In the Consul's unwavering view, Americans envied the political and commercial eminence of Britain and were 'mortified' by their own sense of social inferiority. Yet this was tempered by a pride in a common ancestry, language and literature, so that, in the view of the Consul, there existed no spirit of national hatred strong enough to overbalance considerations of pecuniary advantage.

As to the divisive issue of slavery, Grattan had little sympathy with the idea that war would eventually prove to be the only solution to this volatile topic. He was convinced that there was a sense of general interest among all sections of the Union that was more powerful than any differences of opinion. While he readily acknowledged that slavery was the touchstone that would try the strength of the confederation, he was certain that the time for putting this to a trial was far off: he saw no chance of a speedy collision between North and South on the 'mere merits' of the question. True, the people of New England and New York, he held, did not approve of slavery, but inasmuch as they needed their factories to be supplied with cotton they would assuredly do nothing en masse to check the growth or raise the price of 'this staple of their own prosperity'. That the abolitionist movement was steadily gaining ground he did not deny, but he was certain that were the abolitionists to double their numbers in the next five years, the animosity of their opponents would show the same result. The abolitionists were, after all, the only portion of the populace to desire a dissolution of the Union on grounds of religious principle or moral justice. Against this, he was more than certain that the dread of pecuniary ruin, inevitably following on any such dissolution, would neutralize 'every boast of sectional dignity'.

Turning again to the merits of being born an Englishman, Grattan held that this good fortune extended to the level of education provided to the children of the aristocracy in England that in part accounts for their superiority. But while instruction in America was far less extensive than that devoted to the superior classes in England, the education afforded to the lower classes of the people in the United States was to be noted as a positive fact. That nearly all native-born Americans were able to read, write and cipher was reason for admiration; exceptions to this were to be found among the families of European immigrants who, the Consul stated, brought with them the ignorance that is inseparable from the political systems they left behind. Still, there were notable differences between the educated in England and in America. A 'smart' man can be said to mean the same thing in both countries: a quick, sharp, intelligent individual. But in England, a nation abounding in men of superior talent, the word 'clever' is applied to distinguish these men from the men of mere smartness. These distinctions were to be noted as well, Grattan went on to say, in the sphere of politics, for English politicians were, in well-balanced degrees, also men of business. Americans, he acknowledged, also engaged in this dual role, but what they called politics was 'nothing more than a business of a mean and contracted sort'. Grattan was convinced that the politics of England were of so elevated a level that they influenced all aspects of English life and raised the community 'into a lofty and expansive sphere of thought'.

Turning to the world of literature, Grattan was of the opinion that American men of letters, as a class, were an obscure and insignificant portion of the population, although the papers insisted on 'puffing' them up far beyond their merits. Among those he mentions is Washington Irving, whom he met abroad and considered a friend, while of the few others listed, Grattan signals out William Cullen Bryant as being absurdly eulogized when a local magazine compared him (misguidedly, to be sure) to Shakespeare, Spenser, Milton, Byron and Wordsworth. Certainly it is true that such American classics as *Moby Dick*, *Walden*, *The Scarlet Letter* and *Leaves of Grass* were on the horizon, but they had not yet been published.[8] There were in the 1830s the prose masterpieces coming from the pen of Ralph Waldo Emerson, who himself recognized that America had not yet realized any grandeur in the arts. Though Emerson was a prominent New Englander, he is not mentioned by Grattan, nor does the latter cite the highly popular novel *The Last of the Mohicans*, which was published in 1826 by James Fenimore Cooper and became very popular abroad. Turning to the weakest element in the nation's literature, Grattan points to dramatic writing for the stage, attributing this lacuna to the abundance of excellent material imported from England for the theater as well as making the observation that life in America was not sufficiently 'varied' to be drawn on for comic or colorful characters.

In the field of art, Grattan felt there were doubtless some artists deserving of a good reputation, and he cites about ten names, among them John Kensett, Frederic Church and John Cropsey. He neglects to underscore the accomplishments of John Singleton Copley and Benjamin West, both eighteenth-century artists who gained an international reputation. West was not only the first American-born painter to gain worldwide notice, he also subsequently became historical painter to the King of England. More than passing notice is given to the art of Washington Allston, whom the Consul met. Allston was a South Carolinian by birth but resided in Boston and was the first American painter whose art, stemming from a brooding imagination, explored the visions within his mind. In time, his work lifted American landscape-painting from the level of simple topography to that of the dramatic landscape of mood. The Consul dwelt at some length on his paintings, feeling qualified to make an aesthetic judgment:

> Allston, the foremost among [America's native painters] was a man of rare qualifications, but by no means perfect in his calling. Sentiment, suavity, seen through a rather hazy and vapoury medium, richness of colouring – his leading characteristics – were not combined with correctness of drawing or largeness of conception. Though often classed by American writers among historical paintings, his best works are of a less ambitious character, chiefly consisting of landscapes and ideal heads. The latter especially are of much beauty, and possess great charm both in composition and colour.[9]

It was the considered opinion of the Consul that sculpture was decidedly the branch of art in which American talent, taste and industry were most favorably displayed. He noted the great celebrity achieved by distinguished American sculptural artists in the previous quarter of a century, and went on to admire the work of Hiram Powers, in particular his statue entitled *The Greek Slave*. He could scarcely imagine anyone with an acute feeling for art gazing on it without emotion, as that work of art, in his view, had done more honor to the United States than the Webster–Ashburton Treaty and the annexation of Texas had caused discredit.

Turning to a consideration of a national academy of art or of design, the Consul saw no chances for either the inauguration or the success of such an institution. Both the fostering protection of the government and the private tastes of its citizens were wanting for the establishment of an academy, he held, and the consent of the Western states ('those enormous swamps of semi-culture') would never be obtained. He came to the studied conclusion that the utilitarian principles of democracy were undoubtedly unfavorable to a liberal encouragement of the arts. What Grattan did not recognize was that there was in existence a whole group of artists who made the very experience of the Western frontier their theme; chief among them was George Caleb Bingham. In any case, the Consul was certain that the number of persons in America who were qualified to be connoisseurs was small. Yet the American Academy of the Fine Arts was established as early as 1802 to train artists and to encourage appreciation of the classical tradition, and the National Academy of Design was created in 1826 to encourage American art and artists, while the South Carolina Academy of Fine Arts was formed in Charleston, South Carolina, to foster an appreciation of art. Grattan gave little heed to the fact that there were more than a few specimens of European art to be seen by art lovers on the western side of the Atlantic. Grattan did note that a few cultivated Americans who had traveled to Europe, and were familiar with the works of the great masters, had brought back European specimens – both ancient and modern – of tolerable merit, but rarely could any of them be considered *chefs-d'oeuvre*.

And now for the world of music: Was there a prodigy to be found in America? Not likely. Consul Grattan mentions no particular talent in this field – in either composition or performance – but was happy to report that the progress of musical taste in America had 'of late years been prodigious'. In proof of this, he reproduces a newspaper article attesting to the enormous crowds in New York thronging the newly constructed Academy of Music there.[10] The building had been opened in New York in the fall of 1854 to acclaim for its acoustics and enduring popularity; it shared its audiences with a number of smaller halls in the city that were given over to performances of classical music. Out West, musical recitals of various levels of sophistication were not infrequent, as reported by the newspapers that Grattan must surely have read. Sometime earlier, the British traveler Harriet Martineau had registered her great pleasure in attending a Mozart concert that took place in Cincinnati, one of America's purported 'swamps of semiculture'.

And where did the pleasures of music, art, and literature, as well as all the other positive goods of life such as health, wealth, and domestic affection, lead in this country? It was a question thoughtfully pondered by the British diplomat, who declared that an opinion prevalent in Europe maintained Americans were an unhappy people. He admitted, of course, that happiness is a state of feeling very difficult to define, but nonetheless ventured an answer to the question:

> [Happiness] is an abstraction, out of the reach of measurement or calculation. But all the positive goods of life, health, wealth, domestic affection, and every combination of refinement, will not make happy those who want the buoyancy of spirit and the fullness of heart, that leap and gush forth, to meet the blessings which Heaven has showered on them. It is certain that the American people within the bounds of civilization are strikingly deficient in that elasticity of character. Their moral movements seem without a spring. Those of their physical action are analagous.[11]

Further consideration of this issue led Grattan to an examination of sports in America; to the pleasures of youth (so unlike those of Europe, he felt); to the peculiar habit in America of changing family names; to the curious appellations of towns (most names being patriotic, foreign or Native American); and finally to the depth of originality in Yankee humor. Thoughtful pondering of these very varied issues eventually led him to proclaim that if Americans were not a happy people, still he could not claim that they were the opposite of it.

A topic that was clearly of little interest to the Consul but could not be overlooked was the status of America's Native Indian tribes. Though he acknowledges that Native Americans were a significant part of the New World scene, he deemed them to constitute more a problem than anything else. He viewed them as an unfortunate lot, declaring unkindly that they had nothing inherent in their character that would gain for them an abiding place in the feelings of mankind. True, they had inspired the fantastic imaginings of poets and romance writers – notably in the literature inspired by the seventeenth-century story of Pocahontas, a female Native American who married an English tobacco planter and was presented at court – but the Consul did not subscribe to any of these lofty feelings. In time the British Consul came to believe that Indians were truly an inferior race of beings, incapable of achieving greatness. Accordingly, he issued the extraordinary statement that it would perhaps have been better for the Indian tribes had the white men made slaves of them: then it would certainly have been in the interests of their masters to encourage the propagation of the species. But this he soon dismisses with the statement that, early on, it was discovered that the Indians were as unfit for slavery as they were unworthy of freedom. He declared that there was not a spark of genius or enterprise among them, going further to say that a degraded independence, sloth, dirt and licentiousness formed the sum total of their characteristics. With continuing assurance on the subject, he went on to declare that though he had never lived among them, the Indians of North America had never produced a man of great qualifications for any branch of government, civil or military. No literary talent has appeared among those who have been educated, he claims, and even among those with a smattering of education, the strongest passion seems to have been a longing to relapse into savage life. Despite his insistence on what he believed to be the negative aspects of the Native American character, the Consul finally makes the obvious statement that their treatment by the white invaders of their country constitutes a dark chapter in the history of Christian exploits.

A still more serious issue came under the consideration of the British Consul, to which he devoted a long chapter. Here we have his

perspicacious comments on the overriding political concern that dominated the several years of his tenure – the issue of slavery. Like other
foreign observers, he recognized it as a momentous question affecting
the very existence of the United States as year after year it loomed as
the pivotal topic of debate in Congress, passionately argued on both
moral and economic grounds. He acknowledges that slavery was introduced by England when America was still a British colony, but insists
this was at a time when the true principles of liberty were 'imperfectly'
understood. He wonders why the sagacity of George Washington, the
benevolence of Benjamin Franklin and the shrewdness of Thomas
Jefferson did not subsequently combine to eradicate the practice with
the Declaration of Independence. The third of these leaders did make
such an attempt, he admits, but was overruled since at least twenty of
the signers of the Declaration were slaveholders. (In the first draft of
the Declaration, Jefferson had inserted a clause imputing the existence
of slavery in Virginia to George III, as one of the crimes that proved the
British monarch to be unfit to govern a free people and which accordingly should be eradicated.) But between the initial cupidity of English
merchants and the great stimulus later given to the culture of cotton by
the discoveries of Eli Whitney, who invented the cotton gin, the practice
of slavery, Grattan avows, became firmly rooted in the Southern states.
He recognized that no foreseeable solution was on the horizon in his
day, given the fact that immediate manumission to the several millions
of slaves of the time would spell pecuniary ruin to the territories of the
South. His further views on the matter were that, while inferior to the
white race, the black population was still a portion of humanity and as
such entitled to the common privileges – freedom, equality and the
enjoyment of liberty – stated in the Constitution. (Why, it might be
asked, did he not find this to be true of the Native American population?)
The Consul had made an excursion to some of the Southern states,
and was particularly taken with his visit to Virginia. Although he felt
that the state was then slowly in decline owing to the inherited 'curse'
of slavery, he considered it the 'noble district of the New World, which
excites more than any other the interest and sympathy of England from
the irresistible force of old association'.[12]

It was in Virginia that Grattan witnessed a slave auction and there
pondered the many issues engendered by the unholy practice of

putting black families up for sale. Though he discussed these issues frequently with politicians he admired, he found himself unable to predict the outcome of what was truly the overwhelming American dilemma of the mid-nineteenth century:

> So fluctuating is the character of American politics that it is impossible to foresee what turn any great question may take from day to day. Judging by the strong array of free-soil (or Republican as the party is now called) at the last Presidential election, and the extraordinary display of anti-slavery feeling manifested in the North during the contest, one would imagine that the time was not far distant when every state in the Union would co-operate in the election of a President firmly pledged to resist all further encroachments of the slave power, and that a majority would be found in Congress prepared steadily to oppose the admission of new slave States. But the superior skill and sagacity of the South – where statesmanship is an art and every man able to give his undivided attention to political struggles – has hitherto secured its supremacy in Congress; and the Southern States united as one man on any question involving slavery, has been an overmatch for the divided North.[13]

One of the politicians with whom Grattan discussed the issue of slavery, and a person whom he distinctly admired, was Henry Clay, an 1844 presidential candidate from Kentucky. He was, in the view of Grattan, 'the noblest specimen of a purely American statesman' – and in the later view of Abraham Lincoln the ideal of a great man. The Kentucky politician favored a scheme of colonization on the western shores of Africa as a solution to slavery but when he stated that this would likely take 150 years to accomplish, he left the Consul incredulous; the latter was certain that this would never satisfy the demands of the abolitionists, nor was it within the bounds of reasonable expectations. Still, the British visitor retained a high admiration for Clay and was aware that, as far back as the year 1827, he had made a highly significant speech in the House of Representatives on the issue of slavery. At that time he declared that he would consider it the greatest triumph of his political career if he could be instrumental in eradicating what he called the 'deepest stain' on the character of America.[14]

Alas, nothing but a devastating war, it would eventually prove, could eradicate that stain.

There were many other issues of significance that marked the American political scene during the time of Grattan's tenure as Consul between 1839 and 1846; all of them he followed closely, particularly those that involved a serious dispute between Britain and the United States and called for careful diplomacy. Of the latter, he singles out the 'Northeastern Boundary Question' as being by far the most difficult and dangerous. This represented a political challenge in which the Consul was intimately involved. At issue was the demarcation of the boundary dividing the state of Maine from the British North American provinces and New Brunswick. Because Grattan was assigned by his government to study the documents pertaining to this issue, he offers numerous details beginning with the essential fact that the boundary question rested on the interpretation that would be given to the Treaty of Paris of 1783. In that document was established the northeastern frontier of the newly formed Unites States: it was to be 'along the highlands which divide the rivers that empty themselves into the river St. Lawrence from those which fall into the Atlantic Ocean'. As Britain and America put forward different interpretations as to which constituted the range of highlands so stipulated, the issue became hopelessly entangled and was not resolved until the signing of a treaty in 1842.[15] The very many details that the consul offers make for a revealing glimpse into the winding corridors of diplomacy as well as into the growing might of the new nation as it declared its place on the international scene. But although America had long had its eyes on the annexation of all of the territory to the north as part of its 'manifest destiny', its expanding powers did not lead in this direction.

When Grattan's tenure as British Consul in Massachusetts finally came to an end, he was resolved to publish the record of his stay. Already he had a fair number of novels to his credit, as well as a few travel accounts; eventually he would also prepare his autobiographical recollections, in two volumes entitled *Beaten Paths: And Those Who Trod Them*. Yet he was not at all sanguine as to how the record of his stay in the New World, entitled *Civilized America*, would fall on American ears. The English public, he wrote in the introduction, would take the volumes as they were meant 'because they will understand the author's feelings even if they dissent from them. I am not so confident as regards America. But it is only my imagination, not my conscience, that takes the alarm. I can safely say that the work is faithful and sincere.'[16] Since the volumes were published more than a decade after Grattan's return to England, he had the luxury of reflection (which he admits) on the opinions he accumulated during the course of his diplomatic assignment. Justice was therefore rendered, avowed the author, to the peculiar traits of the population studied at close range over many years. Americans, he averred, were a people 'easy of access, but difficult to understand; offering to the observer a mass of incongruities, and swayed by agitations which defy a steady description'.[17] But Grattan's pen reveals no unsteadiness: he astutely recorded what he considered both the pretensions and the reality of the expanding New World with unwavering diplomatic aplomb.

CHAPTER 10

The First Visit of Charles Dickens to the New World

H E WAS THE DARLING of the media on both sides of the Atlantic, and who can wonder? While still in his twenties, Charles Dickens had conceived five novels abounding in new ideas and teeming with a galaxy of vividly rendered characters as colorful as they were original. Who had not heard of the irrepressible Samuel Pickwick, wandering chairman of the Pickwick Club, or of the gentle Oliver Twist, orphaned and frightened, who dared to ask for more? Or of the villainous Wackford Squeers, the disreputable Sir Mulberry Hawk, the benevolent Charles Cheeryble, the penniless Madeline Bray, the thieving Peg Sliderskew or the talented Miss Snevellicci – all denizens of the wide Nicholas Nickleby circle? Who had not shed tears as they followed the serialized fate of doomed Little Nell, forced to find her way in the cheerless streets of London, begging her creator by mail not to let her die in the final segment? No author wrote with more sympathy for the disenfranchised; no gallery of storied characters is more varied, outlandish or memorable, and each was as familiar to the minds and hearts of a multitude of readers in the early nineteenth century as was the name of the author himself. And now, in January 1842, the 29-year-old Dickens was ready to board a steampacket, brave the winter terrors of the ocean, and meet his American readership. Not only had his good friend Washington Irving assured him that he would receive an enthusiastic welcome, but the novelist had for some time been brimming with curiosity about life in the brave New World.

It was with great excitement, then, that Boz, as Dickens was popularly known, climbed the gangplank of the *SS Britannia* in the company of his wife and her maid. The ship had made her maiden voyage westward across the Atlantic two years earlier, reducing the duration of the crossing to a record fourteen days. The *Britannia* would carry seventy passengers, an impressive gaggle of various farm animals that were being exported, and Her Majesty's mails. Steamers were the newest travel sensation of the time, for it was only in 1838 that a successful transatlantic steam run was made from England to America. Still, a nineteenth-century crossing of any kind could be unsettling – as we learn both from the earlier trip of Charles Augustus Murray aboard the foundering packet *Waverley* and from Boz's spirited account of his 1842 trip, wherein he gallantly coats with humor all that daily befell him. For one thing, he was seasick for most of the eighteen days at sea; for another, he considered his stateroom to be of ludicrous proportions, though it had been specially engaged for the novelist and his wife. Was this 'profoundly preposterous box', he wondered, to be home for two and a half weeks? Surely, it was no more able to accommodate a couple with two large trunks, he declared, 'than a giraffe could be persuaded or forced into a flowerpot'. Rolling seas caused his water jug to leap and plunge 'like a lively dolphin' while, during the entire crossing, he was forced to endure the domestic noises of the ship such as 'the tumbling down of stewards, the gambols, overhead, of loose casks and truant dozens of bottled porter, and the very remarkable and far from exhilarating sounds raised in their various state-rooms by the seventy passengers who were too ill to get up to breakfast'.[1]

Nonetheless, the traveler disembarked in the waters of Boston harbor eager for the heady experiences of a country that, in his understanding, embraced all classes in its utopian politics and measured human achievement with an eye to equality and energy rather than elegance and sophistication. The novelist traveled extensively in North America during a period of six months and, within a short time of his return to England, published an account of all that he experienced. Such a travel book by a highly popular author would be eagerly awaited on both sides of the Atlantic, and of this Dickens was acutely aware. Indeed, Americans would scan every word to determine whether his remarks were laudatory or damaging to the reputation of their new nation. Had not several earlier books, written by English visitors with a discernible Tory bias (Frances Trollope, Basil Hall and Captain Marryat among them) been excoriated and vilified in the American press? More impressively on the other side of that coin, had not Mrs. Trollope, following the torrent of abuse heaped on her book, profited immeasurably from the sensationalism? This unpredictable, if rather fabulous, turn of events for the impoverished Mrs. Trollope is acknowledged with apparent humor by Dickens in *The Pickwick Papers*, written in 1836. There, in chapter forty-five, he has Sam Weller's father propose that the impoverished Pickwick travel across the Atlantic and write a book 'about the 'Merrikins as'll pay his expenses'. Dickens did write his own book on travel in the New World, and it came off the press not long after his return; its seemingly flat title of *American Notes for General Circulation* ingeniously derogated America's vaunted obsession with money. The English were delighted with his account. Not so his readers on the western side of the Atlantic, for Boz's narration proved to be not altogether flattering to America's still fledgling society. It was based on notes that he had taken throughout his trip, and it relied as well on lengthy letters he had sent to family members, friends and his contacts with the press, many of the letters serving as aides-memoire. But his prediction to Pickwick was nicely realized: the ''Merrikins' brought out more than one edition, as did his English publishers.

Boston was the first major stop on the novelist's itinerary. It was a city that Dickens genuinely admired, and it probably set him up in expectations that were never fulfilled in other parts of the country. He responded joyfully to the environment of intellectual refinement provided in the environs of Harvard University, and commented that the public institutions and charities of that city were as nearly perfect 'as the most considerate wisdom, benevolence, and humanity, can make them'.[2] He wrote of the charities at length in his journal, often with great feeling for the individual occupants of the institutions involved. Because he was reform-minded and had once considered becoming a public servant concerned with education, or housing, or the treatment of criminals, he would make a constant effort during his American tour to visit prisons and institutions devoted to the public good. Wherever he went, feeling for the young novelist ran high, admired as he was as much for the wizardry of his pen as for his egalitarianism; his name was on nearly everyone's lips to a degree that overshadowed even the earlier, famed visit of the Marquis de Lafayette. Had his friend Washington Irving not predicted just such a welcome?

Boston gained the novelist's sincere approval, for there he discerned closer ties to an English heritage than were manifest elsewhere. He particularly enjoyed finding himself welcomed among the city's intellectuals and writers, with many of whom – in particular Henry Wadsworth Longfellow and Ralph Waldo Emerson – he became good friends. Enjoying the stimulation of such good company, the novelist was prompted to make some passing remarks on the subject of transcendentalism, a philosophical concept based in turn on a Romantic idealism influenced by the philosophy of Immanuel Kant. An important doctrinal element of transcendentalism, he learned, was a "hearty disgust of Cant." It was then popular among New England's Brahmins, though a mystery to most of the population. The term itself referred to the doctrinal beliefs of the Transcendental Club, which was founded in Boston just a few years before the arrival of the novelist and had for its most distinguished member Ralph Waldo Emerson. The visiting novelist was given to understand that 'whatever was unintelligible would be certainly transcendental' and that an important doctrinal element was a hearty disgust of cant. While not at all sure whether he understood the basic tenets of this new philosophy, Boz announced with aplomb that 'if I were a Bostonian, I think I would be a Transcendentalist.'[3]

There were visits to many of the city's institutions, which Dickens responded to in raptures. So far impressions of the developing country being made on the welcomed visitor were all to the good, almost as if the newspaper prediction of the *New-York Mirror* of 14 February 1842 was of sound origin:

> One thing he [Dickens] cannot fail to see, that men here have a higher, more pervading idea of fraternity and fellowship; that many, very many, social evils are trodden and suppressed by the great, paramount conviction, that all men are born free and equal. Here is a truth that strikes at the heart of much wrong at which he has aimed his trenchant and vigorous pen.

While in Boston, Dickens sat for both a portrait-painter and a sculptor, and made an important move in hiring an amanuensis by the name of George Washington Putnam. The latter proved very amiable, being not only the same age as the author but an ardent abolitionist; much later, he would leave a warm account of the four months spent in the company of the author.[4]

From Boston, the author made an excursion to nearby Lowell that occasioned his first ride on an American train. Overheated and shabby, the train offered no shield – with its open seating arrangement – from strangers who unabashedly struck up a conversation with him, unbidden and unwelcomed. It thoroughly ruffled his English reserve. Lowell itself, however, proved to be a gratifying experience, with Boz lauding the model conditions under which young women were employed in the factories. What made a further impact on him was the appearance of the *Lowell Offering*, a literary periodical conceived and published by workers, 'with original articles written by females actively employed in the mills'. While he was in Massachusetts, a reporter for the *Worcester Aegis* gave American readers a fairly detailed portrait of the young novelist after meeting him at one of the many receptions staged in his honor:

> We found a middle sized person, in a brown frock coat, a red figured vest, somewhat of the flash order, and a fancy scarf cravat. His hair, which was long and dark, grew low upon the brow, had a wavy kink

where it started from the head, and was naturally or artificially cork-screwed as it fell on either side of his face. The nose was slightly aquiline – the mouth of moderate dimensions. His features, taken together were well proportioned, of glowing and cordial aspect, with more animation than grace and more intelligence than beauty.[5]

As he wended south in February of 1842 to New York City, Dickens gained the impression that most of the New England towns through which he had passed were disconcertingly cloaked in an aspect of newness. 'All the buildings looked as if they had been built and painted that [Sunday] morning, and could be taken down on Monday with very little trouble,'[6] he writes at one point. There was no sense of permanence, no welcoming hint of history lurking in ruins, in cemeteries, in buildings or even in old ornamental motifs that tied America to a past – her English past above all – to which European travelers like himself could cling. A lack of historical layering – and the sense of a culture living determinedly in the present – proved to be characteristics of the New World that were ever disturbing to the novelist during the course of his travels. Indeed, this lack of historical perspective would be reiterated by many a visitor, persisting to the end of the nineteenth century when yet another spirited observer – Henry James – would bemoan the lack of what he termed traditional 'forms' in guiding American behavior.

As Dickens continued on to Hartford, Connecticut, his pace did not slacken. There he visited the public institutions that were of interest to him, including the Insane Asylum, and held public court or what was termed a 'levee' for two hours every morning. These constant, staged appearances were both frequent and tiring. It was in Hartford, at this early point in his trip, that Dickens first felt unexpected blows to his ego and the start of a disenchantment with the New World from which he never fully recovered. This was occasioned by the controversy surrounding an international copyright law. At issue was this: sometime prior to Boz's arrival, America had declined to enter into a reciprocal agreement on copyright with Britain; the absence of such an agreement meant that the press in the United States was freely issuing Dickens's novels without paying royalties to him, and without providing compensation to his British publishers. That America steadfastly declined to honor a copyright law rankled the young author, both on his own behalf and on that of fellow writers.[7] Determined to speak out, Dickens had initially done so in Boston following a speech he had given there on the occasion of a banquet staged for him in that city. He then raised the issue with more vigor at a public dinner arranged for him in Hartford. Why shouldn't an author expect a well-earned income, Dickens reasoned, from an audience that devoured his fiction? Were not his novels already as popular here as in England? Indeed, America's steady consumption of British books had long been noted by other travelers, among them Alexis de Tocqueville, who visited the New World a decade earlier and commented on this very fact:

> It is England which supplies them with most of the books they need. Almost all important English books are republished in the United States. The literary inspiration of Great Britain darts its beams into the depths of the forests of the New World. There is hardly a pioneer's hut which does not contain a few odd volumes of Shakespeare. I remember reading the feudal drama of Henry V for the first time in a log cabin.[8]

Yet, not only did the American press refuse to translate adulation into income, most publishers and editors were incensed by Boz's plain-speaking advocacy of copyright. 'I have never in my life been so shocked and disgusted,' Dickens later confided to an American friend, 'or made so sick and sore at heart, with scores of your newspapers attacking me in such terms of vagabond scurrility as they would denounce no murderer with.'[9] We only learn of this heated reaction through letters; Dickens mentions not a word of the copyright affair in *American Notes*. He wanted to wait, it appears, for the protective distance of a fictional account before he gave vent to his bottled-up outrage against the press. 'Charles Dickens has come home in a state of violent dislike of the Americans,' confided Mary Shelley in a letter to a friend, '& means to devour them in his next work.'[10] When *The Life and Adventures of Martin Chuzzlewit* was published a year later, it was abundantly anti-American.

What was Dickens to think of New York, his next major stop? The city was all atwitter with extravagant preparations that included dinners, balls and *tableaux vivants* based on the characters of his novels. Then, New York had many of the characteristics of London: vitality, architectural distinction, crowded streets and shops, theaters, an elegant salon life, slums, institutions of various kinds in public service that he would hasten to visit, and a show of humanity at all levels of desperation. Here was a city that Boz associated with the literary delights of Washington Irving, in whose company he found great pleasure. He was to meet many of New York's leading personalities, some of whom entertained him grandly, and he inspected a good number of its public institutions. Yet, Boz could somehow not take warmly to the city. There were none of the comforting, English distractions or modes of deference to be found in the daily rhythm of Manhattan life. New York was too noisy, too full of rough edges, too palpably commercial, with little of the show of delicacy and sweet temper of New England. Dickens complained of the hideous tenements through which he passed, of the poor audience showing in the Park and Bowery theaters, and of the tobacco chewing and heavy drinking that served as pastimes for much of the population. Also to be excoriated was the presence of spittoons and the odious purpose for which they served. Dark alleys, rotting houses and squalid lanes in so relatively new a metropolis shocked him; such things surely existed in London, but were somehow offset by the abundant charms of the city. The squalid side of New York made him sigh for the colorful street scenes that lend to many a blighted European setting a light-hearted air. He was prompted to ask:

> Are there no itinerant bands; no wind or stringed instruments? No, not one. By day, are there no Punches, Fantoccinis, Dancing-dogs, Jugglers, Conjurors, Orchestrinas, or even Barrel organs? No, not one. Yes, I remember one. One barrel-organ and a dancing-monkey – sportive by nature, but fast fading into a dull, lumpish monkey, of the Utilitarian school. Beyond that, nothing lively; no, not so much as a white mouse in a twirling cage.[11]

Nonetheless, the New York visit ended in an endearing tribute to the friends that Dickens made during his several weeks there. 'There are those in this city who would brighten, to me, the darkest winter-day that ever glimmered and went out in England.'[12] High on that list was

Washington Irving, though he is unnamed, since Dickens made it a practice throughout his *American Notes* not to identify any personalities, whether it be those whom he admired, those he did not, or those who so profusely entertained him with Manhattan dinners and balls. And entertain him they did. Although Dickens and his wife had become accustomed – beginning in Boston – to the exhausting round of parties and 'levees' in which they were forced to participate (often shaking as many as 300 hands a day), they could scarcely have been prepared for The Great Boz Ball, held on 14 February at the Park Theatre. Organized by an enthusiastic group of well-placed New Yorkers, the elaborate affair was attended by 2,500 people whose lavish attire (for which New Yorkers were known) complemented the quite sumptuous decorations, some of which were designs based on scenes from the author's novels. Philip Hone, who was an ex-mayor of the city and on the organizing committee, recorded the event in his diary:

> The agony [of organizing] is over; the Boz ball, the greatest affair in modern times, the tallest compliment ever paid a little man, the fullest libation ever poured upon the altar of the muses, came off last evening in fine style. Everything answered the public expectation. The theater was prepared for the occasion with great splendor and taste. A small stage was erected at the extreme end opposite the main entrance, before which a curtain was suspended. This curtain was raised in the intervals between the cotillions and waltzes to disclose a stage on which were exhibited a series of tableaux vivants, forming groups in the most striking incidents of 'Pickwick,' 'Nicholas Nickleby,' 'Oliver Twist,' 'The Old Curiosity Shop,' 'Barnaby Rudge,' etc. the crowd was immense.[13]

Dickens was truly impressed, as he wrote to friends, but he was understandably to suffer a sore throat for the three days following and was forced to decline several invitations. Subsequently he was able to attend yet another welcoming affair, this time a lavish banquet held in the City Hotel, which was hosted by Washington Irving. Feeling confident in the presence of his good friend, Dickens once more raised the issue of international copyright though fully aware he would be attacked in the press. Of course he was. (Now, advancing slowly and inexorably, there developed a running strain of mutual dislike between himself and the press over the copyright issue during the author's stay in America.) Philip Hone was also to attend this second tribute to the visiting novelist and in his diary leaves us his impression of the honored guest:

> The author of the 'Pickwick Papers' is a small, bright-eyed intelligent-looking young fellow, thirty years of age, somewhat of a dandy in his dress, brisk in his manner and of a lively conversation. If he does not get his little head turned by all this I shall wonder at it. Mrs. Dickens, is a little, fat English-looking woman, of an agreeable countenance, and, I should think a 'nice person.'[14]

Before leaving New York, the 'bright-eyed intelligent-looking young fellow' visited some of the less glamorous places there that were of interest to him, particularly the city's famous House of Detention known as the 'Tombs'. He also managed to make the rounds quite anonymously (with a few friends and two policemen assigned to him) of the city's slums and brothels. The New York visit was now coming to an end and as he prepared to board the train that would take him farther south, Dickens must have drawn a modicum of solace from the fact that an important Manhattan paper warmly supported his efforts with regard to the issuance of an international copyright law. This was the *New-York Mirror: A Weekly Gazette of Literature and the Fine Arts*, which had devoted its entire issue of 14 February 1842 to the arrival of the novelist on American shores and to the welcome prepared for him in New York:

> We trust this occasion will be seized upon by the American people to perform a solemn act of justice to this distinguished writer and his many noble brethren beyond the sea. The occasion is a ripe and becoming one to press the Authors' Bill of International Copyright: and unless this act of an imperial necessity is consummated now, speedily, this great writer must regard all tributes paid to him as a hollow mockery. Impressed with a solemn conviction that the hour for the performance of this great duty, the hour of deliverance and justice is arrived, we repeat again aloud: A welcome to Boz, the Painter

of the Poor! A welcome to Charles Dickens, one of the noblest and foremost republic penmen of the nineteenth century!

Next on the itinerary was Philadelphia, which was to offer the visitor some architectural attractions: the United States Bank building and the still-unfinished Girard College are among those he mentions. He deemed it a handsome city though its geometric street plan (conceived by William Penn in the seventeenth century) struck him as distractingly regular: Boz found himself longing for a crooked street. An important if depressing outing during this brief four-day visit was to the city's Eastern Penitentiary, opened over a decade earlier and then famed for its 'Solitary System'. This was an imposition of silence throughout the institution: regardless of the length of the sentence, each prisoner was forbidden from speaking for the duration of his confinement. Not unexpectedly, Dickens was to decree this estrangement of one prisoner from another nothing less than an unnecessary and intolerable cruelty. Communication was a basic tenet of the human condition in his view and he feared the consequences of a withdrawal from society that was unwisely imposed. During his Philadelphia stay, there was, as one might expect, a levee during which the novelist was obliged to shake hands and smile for over two hours. One visitor to his hotel was the poet Edgar Allan Poe, whom Dickens admired and whom he promised – unsuccessfully as it proved – to find an English publisher. (Poe was also connected as a journalist to the supportive *New-York Mirror.*) Though his stay in Philadelphia was short, Dickens could say that 'what I saw of its society, I greatly liked.' A brief pause in Baltimore, en route to Washington, gave Dickens his first experience of being waited on by slaves, a sensation he did not find palatable. 'The institution exists, perhaps, in its least repulsive and most mitigated form in such a town as this,' was his observation, 'but it is slavery; and its presence filled me with a sense of shame and self-reproach.'

On arrival in Washington, a first impression of the still formless Federal capital stirred little enthusiasm. Though he knew there were ambitious plans for its embellishment, it held out little possibility in the visitor's eyes for any future grandeur. He did not find the Capitol or any of the other existing architecture particularly distinguished, and characterized Washington as a city of 'spacious avenues that begin in nothing and lead nowhere'. While in Washington, Dickens visited both houses of Congress and attended a presidential reception. He did like meeting President John Tyler, whose manner he found 'remarkably unaffected, gentlemanly, and agreeable. I thought that in his whole carriage and demeanour, he became his station singularly well.' It was during the presidency of Tyler that the former large territory of Texas, once belonging to Mexico, achieved United States statehood and spectacularly enlarged the boundaries of the New World. Dickens did not, however, travel this far southwest. While in the capital, the author took the occasion to present two petitions in favor of international copyright; these had been signed by American writers who supported the novelist in what temporarily appeared to be a hopeless endeavor, inasmuch as American newspapers attacked him mercilessly on the subject. As elsewhere, the novelist was flocked by well-wishers and over-zealous supporters of his art; in his letters abroad he now often complained that he was without any rest or peace. Sometime earlier, the *Journal of Commerce*, an anti-slavery weekly, had ridiculed what was seen as a 'Boz mania' and printed a rhyming protest:

> *They'll smother thee with victuals, Boz,*
> > *With fish and flesh and chickens,*
> *Our authorlings will bore thee, Boz,*
> > *And hail thee, 'Cousin Dickens'.*
> *Beware, Boz, Take care, Boz!*
> > *Of forming false conclusions;*
> *Because a certain sort of folks*
> > *Do mete thee such obtrusions;*
> *For they are not the people, Boz,*
> > *These templars of the cork,*
> *No more than a church steeple, Boz,*
> > *Is Boston or New York.*[15]

A night steamer on the Potomac River, followed by a stagecoach and then a train, bore Dickens and his entourage to Richmond, Virginia. It is not clear on which of the three conveyances the traveler felt the most uncomfortable, but in his lengthy dwelling on the torments of the stagecoach, we learn that he managed ten miles in two and a half hours over a series of alternate swamps and gravel pits that passed for roads. Richmond itself, where he was greeted by the seductive sight of peach trees and magnolias in full bloom, offered pitiable contrasts of picturesque villas and deplorable slave quarters. Over and over during his time in the South, Dickens turns to the question of slavery, which sat uneasily on his conscience though there was clearly little in his power to affect a change. At the conclusion of his *American Notes* he was, nonetheless, to devote an entire chapter to the horrors of the slave system, feeling that an outsider could bring a compelling, disinterested point of view. He particularly lashed out at slaveholders, who were inclined to say that Dickens was deceived by the representations of the emancipationists. After all, he was told by more than one slaveholder, 'The greater part of my slaves are attached to me.'[16] Nor was Dickens ignorant of the ambiguous role played by Thomas Jefferson in the annals of slavery. Though he does not mention the name of Sally Hemings in his novel *Martin Chuzzlewit*, there is a passing, denunciatory reference to this indiscretion on the part of the third American president.

There followed trips to York, Harrisburg and Pittsburgh, all located in the south and west of Pennsylvania where, at this time, most of the important rivers in that region were being canalized to provide carriers for the state's output of coal. A three-day journey along the Ohio River to Cincinnati was next on the agenda, aboard a steamboat named *The Messenger*. Cincinnati appealed to the traveler on his very first view: it was declared to be 'cheerful, thriving and animated'. Nor was this fast-rising Ohio city less so on closer acquaintance. Adding to its animation was a Temperance Convention that was in full swing when the novelist arrived, and which provided the kind of street gaiety that he had elsewhere missed. There were temperance parades with fluttering banners of bright colors, marshals on horseback looking smart and lively bands of music intended to raise the spirits of any onlooker. Nowhere is there a mention of pigs (the ubiquitous source of Cincinnati's wealth) grunting in the streets, or of bad manners, or of any of the American habits so offensive to foreigners; the local society in which he mingled was decreed intelligent, courteous and agreeable. Was Dickens determined to see only the fair side of this city, mindful of the storm raised by the unflattering account of Cincinnati published by that earlier English visitor, Frances Trollope? Already at this time Cincinnati could boast distinguished visitors, including Alexis de Tocqueville and Harriet Martineau, who were impressed with the location's rise from a wilderness. And now it would seem from what he wrote that Boz was genuinely charmed by the appearance of the border town and its adjoining suburb Mount Auburn; he was also pleased with the hospitality that was extended to him there.

The itinerary beyond Cincinnati was to take the author via steamboat to St. Louis, the westernmost point in his American odyssey. Travel on the Mississippi held out no pleasures. That mighty river, which he referred to as 'an enormous ditch' or 'this foul stream', offered only desolate scenes of wretched settlements few and far apart, with inhabitants that were 'hollow-cheeked and pale':

> At length, upon the morning of the third day, we arrived at a spot so much more desolate than any we had yet beheld. A dismal swamp, on which the half-built houses rot away: cleared here and there for the space of a few yards; and teeming, then, with unwholesome vegetation, in whose baleful shade the wretched wanderers who are tempted hither droop, and die, and lay their bones; a hotbed of disease, an ugly sepulchre, a grave uncheered by a gleam of promise.[17]

Such was the novelist's reaction to the Illinois community of Cairo, a locality along the Mississippi that would not be successfully settled until the middle of the century. As thoroughly devastating as this description appears, it barely approaches in intensity the brutally frank treatment the city would receive later in *Martin Chuzzlewit*.

The comforts of St. Louis somewhat restored Boz's spirits. He felt less of a stranger in the old French portion of the town, with its narrow, crooked thoroughfares, its quaint houses, its queer little barber shops, its drinking houses and its 'abundance of crazy old tenements with blinking casements, such as may be seen in Flanders'. To satisfy the desire of the English traveler to visit a prairie while out West, a group of young men from St. Louis arranged for a stagecoach expedition to the Looking-Glass Prairie, less than thirty miles away. What could have been the author's impression of a barren area over which he traveled on tracks of mud, with the coach sometimes sinking almost to its windows, and where only wretched cabins, pigs of a coarse, ugly breed, and an occasional community of rough wooden houses interrupted the treeless prospect? Not hard to imagine. 'I felt little of that sense of freedom and exhilaration which a Scottish heath inspires,' he laments, 'or even our English downs awaken. It was lonely and wild, but oppressive in its barren monotony.' Even the much-touted prairie sunset was a let-down.[18]

The push was now to proceed north with the eventual goal of that wondrous tourist attraction, Niagara Falls. It was a raw and miserable day when Dickens arrived in Niagara to behold the roaring cataract from the Canadian side, but this undoubtedly added to the drama. At first, he was too stunned by the vastness of the scene to grasp it in all its full might and majesty, but:

> Then, when I felt how near to my Creator I was standing, the first effect, and the enduring one – instant and lasting – of the tremendous spectacle, was Peace. Peace of Mind: Tranquillity: Calm recollection of the Dead: great Thoughts of Eternal Rest and Happiness: nothing of gloom or Terror. Niagara was at once stamped upon my heart, an Image of Beauty; to remain there, changeless and indelible, until its pulses cease to beat, for ever.[19]

Such a heightened reaction was not dissimilar to that of other early-nineteenth-century visitors who saw in the wonder of the cataract a manifestation of the awesomeness of God, and who were wont to express themselves transcendentally.

The traveler's sojourn on the Canadian side of the border included trips to Toronto, Kingston, Montreal, Quebec and St. John's, but as it was the wish of Dickens to 'abstain from instituting any comparison, or drawing any parallel whatever, between the social features of the United States and those of the British Possessions in Canada', his report on this leg of the journey is appropriately brief. Nonetheless, he viewed Canada most favorably as having nothing of flush or fever in its system, but advancing quietly, full of hope and promise.

It was now late May of 1842, fast coming on the time when Dickens would be heading home to England. During the week that was left, Boz was anxious to see for himself a community of the much-talked-of

Shakers, and thereupon proceeded to the town of Lebanon in New York. But he found the experience bleak and his account of the visit is laced with the word 'grim'. Requesting permission to observe Shaker worship, he was led

> into a grim room, where several grim hats were hanging on grim pegs, and the time was grimly told by a grim clock. Ranged against the wall were six or eight stiff high-backed chairs, and they partook so strongly of the general grimness, than one would much rather have sat on the floor than incurred the smallest obligation to any of them.[20]

What he held against the Shakers was influenced by his characteristic conviction of the need for a full involvement with life: he viewed their withdrawal from society with horror.

Still to come was a stopover at West Point as he sailed south in a Hudson River steamboat, gliding past the lovely highlands of that river. West Point, echoing with memories of George Washington and the Revolution of 1776, offered a nice balance to the gloomy Shaker visit. So, too, did other Hudson River landmarks: the Catskill Mountains, Sleepy Hollow and the Tappaan Zee. All of them were affectionately tied in the mind of Dickens to the literary genius of his friend Washington Irving, and he was pleased that these scenes would be among the freshest of the memories he would take back to England.

A day later, on 7 June 1842, Dickens embarked from New York on the steampacket *George Washington* for the voyage home. He would return to the brave New World again, but it would take some time: twenty-five years to be exact. In 1867, his American publishers persuaded him to cross the Atlantic for a series of public readings, predicting that there would be overflowing audiences in the various cities on each occasion. Indeed there were. If Americans and their country in the post-Civil War era seemed barely more appealing than in times of yore, the author found his sentiments somewhat tempered by the enormous income garnered from his eighty-five readings. After six months of mounting the podium in the New World, Boz boarded the ship back to England with pockets quite full.

CHAPTER 11

William Makepeace Thackeray
Lectures in America

'SHALL I MAKE a good bit of money for you in America and write a book about it? I think not. It seems impudent to write a book, and mere sketches now are somehow below my rank in the world,' confided William Makepeace Thackeray to his young daughters. The letter was penned aboard the steamer *Canada*, sailing out of Liverpool en route to the New World. It was the author's first transatlantic crossing and he was in high spirits: the year was 1852, the author forty-two years old. Indeed, what was Thackeray's rank at that point in his writing career? Rather splendid, it would appear, inasmuch as he had just finished the last chapter of his serialized *Vanity Fair*

and had climbed to the full height of the literary summit. Thackeray's name was now being ranked with that of Charles Dickens and Thomas Carlyle as one of the three major English writers of the nineteenth century. His reputation was given a further boost when Charlotte Brontë dedicated the second edition of *Jane Eyre* to Thackeray, stating that in him she found 'an intellect profounder and more unique than his contemporaries have yet recognised'. Such heightened profiling was new to Thackeray – now a celebrated writer after years of toiling with his pen – and thrilled him to the core. He was anxious to live up to this new stature, conscious that he owed much to the creation of the outrageous Becky Sharp, the likes of whose personality no reader had heretofore encountered in fiction – certainly not cloaked as a would-be heroine. What proved eminently engrossing about the young Becky – who makes her entrance on the page robed in shamelessness, being both intriguing and unprincipled – was her pluck and perseverance: Americans immediately fell in love with her, to the delight of the author.

Armed with an invitation from the Boston publisher James T. Fields, and another from the New York Mercantile Library Association, Thackeray planned a series of lectures in America entitled 'English Humourists of the Eighteenth Century'. The speaking tour would take him to a fair number of cities North and South, and would last for a period of nearly six months. He was by now an experienced lecturer, having survived a bout of nervousness at the podium when he so successfully launched the same series of lectures in England the previous year. He had been helped in achieving a commanding posture at the lectern by the well-known actress Fanny Kemble, who was a good friend. A giant of a man for his time, Thackeray was all of six feet three inches tall, with 'the face and contour of a child, of the round-cheeked humorous boy, who presumes so saucily on being liked, and liked for his very impudence', wrote his contemporary Leigh Hunt.[1] Thackeray certainly exuded charm and goodwill, the latter a virtue he very much needed in preparing to accept with grace the comments in the *New York Herald* of 18 September 1852. There the caption for an editorial commenting on his impending arrival was 'Another Cockney Character Coming Over', with the editorialist going on to berate the Mercantile Library Association for inviting such a 'literary snob' as Thackeray to lecture in the States.

But Becky Sharp's creator was truly neither a Cockney character nor a snob, accepting all such slurs with admirable composure. He was firm in his determination to be open-minded and to appreciate what was both new and daring in the rise to nationhood across the Atlantic of a former British colony, and at the same time keenly aware of the negative remarks published by some previous European visitors. Not only had he come to the States in acceptance of two invitations, but a compelling reason for the transatlantic crossing was his dire need to make money for his family, which consisted of two cherished young daughters and a wife who had long since been pronounced incurably ill. Born in Calcutta and raised in a prosperous Anglo-Indian environment, Thackeray had inherited a modest fortune, which he subsequently lost on his return to England through gambling exploits and the collapse of Indian investments. The unhappy prospect that then loomed before him was the need to earn a living, something rarely expected of an Englishman educated at Charterhouse and Cambridge, and classed as a gentleman. He had become aware of the considerable fortune amassed ten years earlier by Dickens when, in 1842, the latter made the first of his two New World visits on a lecture tour. This was surely the road to his salvation, he believed. Then, too, there was another compelling reason to make a transatlantic crossing: Thackeray had fallen in love with a married woman in England and needed to distance himself for a while from a difficult scene at home.

The author's first stop on American soil was Boston, his ship the *Canada* having initially touched port at Halifax. He had made the Atlantic crossing in the company of his assistant Eyre Crowe, a young artist who would prove a worthy companion. Thackeray found the trip across the high seas tolerable enough though characterized by inevitable bouts of seasickness, much rolling and tossing of the ship and some sleepless nights during which he had entertained himself trying to understand the difference between latitude and longitude (concluding, 'Now I really think I do'). On arrival in Boston, the travelers were to spend just a few days there, lodging at the Tremont House. At this time, the main streets of the New England city were decked with mourning draperies honoring the funeral of Daniel Webster, a politician known for his statesmanship but more particularly for his mesmerizing oratory. As Bostonians held him in high esteem for his memorable dedication of the Bunker Hill Monument some ten years before his death, Thackeray and Crowe went to visit the monument, noting that the newspapers of the time were filled with encomiums attesting to Webster's statesmanship as well as to his stand as a pro-Unionist. This issue, tied to slavery, would dominate American news during the course of Thackeray's stay, whether it was in the North where the cause of abolitionism continued to expand, or in the South where the very economy depended on the slave system.

While in the New England city, the British author had dinner with his friend William Hickling Prescott, an historian whom he had met in London and whose company he enjoyed. (Prescott had gained an international reputation sometime earlier with the publication of his book on the Spanish reign of Ferdinand and Isabella.) During his residence at the Tremont House, Thackeray dined there with several passengers who had sailed with him aboard the *Canada*; he also spent an evening, according to the *Boston Courier* of 13 November, at the Melodeon Theater, where a recital was staged featuring the famed German cantatrice Henriette Sontag. As Thackeray was to lecture at the Melodeon a month later, he took note of the theater's acoustics to ascertain the proper pitch of voice he would then need. Whatever pitch he eventually decided upon proved exceedingly pleasing to his audience, as the press would subsequently report.

Accompanied by Crowe, the British traveler then made his way by rail to New York. En route, he was both startled and delighted to hear a young bookseller on the train call out 'Thackeray's works!' without suspecting the presence of the author; he thereupon found himself rereading his own prose as the train headed south. There were also sold on the train copies of *Uncle Tom's Cabin* by Harriet Beecher Stowe, which was then newly published. It had first appeared in serial installments in the *National Era*, an anti-slavery paper published in Washington; it was exactly during the month of Thackeray's arrival in the United States that it appeared in book form. Crowe bought a copy on the spot (for twenty-five cents) but his mentor refused either to buy it or to read it, having been seriously warned by judicious friends not to commit himself on either side of what was then a volatile political issue.

On arriving in New York, Thackeray wrote to his daughters that he and Crowe were accommodated 'up 3 pair of stairs in very snug rooms at a very good hotel. The people have not turned out with flags & drums to receive me like Dickens: but the welcome is a most pleasant one because there is no speechifying nor ceremony in it.'[2] It was now in New York, where he was staying at the Clarendon Hotel, that Thackeray launched his series of lectures entitled English Humorists in the Eighteenth Century. The lectures were booked in the Unitarian Church of the Unity, an unexpected Manhattan venue that initially startled Thackeray when he gave his first talk, as he gazed on the pillared nave and the oak pulpit generally occupied for religious purposes. While it seemed to him 'very queer' to be lecturing in a Unitarian church, he nonetheless attracted a good-sized audience there, with many notables of the city in attendance. Among them were his chief detractor, James Gordon Bennett of the *New York Herald*, as well as a host of staunch admirers who included Washington Irving and Henry James, Sr. The latter, writing in the *New York Daily Tribune* of 13 November 1852, pronounced Thackeray 'the most thoughtful critic of manners and society, the subtlest humorist, and the most effective, because the most genial, satirist the age has known'. Still more praise was to come from the *New York Evening Post* of the next day, which reported that the lecture (on the humor of Jonathan Swift) was delightful while bemoaning the fact that the room was not large enough to hold the many New Yorkers who sought entrance. Particularly striking, according to the *Post*, was the utter absence of affectation of any kind on the part of the speaker. Not only was the lecture itself a work of art, the paper went on to say, but there was much to admire with regard to the lecturer:

> His voice is a superb tenor, and possesses that pathetic tremble which is so effective in what is called emotive eloquence, while his delivery was as well suited to the communication he had to make as could well have been imagined. His enunciation is perfect. Every word he uttered might have been heard in the remotest quarters of the room, yet he scarcely lifted his voice above a colloquial tone. There has been nothing written about Swift so clever. Though suitable credit was given to Swift's talents, yet when he came to speak of the moral side of the dean's nature he saw nothing but darkness.

The paper noted that subsequent lectures would be held on the satirical writings of William Congreve and Joseph Addison.

Thackeray was, of course, immensely pleased that his public appearances had gotten off to a favorable start, and wrote home to share the good news:

> The lectures are liked hugely: so much so that I think we shall repeat them: and make the £300 into 6. They will do in all probability as well at Boston and I have agreed to deliver 3 at Providence (look out Providence) for £180 a minute! Think of that! […] Almost all the papers praise me hugely – one, & that is the most read confound him abuses me & says I am a Snob and a second rate.[3]

Against any derogatory remarks to which the lecturer had to submit was the happy news that the American publishing firm of Harper and Brothers had entered into an agreement to publish his lectures, the book being scheduled to appear simultaneously with the London edition. Additionally, he was made an offer by G.P. Putnam & Co. for the same rights, which pleased him enormously, leading him to remark that he rejoiced to find how very kindly American publishers were disposed toward him and his 'literary brethren in England'. Still another moneymaking offer was extended by Appleton Press, which was interested in editing the contributions that Thackeray had made to *Punch* magazine. Thackeray had known William Henry Appleton in Paris and was pleased to be introduced by him to the Century Association in New York, which proved to be the visiting author's favorite social club. It had been formed some twenty years earlier to foster interest in the fine arts and literature and counted many distinguished Americans (including Winslow Homer, Asher B. Durand, Frederick Law Olmsted and Stanford White) among its members.

The exalted reference on the part of the *Tribune* to Thackeray's brand of satire extended to the realm of art as well as literature. Unbeknownst to most members of the American audiences, Thackeray was a skilled cartoonist whose work as a 'subtle humorist' graced many pages of *Punch* magazine. In fact, he had once thought of devoting his talents to art but came to the conclusion after studying in Paris that artists were better appreciated in France than in England. (An early disappointment was when he tried to persuade Charles Dickens to take him on as an illustrator of *The Pickwick Papers*.) He then went on to a career as a freelance journalist, contributing to *Fraser's Magazine*, *Foreign Quarterly Review*, *The Morning Chronicle* and *Punch*. Working on the staff of *Punch*, he had honed his skills as a writer, met many of the artists and writers of the day and connected with a large London public. It was subsequently from among this group that Thackeray had chosen the young artist named Eyre Crowe to accompany him as an assistant on his New World trip; though he reminded Crowe that he was not the 'cutest' possible choice, the pair proved to be highly compatible. Indeed, he was to speak of Crowe as the 'kindest, fondest, best-humoured affectionate fellow', who was of the very greatest comfort during all phases of the American tour. Crowe would subsequently publish a book recounting his trip with the author entitled *With Thackeray in America*; it is studded with drawings that are both charming in their sketchiness and valuable as pictorial documents of mid-nineteenth-century America. Moreover, the book itself stands as an account of Thackeray's trip, since the author deliberately refrained from recording and publishing his experiences overseas.

Thackeray was pleased to have the New York audiences shower a good deal of attention on him by applauding his lectures and leading him through a whirl of dinners and parties. 'The pace of London,' he declared in correspondence with his daughters, 'is nothing to the racketting life of New York.' Broadway loomed in his view as being miles and miles long, with a rush of pedestrians like he had heretofore never beheld except perhaps on the Strand in London. Furthermore, he was dazzled by the attire of Manhattan's ladies, who, he declared, were arrayed so magnificently as to invoke comparison with the Queen of Sheba on a state visit. He particularly enjoyed being invited to the Century Association in New York, where he spent many an evening among the Centurions drinking and socializing; at the club he came to know a good number of the city's writers and artists, providing the kind of heart-warming camaraderie that substituted for the lively times that had been spent each week back home bantering with co-workers at *Punch*.

Certainly it was a hectic pace that characterized his stay in New York, as Thackeray never failed to report in his letters home. An average day was spent in receiving a steady stream of visitors soon after breakfast, writing notes or penning addenda to his lectures; attending a dinner before delivering his talk; then going to parties afterwards. He made a fair number of friends among both men and women, and although he found that American young ladies could be forward and commanding, he also admitted that there was an abundance among them who were sparkling in their appeal, calling them 'airy-looking little beings with camellia complexions'. Indeed, there was one who stood out from the crowd. Unexpectedly, he found himself attracted to the young daughter of a new acquaintance named George Baxter; the latter was a warehouse owner of modest means and had been introduced to him by an English acquaintance. Thackeray deemed Baxter's daughter Sally to be a highly intelligent and vivacious member of the local scene; subsequent invitations to the Baxter home distinctly enlivened his stay in New York and, judging from his letters, he very mildly lost his heart to her.

Thackeray deliberately took the occasion, during his lively stint in New York, to pay a generous tribute to Dickens, a fellow author now beloved by millions and with whom he would not always be on the best of terms. When invited to give a talk at a Manhattan charity affair to benefit children, he announced from the lectern that Dickens had paid the most glorious tribute of all to children by writing *A Christmas Carol*; a feat, he averred, that could not be equaled. 'I may quarrel with Mr. Dickens's art a thousand and a thousand times, I delight and wonder at his genius,' he said.[4] (Some years later at a public function in London, Dickens would in turn raise a glass to Thackeray's health, calling him a gentleman who is an honor to literature and in whom literature is honored.) Wherever he went, Thackeray himself was admired for his engaging style at the lectern, his gentleness of manner (invariably contrasted with what was considered his gigantic size) and for his lack of any haughtiness. Still, like most visiting Britons, Thackeray felt himself an outsider among the majority of Americans he encountered, not only in New York but throughout the country. There was frequently an abounding arrogance and show of bad manners to be tolerated from Americans, and always there was the less-than-poetic mouthing of a shared language, alien to English ears.

From New York Thackeray traveled to Boston, where his audience included eminent personages like Longfellow, Lowell, Emerson, Oliver Wendell Holmes, John Greenleaf Whittier, Francis Parkman, and Francis Ticknor. Meeting with the literati prompted him to describe the inhabitants there as akin to 'the Society of a rich Cathedral town in England, grave and decorous & very pleasant and well-read'.[5] Newark was the next stop, followed by Philadelphia; he traveled to the Quaker City by ferryboat and train, and had the good luck of meeting Washington Irving en route. Irving was to comment that the trip passed off delightfully; he had the impression that Thackeray was truly enjoying his trip and that he had entered into American life with great relish. He did hear from the British traveler the negative news that some Boston papers had written of him critically but, according to Irving, this had not ruffled his temper. In Philadelphia, Thackeray was struck by the fact that there were scarcely any poor people, feeling that for hundreds of years to come there would be room, food and work for anyone who made his or her life there. He proclaimed that 'greater nations than ours ever have been' were rising in America and Australia and claimed to feel youthful again as he imbibed 'the young air'. He was further led to remark, in a letter to a friend in England, that he liked 'the equality which characterizes this prodigious republic'.

While in Philadelphia, Thackeray took the occasion to visit Pierce Butler, one of the prominent social figures of that city and the ex-husband of his good friend Fanny Kemble; Butler had inherited sizeable holdings in the South and would prove to be one of the country's largest slaveholders. For the estranged Fanny's sake the visiting author asked to see the two children, but they were not 'shown'. When the Philadelphia lecturing gambit was completed, Thackeray was moved to make the following assessment of the various places in the North of the States where he had been invited to lecture:

> Now I have seen three great cities, Boston, New York, Philadelphia, I think I like them all mighty well. They seem to me not so civilized as our London, but more so than Manchester and Liverpool. At Boston is a very good literary company indeed; it is like Edinburgh for that – a vast amount of toryism and donnishness everywhere. That of New York the simplest and least pretentious.[6]

A three-week stay in Washington did not elicit extended comment. Thackeray attended receptions there and did meet some notables in the capital city, including the outgoing and incoming presidents. Both ex-President Fillmore and incoming President Pierce honored the British author by attending one of his lectures. Among the many invitations he received was one from the Secretary of State Edward Everett, who had been American Minister to England and President of Harvard in turn. (Thomas Colley Grattan, visiting the States some thirteen years earlier, had come to know Everett fairly well when the latter was serving as Governor of Massachusetts, and wrote about him at some length.) There were the usual pilgrimages to both houses of Congress, as well as to the Supreme Court; sketches of the Supreme Court in session, and of the two presidents, were artfully made by Crowe and included in his published account. The two visitors were shown the rooms of the War Department by General Winfield Scott, who had recently been defeated in his bid for the presidency and who would be distinguished, as a Unionist, for his brief role in the upcoming Civil War. Again they were privileged to be escorted through the different halls of Congress by Charles Sumner, one of the two senators from Massachusetts. Sumner was a Unionist, too, and employed his prowess as a powerful orator to lead antislavery forces in the Senate. On the walls of the Congress building, Thackeray was shown the murals commemorating the American Revolution executed by the artist John Trumbull: he pronounced them admirable. (Trumbull's depiction of the Declaration of Independence appears on the reverse of the two-dollar bill.)

However much Thackeray admired certain aspects of Washington and the Northern cities he had visited, it was in the South that the visitor felt somewhat more at home. He visited Richmond and Petersburg in Virginia, Charleston in South Carolina and, finally, Savannah in Georgia. There was a pace and civility in the social climate of these cities that had appeal for a European. He attended many a social function that was conducted with grace as well as unexpected lavishness, and he made many friends. Nonetheless, there was the looming question of slavery, which simply could not be avoided, much as the British traveler attempted to do so. Moreover, the conflict between North and South had lately reached fever pitch in conversations taking place on both sides of the political border, stoked by the appearance of Harriet Beecher Stowe's *Uncle Tom's Cabin*, now selling widely in the States as well as abroad since its appearance in book form. Knowing that he would be expected to discuss its contents and tender his opinion while lecturing and visiting in the South, he had avoided making himself familiar with the book's contents; it was also his considered judgment that stories founded upon such painful themes were scarcely within the legitimate purview of storytelling. Still, the book was clearly making a powerful impact through the very qualities that fiction could command: drama and emotion. Judicious friends had dinned well into his ears the propriety of his not committing himself on either side of the slavery question if he wished his career as a lecturer not to become a burden to him. Nonetheless, as he traveled, lectured and was entertained in the South, the controversy he sought to avoid in conversation with officials and friends was to unfold before his very eyes: from the pen of the artist Crowe we have a remarkable set of sketches attesting to that pre-Civil War period in American history. Two of particular interest that appear in Crowe's account are entitled 'In the Richmond Slave Market' and 'A Negro Ball, Charleston'.

Meanwhile, the Richmond public turned out in good numbers to hear the Thackeray lectures. He himself was well pleased with the attendance, having high expectations following the success of his recent appearance in the nation's capital. Now on Southern territory, he found Richmond a pretty town, noting with satisfaction that the Athenaeum Hall where he lectured was overcrowded and box-office receipts quite pleasing. It was during the course of his stay here that Thackeray penned in a letter to a friend some reflective judgments that he had made thus far during the course of his peregrinations in America; he prefaced his remarks with the dictum that no visitor was qualified to write a book about the New World without spending at least five years there. What could Dickens mean, he asks in the letter to his friend, by writing that book entitled *American Notes*?

> You learn to sympathize with a great hearty nation of 26 millions of English-speakers, not quite like ourselves but so like, the difference is not worth our scorn certainly; nay I'm not sure I don't think the people are our superiors. There's a rush and activity of life quite astounding,

a splendid recklessness about money which has in it something admirable too. Dam the money says every man. He's as good as the richest for that day. I like the citizenship and general freedom. There's beautiful affection in this country, immense tenderness, romantic personal enthusiasm, and a general kindliness and serviceableness and good nature which is very pleasant and curious to witness for us folks at home, who are mostly ashamed of our best emotions. If a man falls into difficulty a score of men are ready to help.[7]

While in Richmond, Thackeray made still another visit, as promised, to the erstwhile husband of Fanny Kemble, in an attempt to see the two daughters and thereby give a report to Fanny on his return to England. Again Pierce Butler made excuses, just as he had done in Philadelphia: the visitor was not permitted to see the two girls. Thackeray reported in a letter to a mutual friend that he found Fanny's ex-husband living elegantly and that he avoided any hospitality from Butler as it would rather have 'choked' him. The same 'pretty' town of Richmond proved to be the scene of a brief encounter with the slave market, recorded in a sketch by Crowe and commented on subsequently both by the press and by Thackeray himself in yet another letter:

> Crowe has just come out from what might have been, and may be yet, a dreadful scrape. He went into a slave market and began sketching; and the people rushed on him savagely and obliged him to quit. Fancy such a piece of imprudence. It may fall on his chief, who knows, and cut short his popularity. The negroes don't shock me or excite my compassionate feelings at all; they are so grotesque and happy that I can't cry over them. The little black imps are trotting and grinning about the streets, women, workmen, waiters, all well fed and happy. The place [is] the merriest little place and the most picturesque I have seen in America.[8]

News of the incident with Crowe traveled north and was reported a few days later in the *New York Daily Tribune* of 10 March 1853.

The lecturer now moved on to the Virginia town of Petersburg and then further south to Charleston in the state of South Carolina, followed by a trip to Savannah in Georgia. While in Charleston, he and his assistant were invited to witness a 'Negro Ball', which resulted in the sketch by Crowe. The latter recorded that the 'striking features of negro evening dress consisted in astonishing turbans with marabou feathers, into which odd accessories of squib shape and other forms were inserted. We went home in high humour.'[9]

Thackeray himself tried his hand at sketching a black girl seated outdoors shelling peanuts: this appears as an enclosure in a letter written (on 11 March 1853) to his daughter while in Charleston. He learned her name (Margaret) and the fact that she sold and shelled peanuts as an occupation; she could read a little but not write, did not know her age (but guessed it was sixteen) and no, she had never had a sweetheart. One can imagine the compassionate Thackeray engaged in conversation with her: his sketch of her is warm and appealing. A high point in the visit to Charleston was meeting the world-famous geologist Jean Louis Rodolphe Agassiz, who was a professor of natural history at Harvard but gave winter lectures in the medical college of the South Carolina city. Thackeray and Crowe attended one of his scientific talks, but the latter confessed that it was shameful to realize that the instructive discourse of such a master of science falls on the non-scientific mind with no responsive chord, from sheer incompetence to assimilate the abstruse matters under discussion.

The most southern point on the lecture tour of the British author was Savannah in the state of Georgia, which was reached by steamer. There the quays were piled high with cotton bales, testifying to the local industry and to the injustices it engendered. The travelers were booked in a hotel made uncomfortable by a constant swarm of fleas in their rooms, until the British Consul who was stationed in the city invited them to share his quarters. They were not long in Savannah, which they admired for its surrounding bucolic areas rather than for the city itself. Crowe attempted to sketch the juvenile slaves whom the two visitors encountered in the streets there, but this he found not altogether easy owing to what he described as their extra restlessness of limb and feature. It transpired that the mere fact of staring at them – so as to draw them with some accuracy – set them off into 'laughter-convulsions'. Here in Savannah fires were more common, the travelers found, than in other locations, because the buildings were largely constructed of wood. They were told that thirty years earlier, whole sections of Savannah had been swept away in the constant conflagrations. At this point in their travels the weather in the South was becoming unpleasantly hot and the voyagers were happy to turn north. En route they revisited Charleston, then went onwards to Northern destinations. Thackeray had read that twelve inches of snow were falling in New England while he sat in Charleston with windows open and peach trees in full bloom. Still he felt that for the most part America was a dreary, unscenic country; he reported that he had thus far not seen a dozen picturesque views throughout his wanderings in the States. As to the question of slavery, he laid his thoughts bare in correspondence with a friend after finding his way north:

> I have come away from the South not so horrified as perhaps I ought to be with slavery, which in the towns is not by any means a horrifying institution […] It is the worst economy, slavery, that can be, the clumsiest and most costly domestic an agricultural machine that ever was devised. 'Uncle Tom's Cabin' and the tirades of the Abolitionists may not destroy it, but common sense infallibly will before long, and every proprietor would be rid of his slaves if he could, not in the cotton-growing States I mean, but in households and in common agricultural estates.[10]

Once more in New York during the month of April 1853, Thackeray felt himself in familiar and appealing surroundings, writing home that he had never seen such luxury, such stupendous suppers, such tearing polkas, and such fine clothes. He was prompted to think of returning to the New World with a fresh set of lectures, as they had proved reliable wage-earners and he was ever anxious to make 'a snug little sum of money' for his two girls. It was fully Thackeray's intention, now that he was north again, to make the much-touted trip to the falls of Niagara, but this was not to be; he made the quite sudden decision to return home. Having seen in the papers notice of a Cunard ship about to depart overseas, Thackeray impulsively decided to board it and was able to secure passage for himself and Crowe. Within a day of this sudden decision, he was homeward bound on the *Europa*. The date of the Cunard sailing was 20 April 1853, nearly six months after his arrival in the New World.

Thackeray could acknowledge that it had been a colorful, invigorating and eye-opening trip; it had also been a bit too long. The author missed his family, his English friends and the proximity of the Continent, where his family was living at the time: it was not long before he was in Paris to visit them. Once settled in London again, Thackeray was determined not to write a book recounting his impressions, though he was tempted by the offers of a publisher to do so. He was well aware of the widely circulated accounts of British travelers before him (many of which were unfavorably received in America) and was resolved to remain a neutral voice. Moreover, being truly of a generous nature, he was grateful to his American listeners for the money that his lectures had earned, which would help him to support his family. He perfectly well knew that he could have doubled his earnings in the States had there been a copyright law to protect him from the unlawful reproduction of his books. But he was powerless to change this situation, though he resented it, and was hopeful that before his demise, such a protective law would be promulgated so as to benefit his children.

Again, the Calcutta-born author refrained from making public pronouncements on the practice of slavery in the United States. However, we do learn about his stand on this issue from letters to his family and friends. In one letter to his mother, he wrote frankly with regard to America's Afro-American population:

> They are not my men & brethren, these strange people with retreating foreheads, with great obtruding lips & jaws: with capacities for thought, pleasure, endurance quite different to mine. They are not suffering as you are impassioning yourself for their wrong as you read Mrs. Stowe, they are grinning & joking in the sun; roaring with laughter as they stand about the streets in squads; very civil, kind, & gentle, even winning in their manner.[11]

And we have already seen that another letter to a friend penned just prior to his leaving the States finds fault with slavery not from a moral but from an economic point of view: he calls it the worst economy that ever was devised, concluding that common sense will put a stop to it before the arguments of abolitionists do.

Alas, it took a disastrous war and not just common sense to see the end of the slave question. While the issue continued to escalate passions between North and South, Thackeray was to come and go a second time long before war finally erupted. In the spring of 1856, a follow-up visit to America was undertaken by the author with a memorable 'Bon Voyage' dinner in London hosted by Dickens. This time, however, Thackeray traveled without the wide-eyed curiosity that had characterized his first crossing of the Atlantic. To begin with, his health was failing so that it was often hard to summon the stamina necessary for constant lecturing as he traveled from one location to another. Then, there was little new for him to experience in the major cities already visited in 1852–3, the foremost impetus for the trip being a good income from his lecturing. Still, he took the opportunity to travel, for the first time, as far southwest as New Orleans and found there a charm much to his liking, though there were many drawbacks. Southerners, he avowed again, were more pleasant to be with than their decidedly aggressive compatriots to the North. Yet, the conditions for traveling in the South and in the West – as often recorded by other travelers – proved appalling to say the least and the discourtesy he frequently encountered en route barely tolerable. These negative aspects of his visit he was careful not to divulge publicly: we learn of them only through his letters home, which were eventually published long after his demise. One of these letters to a friend, written from New Orleans, is particularly graphic:

I wish I had gone to Cuba instead of pursuing this ignoble dollar-hunting in the languid dreary Southern towns between here and Savannah. This is a picture [here Thackeray has drawn a sketch] of 1000 miles of railway that I have passed over – pines marshes – flats – flats pines marshes – wretched huts now and again with squalid negroes sauntering about or holding up great pine torches as we pass through the dreary darkness at 12 miles an hour. Then I had three days up the Alabama from Montgomery to Mobile – O dreary yellow river! O dingy companions of my travels – What an odd dirty scene it was – with dark troops of slaves landing here and there and marching up the dismal bank into the dingy wilderness beyond: with planters waiting to come on board with their cotton bales with starved ragged planters houses shuddering upon the steep river sides.[12]

Clearly, the author was anxious to terminate this second trip and to make his way home. Still, he had earned a fair amount of money while in America and, confident now of his lecturing, looked forward to continuing that art after recrossing the Atlantic. For then, as he wrote to his daughters:

> I shall be in the civilized world again with scores of thousands of miles of railway to carry me whithersoever the dollars call me. It is not wholesome, the process of dollar hunting keeps the mind engaged with a mean excitement; I am ashamed to think how much I think dollars now. But it is only for a season. When we have achieved an Independence, we'll think about them no more.[13]

On Thackeray's return to London in February of 1856, a new chapter of his life began when the prestigious *Cornhill Magazine* welcomed him on board. Here he became a still more conspicuous personality of the London literary scene and, here, he was at home.

CHAPTER 12

Edward Dicey,
Reporter Extraordinaire

THE AMERICAN CIVIL WAR was at full throttle when Edward
Dicey, a London journalist for the *Spectator* and for *Macmillan's
Magazine*, stepped on the shores of the New World in January
of 1862. Firm in his grasp was a thoroughgoing professionalism with
which he would report the war from every conceivable aspect as he
traveled the battle-strewn terrain of the divided nation. Coupled with
a wondrous erudition was the reporter's equally appealing sense of
fairness: all that he wrote as a record of his sojourn during the ensuing six months interweaves an abiding conviction with charm. The
30-year-old Dicey firmly believed in the cause of the North and in the
abolition of slavery. This pro-Union stand set him apart from the views

expressed by most British reporters and was in distinct opposition to the anti-Union cause adopted by the British government and by that country's most influential paper, *The Times*. Although England itself had long since abolished the slave trade (the year was 1807), the stance taken by Whitehall was to distance itself as much as possible from the American conflict while keeping an eye on who was winning. There were, after all, economic considerations to be considered inasmuch as the American South – or the Confederacy as it was then called – was the principal source of the raw material that kept English cotton mills running. Some specific steps that Whitehall did take in recognition of the New World conflict were to proclaim neutrality, and to allow Confederate ships access to British ports for repairs as well as for the provision of goods that could not be classified as military. Of course, this was assuredly not all that the American South sought from Britain during the passionate struggle that was then raging. The Southern states desperately wanted formal recognition of their claim to independence as a Confederacy, as well as a steady supply of arms and ships; to this end, the Confederacy had dispatched two envoys to lobby London in an attempt to gain recognition of its new standing, but the attempt eventually came to naught.

Conditions for the necessary travel across the warring American continent were decidedly less than ideal when Edward Dicey arrived to take up his reportorial duties and so they would continue for the duration of his stay. He managed, nonetheless, to cover an amazing bit of territory after alighting in New York in the wintry month of January 1862. On his return home, he would publish all of his many observations in a volume entitled *Spectator of America* and bequeath to future Civil War historians an indelible portrait of the embattled Abraham Lincoln, whose election in November of 1860 had set in motion a series of events that would lead to the most searing experience in American history. Seven Southern states had already seceded from the Union by the time Lincoln took the oath of office as president. War broke out when Confederate forces opened fire on Fort Sumter, a Federal garrison in the state of South Carolina.

Like other distinguished travelers from abroad, Dicey had important connections wherever he went and was received hospitably against the background of war. There was something wonderfully pleasant about the first flush of American society, he announced, because he found all of his hosts both cordial and frank. This would prove true whether he was traveling in the North or the South. Eventually, he would come to believe that there was likely no other country in the world where an English traveler could meet with so much courtesy and kindness by virtue of his nationality. New York City was his first port of call after a stormy crossing at sea. He was not particularly impressed with the city during the few weeks he spent there, although he was beguiled by its nineteenth-century seaport magic as his steamboat approached the harbor:

> Fairy pilot-boats, with their snow-white sails, darted across our path; vessels bearing the flag of every nation under the sun were dropping down with the flood; English, French, and American men-of-war lay anchored in the bay, where all the navies of the world might ride at pleasure; and the quaint Yankee river steamboats glided around us in every direction. So we steamed slowly on till the Empire City – a sort of Venice without canals – lay before us, half hidden by the forest of masts.[1]

The city itself provoked some interesting observations as he settled into his lodgings, the first being the aura of equality among all classes viewed on the streets and elsewhere, or, as he rephrased it, the absence of inequality. This he found rather astonishing as 'an inhabitant of the Old World'; also astonishing was the absence of any visible segment of the population brutalized by poverty; the latter was a condition, he insisted, to be observed in all the great cities of Europe. What Dicey had expected to find on arrival was a New York on the brink of revolution and ruin, as popularly believed abroad, but he witnessed little trace of either: the port and quays of the Atlantic seaport were crowded with shipping while the neverending traffic of omnibuses, carriages and carts rendered the city streets nearly impassable. At the same time, sable-lined sleighs and ladies expensively turned out astonished the reporter, who felt he had never seen a brighter or gayer city.

Like many another visitor, the reporter was a fascinated witness to the outbreak of a fire while in Manhattan, and was surprised to learn that the many engines brought to the scene, where a store of kerosene oil had caught fire, were all manned by unpaid volunteers. He noted, too, that there was an orderly crowd of volunteers ready to work the pumps 'with might and main'. Though engines were supplied by the government, the whole expense and labor of the firefighting service was borne by the men themselves, and such was the *esprit de corps* among the different fire companies that admission into them, he learned, was sought eagerly. Though he had been witness to many a conflagration in England, Dicey felt that he had never seen a fire extinguished so courageously as by New York's volunteer firemen. Indeed, he was led to remark that the existence in New York of such a unified organization as that of the fire brigades was enough in itself to make one somewhat skeptical as to the truth of the common impression in England about the city's democratic lawlessness. How did the steadily rising American metropolis compare with London? The question was raised, but the newly arrived visitor did not believe, on reflection, that New York could be called a metropolis in the same sense that London could. On this issue, which he esteemed to be a fundamental one, he turned to the city's press as an initial yardstick for comparison. He held that a metropolis's standard of thought and refinement is reflected in its press as well as in its nation's literature, education and conduct, and the absence of a standard in New York's press was striking to him. For him, the most remarkable feature of the American press was its quantity rather than its quality; the conspicuously low standards of the New York newspapers denied the city the appellation of metropolis and accordingly indicated an absence of advanced mental refinement throughout the country. He went on to cite the characteristics of those papers that had the largest circulation in the city as well as throughout the country, the *New York Herald*, the *New York Daily Tribune* and the *New York Times*, to all of which he attributed frequent, unscrupulous reporting. Still, Dicey observed that a far larger, if far lower, segment of the population read the daily papers in the States as compared with England, this having the positive value of rendering the American press a vast engine of national education. Surprisingly, Dicey does not mention the name of William Lloyd Garrison when speaking of the content of American newspapers then in circulation. Garrison, a New Englander by birth, was an American journalist of the time renowned for his press efforts to promote the immediate emancipation of slaves in the United States. As editor of the *Liberator*, a weekly paper, Garrison worked untiringly to advance the cause of abolition, traveling to the United Kingdom for this purpose and repeatedly placing himself in danger at home for the boldness of his views.

While in New York, at the outset of his American experience, Dicey was anxious to experience for himself the standing of the black population in a non-slave state. It was a new sensation for an Englishman, he held, to enter a hotel for the first time and find oneself surrounded by black servants. This took place at the Everett House on the very first evening that the journalist dined in the New World after disembarking from his ship; there he was served by a bevy of black waiters who marched in from the kitchen two abreast and solemnly made their rounds of serving the hotel's diners. He found that in their behavior and in their very movements they were a race apart, and that they had a distinct charm, as he watched them perform their tasks in the hotel's dining room:

> Trivial as the incident may seem, there was in it a love of stage effect, a sort of dramatic talent which belonged to a far different race than that Anglo-Saxon one of ours. So, throughout my stay in America, I could never look upon a Negro face without a strange attraction [...] Living as one does in a bustling, toiling, sallow, washed-out-world of men and women, it is pleasing to the mental as well as to the physical eyesight to turn to the Negro folk, with their unwonted complexion, varying from the darkest ebony to the faintest tinge of saffron, with their strange passion for gaudy colors, assorted somehow with a touch of artistic feeling [...] and, above all, with their indescribable air of physical enjoyment in the actual fact of life. If I were an American painter, I would paint nothing but the peculiar people.[2]

He lamented the fact that the free black person had not a fair chance throughout the North, inasmuch as the legislation of the country was as unfavorable to the status of free black people as was the social sentiment of the people. As for the enslaved black people in the South, he held that not only was slavery a sin against the moral law of God but that it could be charged with one peculiar guilt not ascribable to other modes of oppression:

It is a gigantic, almost an isolated, attempt to reduce oppression to a system, and to establish a social order of which the misery of human beings is the fundamental principle. It is for this reason that every honest man is bound to lift up his voice against slavery as an accursed thing. It is thus that I think of it, let me say once and for all; and thus, as far as lies within my power, that I mean to write of it.[3]

Dicey moved on to Washington for much of his reporting: there, from the window of his lodgings, he looked out on long and muddy Pennsylvania Avenue and found that everything about the capital had an unfinished, temporary look. Pigs could be seen grubbing in the main thoroughfares while the hotels, regardless of their size, could justly be considered shabby. There seemed scarcely an architectural feature to give the town nobility, while the grand Potomac River was too far off to lend its charm to the city's profile. Even Willard's, the main hotel and famous in its day, was without any notable features although it was constantly crammed with the most motley assortment of humans possible: soldiers, congressmen, senators, army contractors, artists, journalists, tourists, prize fighters, and a host of nondescript hangers-about. With the exception of the President, writes Dicey, there was no statesman, general, politician or reporter whom he did not come across at one time or another in the Willard lobby. But it was to the halls of government that the visiting journalist soon took himself, admitting that the two grand palaces of the Treasury and the Capitol, 'frowning at each other like old German castles', redeemed Washington from an otherwise sorry architectural reputation. He was to find that making one's way into a session of the House of Representatives was an 'unduly favorable' experience:

To anyone who has experienced the dreary waiting in the gallery of our own House with a member's order, and the still more dreary discomfort when at last you do make your way into the close, inconvenient pen, the mere facility of access is enough to put you in good humor. I cannot conceive any intelligent being, arrived at years of discretion, subjecting himself to the annoyance of a visit to our own Houses of Parliament except as a matter of business; and I should

think little of the intelligence of anybody curious in such matters who
did not go constantly to the debates in Washington.[4]

He admitted that the absence of any political line of division between
the members of the House – this being the time of secession – gave a
dull air to the assembly, in addition to which there was no speaker who
could match the renowned oratory of Henry Clay, Daniel Webster or
John Calhoun during earlier days of passionate debate. Still he found
that one notable feature was the fluency of the speakers inasmuch as
he never heard an American politician of either house of Congress
stutter, or hem and haw, insisting that 'nineteen-twentieths' of British
speakers do so when in want of a word.

By that year of 1862 American politicians of both Houses of
Congress, whether voluble or eloquent, had long taken a stand with
regard to the burning question of secession and to the related issue
of slavery. The discussion had been brought to the fore during the
previous presidency of James Buchanan, who had earlier served as
Minister to the United Kingdom and who was opposed to slavery on
the grounds that it was a great moral evil. Buchanan acted for a time
as a breakwater between the North and the South but his attempts
to pacify both sides of the Union failed. In December of 1860, when
it was known that Abraham Lincoln would ascend to the presidency,
the state of South Carolina was the first to declare withdrawal from the
Union of the United States; when other Southern states followed this
example, there was formed in February of 1861 the Confederate States
of America. Subsequent to an attack by the government, two months
later, on Fort Sumter in the harbor at Charleston, South Carolina, Civil
War was declared. Dicey had often heard it asserted in England that
slavery had nothing to do with the issues between North and South,
that it was all a matter of the right of secession. But as a reporter, as a
visitor and as a resident in the States at that time, he heard nothing but
the issue of slavery in conjunction with the political platforms of both
North and South. This enforced condition of America's black population was heinous in the eyes of Dicey who felt that no nation had the
right to maintain a system that, as he had already and most forcefully
declared, was an outrage on the laws of both God and man. Because
the Southern States hotly maintained that the Federal government

lacked constitutional authority to remove slavery within state limits, the cause of the abolitionist movement to remove slavery had gained only limited ground.

At the time of Dicey's arrival, the core of all discussions taking place in the press, in public or in private was whether the Federal government would ultimately abrogate states' rights and abolish slavery. So it was that when President Abraham Lincoln issued what was called his Emancipation Message in the spring of 1862, many – including Dicey – believed that it did not go far enough to placate those rallying to the abolitionist cry of the North; what it offered was pecuniary aid to those states that contemplated the abolition of slavery. It was, however, the furthest step that could be taken in line with the Constitution and in time it did lead to the powerful Emancipation Proclamation, promulgated on 1 January the following year. By that date, Dicey had long since left American shores, but meanwhile he had made the acquaintance of Abraham Lincoln himself and was able to give his readers an indelible impression drawn with the verbal chalk of a Picasso:

> Fancy a man six-foot high, and thin *out of* proportion, with long bony arms and legs, which, somehow, seem always to be in the way, with large rugged hands, which grasp you like a vise when shaking yours, with a long scraggy neck, and a chest too narrow for the great arms hanging by its side [...] Clothe this figure, then, in a long, tight, badly-fitting suit of black, creased, soiled, and puckered up at every salient point of the figure [...] put on large, ill-fitting boots, gloves too long for the long bony fingers, and a fluffy hat [...] then add to all this an air of strength, physical as well as moral, and a strange look of dignity coupled with all this grotesqueness, and you will have the impression left upon me by Abraham Lincoln. You would never say he was a gentleman: you would still less say he was not one [...] there is about him a complete absence of pretension, and an evident desire to be courteous to everybody, which is the essence, if not the outward form of high breeding.[5]

Because many English papers, including *The Times*, did not share Dicey's reading of the Lincoln persona, they continued throughout the war to view the American president as a country bumpkin. Lincoln was to pose several questions to the British reporter about the state of public feeling in England, presenting his queries in a fair and candid way. He mentioned that he was at a loss to understand, like most Americans, what promoted the hostility shown by the majority of the English population to the cause of the North. Ah, but this was not an attitude easily explained away by a representative of the British press. In Dicey's view – a view not shared by the President – the fact that England recognized the Confederates as belligerents inflicted incalculable injury on the North by raising the hopes of the insurgents of attracting foreign intervention. The reporter for the *Spectator* also believed that England's attitude gave the rebellion a tenacity that it could not otherwise have acquired.

Dicey eventually left Washington for a tour of the States, including some army camps, which was undertaken for a short while at the beginning of the trip in the illustrious company of the novelist Nathaniel Hawthorne and the writer Nathaniel P. Willis, both Northerners and both pro-Union advocates who had become the visitor's cherished friends. Their departure was on the day that the President signed a measure for the emancipation of the slaves in the District of Columbia, with the reporter recognizing this as a good omen – as indeed it proved – of a brighter future for the whole country. In viewing the steady parade of soldiers throughout the areas in which he traveled, Dicey was led to make some military comparisons:

I have seen the armies of most European countries and I have no hesitation in saying that, as far as the average raw material of the rank and file is concerned, the American army is the finest. The officers are, undoubtedly, the weak point of the system. They have not the military air, the self-possession which long habit of command alone can give; while the footing of equality on which they inevitably stand with the volunteer privates, deprives them of the *esprit de corps* belonging to a ruling class. Still, they are active, energetic, and constantly with their troops [...] At the scene of war itself there was no playing at soldiering. No gaudy uniforms or crack companies, no distinction of classes. From every part of the North, from the ports of New York and Boston, from the homesteads of New England, from the mines of Pennsylvania and the factories of Pittsburgh, from the shores of the Great Lakes, from the Mississippi Valley, and from the faraway Texan prairies, these men had come to fight for the Union.[6]

As he slowly made his way southwest, traveling for hundreds of miles through unsettled and half-settled territories, the British visitor found it somewhat strange suddenly to find himself in a thriving metropolis filled with the luxuries and comforts of an Old World city.[7] This was Cincinnati, located on the strategic Ohio River, which proved to be as much a German metropolis as it was American with most inhabitants comfortably bilingual. There were German operas, German concerts and the diversions offered by several German theaters to be enjoyed here; such a heightened cultural ambiance understandably earned the city the appellation Queen City of the West. Apparently the city was flourishing during Dicey's visit, to an extent that Frances Trollope, visiting some thirty-five years earlier, would not have recognized. Dicey felt that the music shops, print depots, and bookstands to be seen everywhere reflected the city's wealth, education and refinement. His next major stop was Louisville, capital of the state of Kentucky, also located on the Ohio River with its important access to the Gulf of Mexico. The famous declaration of neutrality, issued by the government of that state sometime earlier, proved of no service to the South and was disregarded by both political parties. Still, Dicey noted that there was a very noisy secession element during the time of his visit and was surprised to find that the bitter animosity toward the Lincoln government was openly expressed in the public barrooms. At this point in the war, the pork trade with the South, one of the staples of Louisville commerce, had completely fallen off while trading on the Ohio had come to an end except for government stores. The very life of the Western states, Dicey noted, flows with the course of their rivers, their unfettered entry to the Gulf of Mexico being imperative to urban development. Still, he remembered Louisville as a rich city; he enjoyed being there because it had one of the best hotels in all of America and he was intrigued by the indeterminate attitude toward the war shown by both the city and state. Kentucky, one of the border slave states, was then still halting between the North and the South; its political sentiment drew it toward the latter, and its commercial interests toward the former.

As he continued on his journey, Dicey found that the road from Louisville to Nashville in Tennessee lay directly on the track of the war and he observed continuous damage, particularly to the roads, made by the troops. Nashville seemed at first so picturesque that he thought of it as a New World version of the city of Bath, but on closer inspection afforded by the length of his stay, he found its streets, hotels and public places quite dirty. He then laid it down as a rule that in America, wherever you find slavery, you find dirty conditions. Despite this remark, Dicey was to be pleased with his subsequent stay in St. Louis, a city that was a constant marvel to him in terms of its cultural offerings. Dubbed the Capital City of the West, it was both civilized and luxurious, with marvelous hotels, beckoning shop windows, numerous bookstalls and – *mirabile dictu* – nine newspapers, of which three were German and one French. Of all the slave cities the reporter had seen, this capital of the state of Missouri was the only one where he could not observe the outward effects of what some called 'the peculiar institution', meaning slavery. Ever since the war broke out, the state had been a battlefield between North and South, yet it was the only city in a slave state where the Federal flag was frequently hung out of private dwellings.

Moving by rail and water as he went west, the British journalist was led to remark that the single prominent feature of American scenery is its vastness. This did not imply grandeur in his view, inasmuch as such beauty as one finds is so protracted that it becomes monotonous by repetition. Cairo was the next city stop, a location often underwater, marking, as it does, the confluence of the Ohio and Mississippi rivers in the southernmost sector of Illinois. Was this not, the reporter mused, the original location of the 'valley of Eden' featured in *Martin Chuzzlewit* by Charles Dickens? Yes, it was, and the city could boast of this exceedingly dubious fame. As the great river steamboats were then constantly docking in Cairo with cargo loads of sick and disabled soldiers, the reporter hurried on to the city of Racine in the state of Wisconsin, located north of Chicago, where friends of his had settled. Although the town had been founded at about the same time as both Milwaukee and Chicago – all three on the shores of Lake Michigan – Racine had not soared to the level of prosperity that marked the other two. Still, so conspicuously rapid had been the growth of cities in the far-flung West that the traveling journalist proposed the motto '*Veni, vidi, edificavi*' ('I came, I saw, I built') as appropriate to a description of Western settlement in America. Despite the war, he reported, the great march of civilization was, as ever, tending westward, building railroads, clearing forests, reclaiming wild lands, raising cities and converting the wilderness into fertile territory. Indeed, he insisted that the great fact of American history is the progress westward across the prairie, and that those who wanted to understand the real character of the present Civil War should keep in mind that this progress continues without ceasing. Like many towns in the steadily developing West, the town of Racine was doing its best for the war effort. Street advertisements urged ladies to attend the Friday sewing meetings in the town hall, where they could sew bandages for the Union soldiers (each lady bringing her own sewing machine); additionally, there was a call by the governor for recruits to fill the gaps left by wounded and dead soldiers in the ranks of the Wisconsin regiments, and meanwhile the mayor was heard to announce that a great battle was expected daily. As for some of the scant entertainment offered to the citizens of Racine, a German *Choralverein* offered weekly performances of sacred music.

Not much farther south along the shores of the great Lake Michigan, Dicey made his way to the bustling city of Chicago, which he deemed the handsomest of all America's commercial cities. Although not a house had been standing there just decades earlier, the city could boast a bustling economy, endless canals and docks, seventy churches and rows of stately mansions. Did it not seem that a transatlantic Liverpool had been raised upon the swampy shores of Lake Michigan within a quarter of a century? So it appeared to the reporter, who observed that in this teeming metropolis of the West, all men were equal, as a matter not of abstract theory but of solid fact. It was true whether one was rich and the other not, for there were no aristocratic families here, he reports, as there were among the first colonists in Virginia, or Maryland, and even in some measure in Kentucky or Tennessee; there was no original Dutch settlement as in New York and there was no dominant religious leadership as in the New England states. As to the general feeling of these new and expanding areas with regard to the war, Dicey reports:

The West means to preserve the Union and is as determined as the North – perhaps more so, though on different grounds [...] There was much less of regard for the Constitution as an abstraction, much less of sentimental talk about the 'fathers of the country,' or the wickedness of Secession. On the other hand, there was a greater regard for individual freedom of action, and a greater impatience of any Government interference [...] With the New England states, Abolition is a question of principle and of moral enthusiasm [...] Now, in the West, Abolitionism is practical, not sentimental. Two propositions with regard to slavery have established themselves firmly in the Western mind [...] The first is that slavery in the West is fatal to the progress of the country, the second, that existence of slavery at all is fatal to the peace and durability of the Union.[8]

Dicey felt that as he traveled he could not forget the war even if he had wished to, for as he took to the railroads for travel, every carriage was laden with sick or wounded soldiers. In his estimation, the West had done the hardest part of the fighting and still appeared ready to fight on to the end.

Eventually, the ever-vigilant journalist for the *Spectator* looked forward to his return east. He admitted to a feeling, on arriving in Boston, that he had returned to an Old World civilization. Having wandered as he did for months through new states, new cities and various new sites, he was pleased to find himself back in a region where there was something (a street, a building, a monument) that was older than himself! There was the pleasure, too, of mounting a streetcar that would take him to Cambridge, Charlestown, Roxbury or Watertown — places with familiar-sounding English names that indicate something about their several histories. And somehow, too, it was less annoying for him to lose and find his way in Boston than in St. Louis or Chicago. He even confessed (with a sense of guilt) to the pleasure of being received at a hotel where the waiters wore white neckties and were pompous as well as civil. In the outksirts of Boston during his drives in the countryside, there appeared to him no signs of poverty, and while the poorest cottages were always those of Irish immigrants, there was 'hardly one of them which was not a palace compared with the cottage of an ordinary English laborer, to say nothing of Ireland'.[9]

It seemed to the reporter that the cause of abolitionism was strongest in the rural districts of New England and the North. Yet the Abolitionist Society had not only gained very little ground throughout America, its members often feared to acknowledge their status with the society. (This was indeed true of the British sociologist Harriet Martineau when she visited America in 1834 and received death threats for her known abolitionist views while visiting in the South.) Dicey himself did not believe that justice was done in England to the distinction between the anti-slavery and the abolition adherents. The chief tenet of abolition, he carefully explained, was that any union or partnership with slaveholding communities was to be considered a crime and therefore all commercial or social relations with slaveholders were to be regarded with moral disapproval. Accordingly, the North was duty-bound in this view to suppress slavery in the slave states at the risk of breaking up the Union, although it could not be ignored that the United States Constitution rests upon the assumption that slavery, even if an evil, is not a crime open to punishment by the government. Clearly the issue was fraught with complications, as the reporter for the *Spectator* acknowledged; he went on to cite the names of Wendell Phillips, William Lloyd Garrison, and Henry Ward Beecher (father of the author Harriet Beecher Stowe) as among those names best known in Europe as abolitionists. Nonetheless, he admits that he was not favorably impressed by what he heard and saw of the Beecher Stowe adherents, although he did admire the startling eloquence of Wendell Phillips. Then, while the reporter acknowledged the phenomenal success of *Uncle Tom's Cabin*, published by Harriet Beecher Stowe a decade earlier, it was his judgment that the book did harm in transferring the cause of emancipation from the domain of fact into that of fiction. Still, it was his good fortune, Dicey declares, to have seen a great deal of the members of the abolitionist party while in New England, for here was a set of people whom he both respected and warmly admired. It was also a section of the country where he found himself in the liveliest conversations, whether with regard to the war or otherwise. He came to an impression that his Boston friends often knew more about England than they did about America. And although New Englanders resented the pro-South commitment of the mother country, Dicey noted that an old love for England continually surfaced. Indeed, there was to him an almost touching cordiality with which an Englishman was received on arrival in America, particularly in the North. He was led to say that:

> Just as the artist world of Europe, willingly or unwillingly, turns to Italy as the home of Art, so the mind, and culture, and genius of America turns, and will turn for many long years yet, to the mother country as the home of her language, and history, and literature. That this should be so is an honor to England, and, like all honors, it entails a responsibility.[10]

Part of the visitor's admiration for this area of the States was the proximity of Harvard College to Boston; he thoroughly enjoyed the acquaintances he made at Harvard as well as the short trips on the 'street-railroads' that took him to the campus from the city, past the site of the famous Boston Tea Party. The crowded conveyance traveled a picturesque route along the creek leading from the Charles River; invariably the reporter would be obliged to surrender his seat to a female passenger who, more often than not, would chance to be 'young and pretty'. In June of each year Class Day was held at the college, and Dicey had been invited in that year of 1862 by the poet James Russell Lowell, a Harvard professor. He found the scene full of merriment despite the war, with speeches, a band, lots of food (lobster salads, raisin pies, ice cream) and a throng of young ladies 'with the brightest of bonnets and the prettiest of faces'. Dicey was thoroughly pleased to be among a group of scholars by whom he was welcomed with a cordiality that he deemed was 'so universal a characteristic of American hospitality':

> Let me say, that of all academical dignitaries whom I have known – and I have known a good number – I should say that the Professors of Harvard College were, as a body, the pleasantest. They are all men of scholarly education, some of them of European repute, and yet, in one sense, they are men of the world. There is nothing amongst them of that pedantry and that exaggerated notion of their own importance which is almost an invariable characteristic of our own University dons. Living near a great city, almost all of them married men, with

moderate incomes, they form a sort of family of scholars, such as I
never met elsewhere.[11]

While in Boston, Dicey met several Americans authors in the nearby
town of Concord, which, he acknowledged, was known to most
Englishmen not with affection but as the site where the American
Revolution sprang into being from the defeat of British troops. His own
memories of Concord, which he described as an old-fashioned, sleepy
New England village, would forever be linked – he reverently insists –
with the names of the American authors whom he came to know and
deeply admire on visits there: Ralph Waldo Emerson and Nathaniel
Hawthorne. Both writers, he declared, had won 'fresh triumphs' for the
English language. In praise of contributions to American literature, he
also includes the names of James Russell Lowell and Oliver Wendell
Holmes, predicting that the two had a far greater career still ahead
of them in continuing their accomplishments. What impressed the
reporter was the degree of intimacy and cordiality that marked the
relationships of these varied creative personalities with one another
and, once again, he took the time to proffer his admiration:

> To anyone who knows anything of the literary world in England, it
> will seem a remarkable fact that all men of intellectual note in Boston
> should meet regularly once a month, of their own free will and pleas-
> ure, to dine with each other; and still more so, that they should meet
> as friends, not as rivals. No doubt, this absence of jealousy is due, in
> great measure to the literary field of America being so little occupied
> that there is nothing like the same competition between authors as
> there is with us; but it is due, I think chiefly to that general kindliness
> and good nature which appear to me characteristic, socially, of the
> American people.[12]

Added to this praise of the New England scene, the reporter found
there a reverence for the Constitution, a respect for law and a strong
attachment to local independence. It was in this area of America that
he acquired the conviction that the effect of the Civil War would be to
consolidate the country. It had taken a while, he observed, for the belief
to gain ground among most Americans that the road to preserving

the Union was the destruction of slavery, but when love for the Union became inextricably linked with the destruction of slavery, he saw a powerful force unleashed, one that would lead to the reuniting of North and South. The US government would at last be made to declare that the war for the preservation of the Union was a war also for the abolition of slavery. If Englishmen would once make up their minds that the Anglo-Saxon race is much the same on both sides of the Atlantic, Dicey interjected, and that the resolution of the North to suppress the insurrection at all costs and hazards was much the counterpart of English feeling with regard to the Indian Mutiny, that conviction would be a valuable one for both England and America. He found it curious to hear Englishmen, who looked on the Indian Mutiny as an act of unparalleled ingratitude, now advocating the sacred right of revolution with regard to the American South. Success of the North, he was told, would inevitably lead to a war between the United States and England, yet it was Dicey's conviction that that success could only be viewed as in the interest of the countries on both sides of the Atlantic.

It was now time, in the month of July 1862, for Dicey to return home and to report, in the published record of his American stay, that he had not been prepared on crossing the Atlantic westward to find a people so kindly and easy-natured. Nor had he been prepared on leaving England, we also learn, to find a country so like his own. Ever anxious to strike a neutral, friendly note, he worried lest any friends of his on either side of the Atlantic would find his account jarring. 'I can only beg them,' he wrote, 'to believe that I have stated simply what I conceive to be the truth, in the earnest hope that, by so doing, I might render some little service towards creating a more friendly feeling between the two great English-speaking nations of the world.' His book, *Spectator of America*, stands as the document of an enlightened journalist.

 CHAPTER 13

Oscar Wilde Brings the New Aesthetics to America

WHEN Oscar Fingal O'Flahertie Wills Wilde set foot on American shores in early January of 1882, he was young (twenty-seven years old), arrogant as well as beguiling, an ascendant poet and a self-declared man of genius. What the essence of that genius was, no one in America – during the many months to come – would be able to define, with Wilde himself quite willing to characterize it as having a 'peculiar quality'. Few beyond the French, he was later to acknowledge, understood it. Still, with all the aplomb that he was characteristically able to muster, the young poet announced to the customs inspector on arrival on the Hudson River shore that he had nothing to declare but his genius. Did he really make that extraordinary declaration? Indeed that is the legend, though the statement, so often repeated, has never been authenticated. Surely it need not be, for such a saucy witticism belongs to the profile of an imposing young visitor teeming with ideas, sparkling banter and goodwill. Eager to court fame, the Oxford graduate was ready to share with the world on the far side of the Atlantic his innovative concepts in the field of art. And he was to do so in a series of lectures delivered across the American continent with an assurance and aplomb that was irrepressible.[1]

Up to this time, the young Irishman had not done much traveling beyond a brief visit to Italy and Greece, nor had he yet written any of the theatrical masterpieces that would ultimately bring him worldwide fame. He had published a volume of his poems, copies of which he had sent off proudly to Matthew Arnold, William Gladstone, Algernon Swinburne and Robert Browning; though it was reviewed in the *Lady's Pictorial* of 9 July 1881 it received little fanfare. Earlier, he had conceived a lyrical drama called *Vera; or the Nihilists*, but that was yet to be staged. His major preoccupation at this time was a passionate embrace of what was termed the new aesthetics, a creed to which the British public had for some time been reacting with mixed emotions if not outright hostility. Because the populace at large had little understanding of its tenets, there began to appear in the London press a parade of caricatures mocking the would-be aestheticians. Wilde himself acquired a cartoon persona in the pages of *Punch* and was singled out as one of the leading proponents of what became popularly known as the 'Art for Art's Sake' movement. It was also considered the latest form of fashionable madness as well as a dangerously foreign notion. Wilde's reaction to press comments (regardless of whether they were flattering or not) was to relish the publicity and brush off the ridicule: for him satire was the tribute that mediocrity paid to genius. And it was his genius to transform scornful satire into applause.

The basic tenets of the new aestheticism, though considered vague and incoherent by the public, could be traced back to ideas then being propounded by the scholar Walter Pater, whom Wilde came to admire abundantly. Pater was at the center of a small circle of intellectuals in Oxford and wrote at length about the cult of beauty as opposed to sheer asceticism, extolling the pursuit of beauty as an ideal of its own, independent of any didactic aims. He felt that the vigor, as well as the significance, of any creative effort should extend well beyond the purpose of its creator and be augmented in turn by the very impact that it had on the beholder. Further still, the Oxford scholar esteemed that art – whether it be music, poetry or painting – should not only offer an intense experience but that its impact should be disassociated from any moral or hortative aims. This insistence was a basic tenet of the new aestheticism. Among the writers and artists making up the canon of new aestheticism were Baudelaire, Whistler, Poe and Whitman, and the earlier Romantic poets Keats and Shelley, as well as other nineteenth-century creative visionaries. In all of their output, there resonated the notion that the aesthetic should make no bow to the ethical. Such an outlook was a departure from the theories of the reigning art critic John Ruskin, who held the title of Slade Professor of Art at Oxford. It was when Ruskin criticized the 'art for art's sake' paintings of Whistler – prompting an acrimonious lawsuit launched by the American artist who was then residing in London – that the rarefied subject of aesthetics became a newspaper topic. Ruskin had been one of Wilde's most admired instructors at Oxford: it was through his teachings that Wilde came to appreciate the nobility of work and the dignity of art in the service of labor. Still, the brilliant Oxford student could eventually not accept Ruskin's basic premise that the rule of art is the rule of morals. Wilde was convinced that music, art and painting were disciplines that enjoyed what he termed a sensuous life of their own and were not beholden to moral, political or religious scrutiny. He was to hold Ruskin in the highest esteem for illuminating his Oxford days, though eventually he shifted his aesthetic allegiance to the younger Walter Pater. The latter urged his students to 'cultivate each moment to the full'.

By 1882, Wilde was bursting with a range of views bearing on the 'new aesthetics', which he planned to share at length with audiences both in his writings and in lectures. It is to be understood that he did not represent the leadership of a 'movement', nor was he a member of a defined group of aestheticians who had distinctive aims. Artists and writers of the time such as Walter Pater, William Morris, Whistler, Edward Burne-Jones, Swinburne and Dante Gabriel Rossetti could

all be identified as taking part in some way in the rebellion against
the conventional tastes of the Victorian era. Their beliefs ran counter
to a basic insistence that art be morally uplifting and in this regard
they could be said to have collectively left an impact on the creative
generation of later decades, as explained by a current scholar of the
Victorian era:

> The 'aesthetic' regard for craftsmanship remained the controlling
> force behind many a serious and powerful work of art, from the
> subtly moral geometrics of [Henry] James to the enormous intellec-
> tual labyrinth of Joyce. And – apart from all formal concerns – there
> persisted the 'aesthetic' concept of the artist as specialist, working
> with his own symbols in his own difficult medium, defiant of the
> wide and widening public that was ever less prepared to fathom his
> particular intention.[2]

What could be identified with the concepts of the young Oscar Wilde
in particular was that his embrace of the beautiful during the decade of
the 1880s extended in a wide arc – beyond art, music and literature –
to all that came within the circumambience of a human being and his
needs: to the satisfaction of being served with fine china at table; to
home furnishings in every detail (including the very placement of
rugs and furniture); down to the craftsmanship in fashioning a working man's tools. Ideas that now broadened the scope of art, such as
Wilde advocated, that distanced it from its former lofty, if sacred, level,
had slowly taken root in the second part of the nineteenth century
following the Great Exhibition of 1851 in London. The very building
in which that exhibition was held was considered an architectural
marvel, being made almost entirely of glass with cast-iron supports;
it was popularly known as the Crystal Palace. Visitors were there
introduced to products that were created for practical purposes but
yet offered an appeal of their own and, in so doing, enhanced the
quality of everyday life itself. In turn this spawned a more appreciative
attitude toward what had been considered the minor arts of ceramics,
textiles, furnishings, interior decoration and the like, augmented by
an upturn in the quality of illustrated books and catalogues that now
proliferated and circulated widely. The middle classes were thereby

invited to expand their artistic horizons beyond the museums to their very homes, and it was in the years following that the term 'Art for Art's Sake' slowly gained ascendancy. The expression itself was taken from the original French saying – *l'art pour l'art* – which had been popularized by Théophile Gautier in the preface to his highly provocative novel entitled *Mademoiselle de Maupin*. Gautier, who was a man of many talents (novelist, poet, dramatist, art and literary critic), was elected in 1862 as Chairman of the Société Nationale des Beaux-Arts and was highly regarded in his day for his opinions on art as well as for the many other productions of his pen. While *Mademoiselle de Maupin* itself has little to do with aesthetics, the expression introduced in the novel's preface gained almost immediate currency since Gautier would further the doctrines allied to the Art for Art's Sake concept. This he did in the influential review entitled *L'Artiste* of which he became the editor.

Interestingly enough, an argument against didacticism in the creation of either poetry or fiction had been advanced some time earlier by the American poet Edgar Allan Poe. He contended in a lecture given in the year 1850 that:

> We have taken it into our heads that to write a poem simply for the poem's sake, and to acknowledge such to have been our design, would be to confess ourselves radically wanting in the true poetic dignity and force, but the simple fact is that would we but permit ourselves to look into our own souls we should immediately there discover that under the sun there neither exists nor can exist any work more thoroughly dignified, more supremely noble, than this very poem, this poem per se, this poem which is a poem and nothing more, this poem written solely for the Poem's sake.

It is not certain whether this declaration by Poe was known to the newly emerged apostle of the Art for Art's Sake movement in England but unquestionably it would have been espoused by Wilde had he been familiar with the works of the American author.

Certainly the young Wilde kept himself abreast of the aesthetic concepts propagated in French reviews (and perhaps in American reviews as well) for it was a topic of more than passing interest to him.

He was delighted that in London a new art venue had recently been opened, named the Grosvenor Gallery, that was sympathetic to the tenets of the new art movement and followed few of the conventions that clung to the annual Royal Academy exhibitions. An intense interest in the inauguration of this new gallery led Wilde to write a review of the opening that was published in the *Dublin University Magazine* of July 1877. In it, Wilde praised Walter Pater for his part in the 'revival of culture and love of beauty' in England, sending his former mentor a copy of the review. Among the works of art displayed at Grosvenor's were the appealing creations of Wilde's friend, the artist James McNeill Whistler, who was one of the painters at the forefront of the Art for Art's Sake movement. Given to a certain flamboyance and dandyism, the American painter evinced unflagging hostility to authority on any level. One of the paintings he exhibited at Grosvenor's was to incur the disdain of Ruskin, who attacked the American artist as impudent in asking 200 guineas for flinging a pot of paint in the public's face. The outraged Whistler thereupon initiated a lawsuit that promptly became a cause célèbre. (Technically the American artist won, but it was a Pyrrhic victory since it brought terms of bankruptcy.) That Wilde and Whistler were kindred spirits is reflected in the autobiography of the actress Ellen Terry, who spoke of the two connoisseurs of art as 'the most remarkable men I have ever known. There was something about both of them more instantaneously individual and audacious than it is possible to describe.' Her terms 'individual' and 'audacious' have clearly been very precisely chosen.

During the opening exhibition at the Grosvenor Gallery, it would become evident that Whistler was a painter as attentive to the manner in which his work was shown as to the beauty of the work itself; he emerged as a forerunner of the notion that the new art deserved a new presentation, not something borrowed from the past. The exquisite simplicity of the frames he went on to design enhanced the art that was displayed within them and started a pleasing trend. Wilde meanwhile went a step further in the cause of the new aestheticism: he declared that the concepts of a new art that denied morality as its basis extended not only to aesthetic creations but also to what one chose to read and assuredly to how one spoke; possibly more importantly still, it extended to the presentation of one's very self. Accordingly, sartorial considerations – inspired by the breeches and stockings worn by members of the Masonic Lodge that he joined at the age of twenty-two – were of the utmost importance to the ascendant Irishman in creating his persona. Indeed, it can be said that his penchant for a certain sartorial precocity had surfaced much earlier in a letter to his mother, written at the age of thirteen, in which he spoke of his flannel shirts among which one was 'quite scarlet and the other lilac'. That he eventually became a flamboyant dandy with a penchant for sunflowers and lilies is not surprising given these early aesthetic tendencies, nor is there any astonishment in his becoming a favorite of the satirical press both in Britain and in America. His dramatic arrival in New York with cascading hair, knee breeches, silk stockings, fur-lined coat, modish cravat and elegant walking stick sent the city's reporters and cartoonists scrambling to their desks.

Surprisingly, the idea for an American visit did not originate with Wilde himself. Rather, it was the brainchild of a theater manager in the employ of the entrepreneur Richard D'Oyly Carte: the latter, already well known for launching the lively operettas conceived by William Gilbert and Arthur Sullivan, now planned to expand his operations abroad. It did not go over well with D'Oyly Carte that stage producers in the United States were purloining his works and unwilling to share the profits. His latest operetta, Gilbert and Sullivan's *Patience, or Bunthorne's Bride,* was enjoying quite a success in London after it opened in April of 1881 at the Opera Comique; it also made theatrical history of a different kind when it moved from there to the brand new Savoy Theatre just off the Strand. The latter became the first theater to offer electric lighting. 'As if by the wave of a fairy's wand,' enthused a local newspaper, 'the theatre immediately became filled with a soft soothing light, clearer and far more pleasing than gas.' As a successful entrepreneur, D'Oyly Carte had no intentions of having any of his productions appropriated abroad in the absence of copyright laws to protect him. Accordingly, D'Oyly Carte arranged to stage the operetta – a delightful spoof of the new aestheticism – in a number of American playhouses with a London company; it was to make its initial appearance in New York, and the idea of sending Wilde to promote the play with concomitant lectures on the new aestheticism was subsequently promoted by D'Oyly Carte's manager William F. Morse.

The latter then contacted an American booking agent explaining the choice of Wilde:

> My attention was first drawn to him for the reason that while we were preparing for the opera 'Patience' in New York, his name was often quoted as the originator of the aesthetic idea and the author of a volume of poems, lately published, which had made a profound sensation in English society. It was suggested to me, that if Mr. Wilde were brought to this country with the view of illustrating in a public way his idea of the aesthetic, that not only would society be glad to hear the man and receive him socially, but also that the general public would be interested in hearing from him a true and correct definition and explanation of this latest form of fashionable madness.[3]

Morse knew that the pairing of Wilde with an operetta that ridiculed what was essentially a vague movement, non-existent in America, would have the result of creating interest in the D'Oyly Carte production, even if this subjected Wilde to ridicule. It was then of little matter to Wilde how he attracted attention.

Wilde was subsequently engaged to travel widely throughout a country where the new aestheticism was most unlikely to be taken seriously. He would eventually deliver over 140 lectures in 260 days while touring the New World, captivating his audiences with both his finesse and his flamboyant appearance, though rarely with his artistic message. Of course, there was always room for snickering and ridicule as well during his rounds of the country, but he handled it all with admirable aplomb. As he traveled west, his audiences were in large part farmers, cattle ranchers and miners who had little acquaintance, if any at all, with aesthetic arguments or indeed with the very notion of aestheticism. But wherever he went to introduce the new aesthetics, he held to his commitment to D'Oyly Carte, which was to enlighten the general public as to the nature of this 'latest form of fashionable madness' that was then mesmerizing the English public.

By the time that Wilde disembarked on American shores, *Patience* had been running for about four months on the western side of the Atlantic; it was proving to be a hit with American audiences as it had been with the English public. This was the sixth musical collaboration between Gilbert and Sullivan and proving more popular than even *HMS Pinafore* had been. The central plot of the operetta derides what were considered to be the pretensions of the prevailing group of English creative artists – painters, poets, musicians, illustrators and designers of every stripe – whose work would culminate in the Art Nouveau movement. Interestingly enough, Gilbert's original idea for the play was to satirize not the new aestheticians with their fashionable madness, but certain factions of the English clergy. After some sleepless nights mulling over the consequences of such theatrical daring, however, Gilbert shunted that idea aside and resolved to focus his satire on the so-called new aestheticism. The program for the opening night of *Patience* in New York was embellished with an essay ridiculing the new art movement in England. As members of the Standard Theatre in Manhattan settled in their seats on the night of 22 September 1881, they were offered a program that read in part, 'We do not yet understand quite what it all is. Quite what had produced in England, the feeling that Intensity must be expressed in one's garments, one's literature, one's walls and carpets.'[4] According to the program, the principal inspiration for the character of Bunthorne was 'a certain clever Oxonian poet whose verses once took the "Newdigate" and whose interests in society now are of the "High aesthetic line"'. It is likely that not very many Americans of the time would have known that Wilde had been a brilliant scholar at Oxford who had won the prestigious Newdigate prize for his poetry (nor were they likely to have heard of the Newdigate). He was also awarded the Berkeley Gold Medal, which was the university's highest award in Greek, as well as the top classics scholarship to Magdalen College in Oxford, which he entered the day after his twentieth birthday.

Gilbert conceived as the three principal characters in his play an impossibly innocent milkmaid named Patience, the 'fleshly' poet Reginald Bunthorne as a would-be suitor, and the 'idyllic' poet she eventually marries named Archibald Grosvenor. The ladies who attend Patience scoff at her innocence and persuade her that true love does not mean truly loving her favorite, being clearly all caught up in the dazzling dialectics of the new artistic creed. By this time, following the long run of *Patience* in England, the character of Bunthorne had become securely fastened in the public's mind to the young Wilde, as had the constant references to the sunflower and the lily – both emblematic of his dandyism. That he also came frequently to be cited as the 'Apostle of Aestheticism' has its origins in the lyrics of the operetta, as we find in one of the refrains of a song assigned to Bunthorne:

> *Though the Philistines may jostle,*
> *You will rank as an apostle in the high aesthetic band,*
> *If you walk down Piccadilly with a poppy or a lily*
> *In your medieval hand.*

Accordingly, it was as an 'apostle' of the new aesthetics that the ascending poet now made his rounds of United States cities and towns. At each stop of his tour, D'Oyly Carte's representative would inevitably be heralded with great excitement in the local newspapers, and though he was to receive a fair share of ridicule, he was admired and recognized by large numbers as an intellectual well versed in the classics, in history, in literature and in art. Wilde conducted himself throughout the tour with his usual equanimity and with an intuitive understanding – regardless of whether he was laughed at or applauded – of the fame it would accord him.

On disembarking from the *SS Arizona* that had sailed from Liverpool on 24 December 1881, Wilde checked in at the Grand Hotel located on Broadway and 31st Street and had his first American breakfast at the famous Delmonico's Restaurant. A few days prior to sailing, he had written to the American poet James Russell Lowell, then serving as the American Minister to London, asking for some letters of introduction, which were given him. It was in New York City's Chickering Hall, located at Fifth Avenue and 18th Street, that the young aesthetician made his first appearance on an American stage for the planned series of lectures. Tickets quickly sold out. His dramatic appearances in knee breeches, a coat lined with lavender satin, a frill of rich lace at the wrists and a waterfall of hair invariably caused a sensation. That he showed laudable self-possession would later be commented on by the press; indeed, throughout the tour, he conducted himself with a remarkable youthful insouciance. He was very pleased with the success of his initial delivery at the podium, writing to a friend that he had an audience that was much larger 'and more wonderful than even Dickens had'. The basic tenets of the speeches that the 27-year-old intellectual delivered to his New York audience – and would deliver elsewhere – had been carefully prepared by him; they were published, following his arrival, in the form of a preface to a book of poetry written by his friend Rennell Rodd. The design of that little volume printed in the United States was undertaken by Wilde himself, who wished to render it an exquisite example of book art: it is considered to this day one of the choicest specimens of applied aesthetics in bookmaking. In the volume's preface, which he entitled 'L'Envoi', Wilde writes:

the meaning of joy in art [is] that incommunicable element of artistic delight which, in poetry, for instance, comes from what Keats called the 'sensuous life of verse'. [It is] the element of song in the singing [...] and in painting is to be sought for, from the subject never, but from the pictorial charm only: the scheme and symphony of the colour, the satisfying beauty of the design: so that the ultimate expression of our artistic movement in painting has been, not in the spiritual visions of the pre-Raphaelites [...] but in the work of such men as Whistler and Albert Moore, who have raised design and colour to the ideal level of poetry and music. For the quality of their exquisite painting comes from the mere inventive and creative handling of line and colour, from a certain form and choice of beautiful workmanship, which, rejecting all literary reminiscence and all metaphysical idea, is in itself entirely satisfying to the aesthetic sense [...] Now, this increased sense of the absolutely satisfying value of beautiful workmanship, this recognition of the primary importance of the sensuous element in art, this love of art for art's sake, is the point in which we of the younger school have made a departure from the teaching of Mr. Ruskin [...] for the keystone to his aesthetic system is ethical always [while a painting] affects us [...] by its own incommunicable artistic essence – by that selection of truth which we call style, and that relation of values which is the draughtsmanship of painting, by the whole quality of the workmanship, the arabesque of design, the splendour of the colour, for these things are enough to stir the most divine and remote of the chords which make music in our soul. [We derive joy in] watching a handicraftsman at his work, a goldsmith hammering out his gold into those thin plates as delicate as the petals of a yellow rose, or drawing it out into the long wires like tangled sunbeams.[5]

Wilde concluded his preface (which runs to about fifteen pages) by stating that 'art cannot be described in terms of intellectual criticism; it is too intangible for that.'

The newspaper reviews in New York – and elsewhere in the country – of Wilde's first lecture were many and they were mixed: there was praise and ridicule, and there was skepticism as to the vigor of his theories. But two important consequences were not lost on the young orator: the box-office receipts were healthy, and he was being very widely noticed. For Wilde, there was only one thing in the world worse than being talked about and that was *not* being talked about. Autograph hunters pursued him and the many celebrity portraits of him that were taken in the renowned Manhattan studio of Napoleon Sarony were widely distributed. (Young Wilde would have been thrilled to know that several of the Sarony portraits would in time become valuable holdings in London's National Portrait Gallery.) Notables of the city entertained him in their gilded drawing rooms, where every *bon mot* from his lips was accordingly repeated. It was during the course of this maiden lecture that Wilde referred to the satirizing of the new art movement in *Patience*: 'You must not judge our aestheticism,' he admonished his American audience, 'by the satire of Mr. Gilbert any more than you can judge of the strength and splendour of the sun or sea by the dust that dances in the beam or the bubble that breaks upon the wave.'[6] He also made certain in his lectures to underscore the importance of personal appearance, declaring that there was nothing more indicative of moral decline in a society than 'general squalor and an indifference to dress'.

Wilde left New York in high spirits in preparation for his lecturing in Philadelphia. He exulted in a letter to a friend that he was experiencing

great success here; nothing like it since Dickens, they tell me. I am torn in bits by Society. Immense reception, wonderful dinners, crowds wait for my carriage. I have [...] two secretaries, one to write my autograph and answer the hundreds of letters that come begging for it. Another, whose hair is brown, to send locks of his own hair to the young ladies who write asking for mine; he is rapidly becoming bald.[7]

The stop in Philadelphia was of particular importance to the aspiring poet for he would have the opportunity to meet the aging Walt Whitman who resided nearby. He knew well the work of the American writer, feeling that his poetry was no less than Homeric in its wide embrace of humanity, particularly Whitman's celebrated *Leaves of Grass*, which came under government censure. Then, too, Whitman's work was breaking the boundaries of poetic form, using unusual images and symbols and frequently bypassing rhyme and meter in favor of free verse. Wilde told the aging poet that his mother had read *Leaves of Grass* to him as a youngster and that his Oxford friends held his work in great esteem. The two poets took an immediate liking to each other and as the *Philadelphia Press* of 19 January reported, Whitman found the visitor 'like a great big, splendid boy. He is so frank, and outspoken, and manly. I don't see why such mocking things are written of him.'[8] Wilde made certain to leave with Whitman one of his photographs newly taken by Sarony in New York and, as he wrote to the aging poet (in a letter now held in the Library of Congress), he hoped to see Whitman again before leaving America for 'there is no one in this wide great world of America whom I love and honour so much.'

The young lecturer experienced some unexpected mockery while journeying from Philadelphia to Baltimore. On the train en route he encountered the ridicule of a Scottish journalist and war correspondent named Archibald Forbes, who was also lecturing in the States at this time and who held the aesthetic movement – and indeed Wilde himself – in low esteem. The latter was somewhat unnerved by the train confrontation and wrote to D'Oyly Carte that he would not be able to endure many more attacks of this nature. But while there would be more mocking things to come, there would also be praise as Wilde embarked on a grueling tour of America, traveling by train to small towns and large cities during the next eight months, delivering lecture after lecture in locations stretching across the still unformed country to California. While still in the East, he had occasions when he commanded large audiences, such as happened when he lectured in Chicago. He wrote enthusiastically about his appearance there in a letter to his Oxford friend George Curzon:

Well, it's really wonderful, my audiences are enormous. In Chicago I lectured last Monday [during February of 1882] to 2,500 people! This is of course nothing to anyone who has spoken at the Union, but to me it was delightful – a great sympathetic electric people, who cheered and applauded and gave me a sense of serene power that even being abused by the Saturday Review never gave me.[9]

An instance of 'abuse' came unexpectedly from an Illinois scholar whose negative remarks, published in a paper called the *Alliance*, solicited a reaction from Wilde that he tossed out with his usual aplomb. Wilde told the reporter from the *Chicago Tribune* of 5 March 1882 that he looked forward to reading the attack for 'next to a staunch friend, the best thing that a man can have is a brilliant enemy. There is nothing more depressing than to be attacked by a fool, as one cannot answer and does not fight with the same weapons.' A month or so earlier, a journalist writing for the *Chicago Inter-Ocean* of 10 February 1882 had reported that the young lecturer was often misrepresented in the press. She held him to have more than average intelligence and without being a genius 'is yet remarkably assimilative of genius. He is one of the people who produce the right atmosphere for art.'

Indeed, not only was the subject of art always foremost in the lectures of the Irish author, it figured largely in his conversations as well wherever he traveled. On his arrival in Cleveland, Ohio, he discussed with a reporter in that city America's need to establish good local art schools and academies of design throughout its wide territory, emphasizing the need for them to be locally fostered as he did not believe there was such a thing as a 'national' school of art. He would often invoke the various regional schools of art established in Renaissance Italy as an example. In Cincinnati, the town made famous (or infamous) by Frances Trollope in 1827, Wilde was deemed by the reporter for the *Cincinnati Gazette* to possess an elegant bearing; the reporter also noted that the traveler wore a large seal ring bearing the figure of Mercury cut in amethyst, with which he sealed his letters and billets-doux. In that Ohio city, Wilde found occasion to express his delight with the West, finding it 'so new and fresh', with its citizens free of prejudice. Whenever led into the subject of the new aestheticism, he explained that that recent movement had changed the whole character of English art by giving to every handicraftsman in England beautiful designs. For it was at this very basic level of the handicrafts, he would always insist, that the foundation of all good art was to be established.

A major stop as the traveler proceeded due west was the city of St. Louis, where an astute reporter for the *St. Louis Republican* of 26 February 1882 described the apostle of the new aestheticism as a thoroughly well-bred and well-educated young gentleman with a large share of good humor and keen flashes of wit in his conversation. The two discussed British and American poetry, among other subjects, with Wilde once more finding the occasion to praise the art of Walt Whitman. He declared the poetry of Whitman to be Homeric in its large, pure delight of men and women; there was more of the Greek residing in Whitman, he held, than in any other modern poet. The *Republican* reporter, who conducted the interview with Wilde in an admirably serious manner (not always practiced by other American newspapermen), terminated the talk 'with a feeling that there was something under the sunflower and lily strangely akin to that practical system of metaphysics so unaesthetically styled as "horse sense"'. The British traveler left St. Louis remarking that it had the best-arranged museum of art he had yet seen in America; though it could not boast of many holdings, all it did contain was 'excellently and brilliantly chosen'.

On his arrival on the west coast, the Oxford poet was to find an exuberant audience, being welcomed in March of 1882 by the *San Francisco Examiner*, which had published a poem in anticipation of his visit:

> *Hail! brother hail! from o'er the seas,*
> *How glad I am to greet you!*
> *Although your pants but cap your knees,*
> *I'm highly pleased to meet you.*
> *Although your locks to some give shocks,*
> *To you I now extend*
> *A hearty hand of fellowship,*
> *My brother, poet, friend.*

He thought San Francisco a truly handsome city and in general considered the West the most beautiful part of America. Several California papers sent their newsmen to the train to greet his arrival and invariably reported their subsequent interviews with him at length. Wilde was always quick-witted, straightforward and kind in responding to the innumerable questions put to him; more often than not, reporters who interviewed him face-to-face were impressed with both his deportment and his erudition. When told by a Sacramento newsman that *Harper's Monthly* (of April 1882) had printed its dislike of the British traveler's eccentricities and extravagance, the Irish wit was quick to retort that there was no limit to the nonsense some men will write if it raises the circulation of the paper from one to two. Of course, Wilde had been well accustomed to the satirical attacks directed at the new aestheticism and its adherents in the pages of *Punch*.[10] Then in England, as now in America, he relished the attention. A stop in the area of the Rocky Mountains brought the lecturer to the mining town of Leadville in Colorado, at that time the second most populous city in the state; silver-lead deposits had only recently been discovered in the area, causing the population to jump to a figure over 40,000. There, at the Tabor Opera House, Wilde delivered his lecture and was subsequently invited by the mayor to tour the silver mine.

> Then I had to open a new vein, or lode, which with a silver drill I brilliantly performed, amidst unanimous applause. The silver drill was presented to me and the lode named 'The Oscar.' I had hoped that in their simple grand way they would have offered me a share in 'The Oscar,' but in their artless untutored fashion they did not. Only the silver drill remains as a memory of my night at Leadville.[11]

While touring several Western locations, young Wilde wrote to a friend that 'I am among canyons and coyotes, I have met miners who are nearly as real as Bret Harte's and I have lectured, and raced, and been lionized, and adored, and assailed and mocked at, and worshipped.'[12] When asked, as he so often was, how he liked America, he now felt the question too broad, for, in his view, America was not a country but a world unto itself with one region vastly different from the other. Europeans who were watching the expansion of the young republic were more interested in the civilization developing in the West, he insisted, because the East had imported too many Old World ideas, absurdities, and affectations.

Making his way to Southern locations, Wilde noticed that elderly inhabitants there always invoked dates in terms of the Civil War, and it was presumably in Southern towns that he was addressed as 'Colonel'. 'When I went to Texas,' he later wrote in his essay 'Impressions of America', 'I was called "Captain"; when I got to the centre of the country I was addressed as "Colonel," and, on arriving at the borders of Mexico, as "General."' During these months of travel in the year 1882, reports coming from the local newspapers were scrutinized by the eminent American cartoonist Thomas Nast, who recorded his inimitable response to phases of the Wildean tour in the pages of *Harper's Bazaar*.

When Wilde returned to New York, he no longer gave lectures but continued to be a personality of interest to the newspapers. A final dictum that he issued to the New York *Sun* of 20 August 1882 was that one of the most serious problems for the American people to consider was the cultivation of better manners: 'It is the most noticeable, the most painful defect in American civilization.' Soon after returning east, the busy lecturer traveled to Canada, followed by a return visit to New York from where he finally sailed home on 27 December 1882 aboard the steamer *Bothnia*.

All England was, of course, eager to learn of Wilde's reaction to the New World and he was equally eager to make his views known. The indefatigable hierophant of the new aesthetics accordingly prepared yet another speaking tour, this time for an audience back home with his lecture 'Impressions of America'. This is what he told his English audiences:

> I fear I cannot picture America as altogether an Elysium [...] The first thing that struck me on landing in America was that if Americans are not the most well-dressed people in the world, they are the most comfortably dressed [...] The next thing particularly noticeable is that everybody seems in a hurry. [It] is the noisiest country that ever existed [...] All Art depends upon exquisite and delicate sensibility, and such continual turmoil must ultimately be destructive of the musical faculty [...] All the cities that have beautiful names derive them

from the Spanish or the French. The English people give intensely ugly names to places. One place had such an ugly name that I refused to lecture there. It was called Grigsville. Supposing I had founded a school of Art there – fancy 'Early Grigsville'. [It] is a country that has no trappings, no pageants and no gorgeous ceremonies. I saw only two processions – one was the Fire Brigade preceded by the Police, the other was the Police preceded by the Fire Brigade.[13]

If there were some negative sentiments mixed with occasional praise in Wilde's impressions of America, the lecture ended on a resounding note: 'It is well worth one's while to go to a country which can teach us the word freedom and the value of the thing liberty.'

Wilde did cross the Atlantic once again, in 1883, this time visiting New York briefly for the opening of his play *Vera; or the Nihilists*. Though this first of his theatrical plays was not a hit, it signaled the start of the brilliant career in London and Paris that awaited him on his return. It was as he had predicted while still a university student. 'I won't be a dried-up Oxford don,' he told a friend in a conversation about his future. 'I'll be a poet, a writer, a dramatist. Somehow or other I'll be famous, and if not famous I'll be notorious.'[14] His fame was to exceed his notoriety.

 CHAPTER 14

Peter Ilich Tchaikovsky
and the Birth of Carnegie Hall

'NEW YORK, American customs, American hospitality – all their comforts and arrangements – everything, in fact, is to my taste,' declared the celebrated Russian composer Peter Ilich Tchaikovsky in a letter to a friend following his first transatlantic crossing. Soon after, he would write exultantly to another correspondent that he could boast of great success in New York and was spoiled by everyone. To his diary he confided that 'one must do justice to American hospitality; there is nothing like it,' and then to another friend he declared with some surprise: 'I am a much more important person here than in Russia. Is that not curious?' New York certainly did treat the newcomer lavishly, almost to the point of exhaustion, though he bore all of the attention with grace. 'If only I were younger,' he sighed.[1]

In the spring of 1891 when Tchaikovsky disembarked on American shores, New York was eminently poised – though a city then still busy inventing itself – to welcome an exalted visitor. In place were beckoning hotels offering lavish rooms and even more lavish amenities, an array of restaurants boasting international cuisines and impeccable (if not fawning) service, a new Metropolitan Opera House to rival the musical temples of Europe, a grandiose park spread like a welcoming carpet in the center of town, and theatrical entertainment of all kinds that was both sparkling and – it was said – risqué enough to make even a parasol blush.[2]

Now there would be an added attraction of especial interest to the awaited visitor, something quite grandiose, indeed a perfect gift to offer for the display of his acclaimed musical virtuosity: this was the newly constructed Carnegie Hall.

Prior to the arrival of the Russian composer, the principal venues for concerts in New York were some small, scattered music halls that proved clearly inadequate by the closing decade of the nineteenth century to serve the flourishing aesthetic interests of the swelling population. Concerts were additionally held in the showrooms of the leading piano companies, in the salons of the wealthy and in some minor concert venues like Tripler Hall (located on Broadway opposite Bond Street), in which the acclaimed Jenny Lind and other artists performed. Following the surge of interest in classical music that had been sparked by a large German immigration, informal concerts were very often held on the streets. Indeed, music in New York, as elsewhere in America, was heavily promoted by German settlers who surprised visitors traveling to Western sites like Cincinnati with sophisticated programs of Bach, Mozart and other revered composers. During the Civil War, a British journalist covering that tumultuous event remarked on the daily sound outside his windows 'of some military band, as regiment after regiment passed, marching southward. The Germans have brought with them into their new fatherland the instinct of instrumental music, and the bands are fine ones, above the average of those of a French or English line regiment.'[3] Subsequently, at the centenary in

1889 of George Washington's inauguration as president, large groups of German singing societies staged most of the music for the event. For the poor in New York, there was music, too, with the appearance of the outdoor organ-grinder whose portable machine poured out popular songs and snatches of opera. That New York was ever-anxious to promote classical music in its midst was made evident by the inauguration of several professional schools of music, all of which came into being not long after the Civil War. The first of these was the Grand Conservatory, followed by the New York College of Music and the National Conservatory of Music. But a concert setting more worthy of the city's widening interests in classical music was clearly overdue as the nineteenth century moved toward a close. The money and backing for so ambitious a project – ah, where would that come from?

The fairytale saga (for a magic wand was truly waved) of how Carnegie Hall finally emerged as a palatial auditorium rightfully begins with the passions and dreams of a talented musician named Walter Damrosch, born in Germany into a notable musical family. His father Leopold had served as the leading violinist in the Weimar court orchestra and because of his virtuosity became known to both Franz Liszt and Richard Wagner. While still in his twenties, he assumed the role of conductor and just a few years later founded a symphony orchestra with eighty musicians. Both Liszt and Wagner accepted invitations to conduct this new group, while Lizst dedicated a symphonic poem to the talented violinist who in time became a composer as well. In 1871 Leopold immigrated to the United States with his family and proceeded to invigorate the musical life of his adopted metropolis: he had come at the invitation of a New York musical organization called the Arion Society. Before the close of that decade, he was being hailed by the *New York Times* as the most highly qualified musician in the country. He had formed the New York Symphony Society in 1878 and was praised for his inspired conducting of German opera. His son Walter, all of nine years old when he crossed the Atlantic with his father to face a new life in America, continued the studies in piano and composition that he had begun under his father's tutelage in Germany. In time as his talents flourished, Walter served in several musical posts, among them as director of two musical units – the Philharmonic Society and the Oratorio Society – and as assistant conductor of the Metropolitan

Opera Company. In these several capacities as a notable musician, the energetic Walter yearned for the city of New York to acquire a sizeable stage for concert-hall performances as it had for the opera. In time he would see his yearnings realized.

Ever ambitious about his musical career, young Damrosch had booked passage on the *SS Fulda* in the summer of 1887 for a visit to his native Germany, where he planned a course of study with the conductor Hans von Bülow. Aboard the steampacket, which was making several transatlantic stops, the 25-year-old conductor found himself in the company of a distinguished fellow passenger named Andrew Carnegie. The renowned industrialist was sailing to Scotland for an extended honeymoon with his young wife Louise Whitfield, and it chanced that the bride was already known to Damrosch, for she had been a singer who performed in one of his choral groups. Indeed, both Carnegie and his bride were aware of the essential roles played by the Damrosch family – beginning with the elder Leopold – in expanding America's musical horizons. It was from his father that Walter had come to understand the need for a proper auditorium to parallel that expansion. (And was it not from Louise Whitfield that Walter learned of the sailing aboard the *Fulda* that would prove so fortuitous?)

The young musician now found himself in an ideal setting for the delicate matter of soliciting support for a grand music hall. The calm of an ocean voyage, the beauty of the sea, the sympathetic ear of Whitfield as well as her husband, and the lack of constant interruptions all augured well for the success of a sensitive mission. Besides, the 52-year-old Carnegie was surely in a radiant mood aboard the *SS Fulda* with his bride: he had courted her on and off for eight years and was finally married on the very day that the two set sail for Scotland. Fellow passengers Damrosch and Carnegie shared several common experiences: both had immigrated to the New World as youngsters from different countries in Europe, both had made New York their home, and both were contributing their talents to public enlightenment, Damrosch in the sphere of music, Carnegie in the world of social and educational advancement through his awesome network of libraries and other benefactions. (He ultimately financed 2,505 library buildings.) The young Scotsman had come from Europe with his father when he, too, was a youngster (then thirteen years old), inaugurating his working life at that tender age as a bobbin boy in a cotton factory. While the tale of his growing up is not quite Dickensian, poverty nonetheless had loomed large on his early horizon: for example, the family could not afford the passage to the New World and was forced to borrow. By the time he was thirty, he had revolutionized steel production in America and amassed a fortune. Carnegie now resolved to attend to the cultivation of his mind with as much intensity as he gave to increasing his wealth and steadily looked to the eighteenth-century Scottish poet Robert Burns as a philosopher, guide and mentor. He began to read omnivorously and eventually authored several books, one of which is a political and economical study entitled *Triumphant Democracy*, which enjoyed several editions soon after publication in 1886. Aboard the *Fulda*, Carnegie and Damrosch developed a friendship, and by the time the steel magnate disembarked for Perth in Scotland he had extended an invitation to his talented fellow passenger to visit him on his Scottish estate. When his sessions with von Bülow had come to an end some months later, Damrosch hurried to Scotland. There, amid the opulent surroundings of a rented castle with fifteen or so other guests, the musician enjoyed a sojourn of grouse shooting, trout fishing and elegant dining. In the evenings, the young and handsome musician played the piano to the delight of Carnegie and his guests, and even beguiled the castle's Scottish owner into learning how to play 'Yankee Doodle' on his bagpipes as he led them to dinner. Carnegie could not help but be charmed by the talents of his youthful friend and invited him again to Scotland the following summer. It was in these splendid surroundings of his vacation estate that the steel magnate, no doubt encouraged by his young wife, lent more than a sympathetic ear to the financing of a new concert hall for New York. Over the years Carnegie had already evinced an interest in music that prompted him to fund the construction of no fewer than several thousand church organs.

The young Damrosch now saw his fondest dream realized, for the magic wand was waved. Not long after this second visit to the Scottish estate of the American steel magnate, Carnegie formed a stock company named The Music Hall Company, Ltd., conceived for the purpose of designing and erecting a massive auditorium; he appointed the seasoned entrepreneur Morris Reno as its business director. Seven parcels of land were in due course acquired by the company, following an intensive search in Manhattan to locate the area best suited for a structure of cultural significance. While the site in what is now mid-Manhattan eventually proved to be exceedingly well chosen, in that year of 1878 the land purchase comprised a fairly barren stretch on the west side of the city between 56th and 57th Streets, bordering on Seventh Avenue. There was not much then to recommend the area, yet in time the new hall would lead to yet another remarkable birth: the emergence of 57th Street as one of Gotham's most aristocratic thoroughfares. With regard to the design of the six-story music hall that would rise on this street, William Burnet Tuthill was chosen as chief architect with several prominent architects – Richard Morris Hunt and Dankmar Adler – brought in as consultants. Tuthill was at this time probably better known in the world of music than in architecture for he was a cellist and had served on the board of the New York Oratorio Society, then under the baton of Walter Damrosch. Within the sphere of architecture, Tuthill had a strong interest in the dynamics of sound, as did Dankmar Adler; the latter had recently participated in the building of Chicago's famed Auditorium Hall. It is not astonishing then, with the two men working in tandem, that the 57th Street building would become known for its extraordinary acoustics as well as for the elegance of its exterior. Such a distinctive edifice would underscore the emergence of New York City as one of the world's major musical centers. Designed in an Italian Neo-Renaissance style of terracotta and iron-spotted brick, the plans called for the structure to accommodate three music chambers: a main hall seating 2,800; a recital hall seating less than half that number; and an auditorium for chamber music with places for 250 patrons. Curiously, the name of the building itself would not reflect the donor's generosity: it would be called simply the Music Hall. Only three years later would the name be changed to Carnegie Hall – this was intended not only to reflect the name of the donor who brought the building into being but to distinguish it from the less exalted status of an ordinary music hall.

As work progressed on what would emerge as an acoustical marvel, newspapers in and out of the city busied themselves reporting in detail on the building's architectural properties. 'The ceiling of what we have loosely called the proscenium has evidently been modeled with great care with reference to acoustics,' commented the *New York Times* on 2 May 1891:

> The arch of the stage is elliptic, is carried upon rich and heavy pilasters, and is decorated in relief, both on the face and in the soffits. The ceiling of the stage may be called a semi-dome though very inaccurately, for it is again evident that its surface has been most carefully varied, and the general form is much more nearly a quarter of an ovoid than a quarter of a sphere. The general tone of the house is a pale salmon-color, produced by a stenciling of white upon a background of purplish pink, officially described as old rose. The seats throughout are extremely comfortable, though the chairs now in the boxes are only provisional. The seating capacity of the house is officially given at 3,000 with standing room for 1,000 more.

These particulars and more found their way into papers circulating throughout the country – not only those with a readership interested in musical developments but those with readers interested in the country's cultural advancement. *Harper's Weekly* of 9 May 1891 was keen to point out that the new recital hall, constructed thirty feet below the level of the street, was the first attempt in the country to convert the basement of a building into a forum appropriate for entertainment purposes. This notion, the paper divulged, was borrowed from Wyndham's Criterion Theatre in London. The newspaper went on to extol the design of the main auditorium, pronouncing it 'a radical departure from the stiff, barren-looking rooms that we have been accustomed to, in that it has two tiers of boxes rising above the main floor'. *Harper's* acknowledged the commanding roles taken by Walter Damrosch and Morris Reno in the realization of the hall while extending recognition to the source of the finances behind it. 'Backed up by Mr. Carnegie's unselfish public spirit, [the two men] have had erected a music hall capable of meeting any demands that can be made upon it.' The fact that so distinguished a musician as Tchaikovsky was invited for its inauguration led *Harper's* to a prophetic statement: 'The music festival with which it opens its doors is a promise of generous endeavor for its future life and prosperity.'

It was not until work on the hall had somewhat progressed that the positioning of the front entrance aroused curiosity. In time it was divulged to the public that the larger though subordinate front of the building was designed to face west on Seventh Avenue, while the smaller or principal front, with its ornate cornices, decorations and tracery in terracotta would lend a distinct presence to 57th Street. There was little doubt that the latter street would rapidly become an address of distinction once the imposing edifice threw open its doors. That the new structure would prove a public auditorium of easy access from various parts of the city was yet another feature duly lauded by the press. It was also noted in the press that although the new edifice was large, if not imposing, it would not take its place among the towering buildings that were beginning to dominate lower Manhattan. (Less than fifteen years later, the distinguished author Henry James would bemoan the fact that time-honored structures in the city were mercilessly deprived of their visibility by the ever-multiplying skyscrapers.) In time, another important step was taken to ensure the success of the hall: young Damrosch happily announced that the building's benefactor had agreed to underwrite the hiring of the city's first permanent orchestra. With this increased show of generosity, New Yorkers could now be assured that truly professional musicians would ensure the success of the new hall in their midst, for did not the new auditorium underscore the emergence of New York City as one of the world's major musical centers? By the spring of 1891, construction of the building was completed and by that time Peter Ilich Tchaikovsky had been persuaded to grace the five-day opening festival with his presence.

Tchaikovsky announced in February of 1891 to his brother Anatoli that:

> I am invited to conduct at three concerts which will take place in con-
> nection with the opening of a new Concert hall in New York. At one
> of them I shall conduct a symphony, at another the Piano Concerto,
> and at the third a chorus; the fee they offer me is quite sufficient –
> 2,500 dollars – and I shall go with pleasure as I am very interested
> in the journey itself.[4]

Indeed he was. As a sophisticated traveler, Tchaikovsky was truly curious about the New World, as he had been about Paris and the many
other capitals he visited. Moreover, an American tour loomed on his
horizon as something altogether challenging and exotic. 'There is a
prospect of a tour in Scandinavia and also in America,' he had written in
a letter two years earlier. 'But nothing is decided as to the first, and the
second seems so fantastic that I can hardly give it a serious thought.'[5]
Then, as the prospect became a reality, he admitted that an American
tour had long been one of his dreams.

The Russian composer sailed for America from Le Havre aboard
the *SS Bretagne* on 18 April 1891; he described the ship as a veri-
table floating palace, being impressed with both the accommodations and the fact that so large a vessel moved so quietly that one
could hardly believe oneself on the water. It was most certainly a
far cry from the experiences of earlier nineteenth-century travelers. (Charles Dickens had described his diminutive stateroom in
1842 as a profoundly preposterous 'box', while rolling seas caused
his water jug to leap and plunge like a lively dolphin.) On disembarking in New York, Tchaikovsky was met by Morris Reno and
his daughter Alice, who was at first mistaken by the press for the
composer's wife. Alice proved not only delightful but, because of
her fluent French, a great help, since Tchaikovsky's English was
virtually non-existent. As he was to say during the course of his
five-day New York visit, conversations are held in 'the queerest
mixture of English, French and German'.[6] He was fluent in the
latter two languages.

Immediately on arrival, the composer was taken to the Hotel
Normandie, located on Broadway at 38th Street, and the next day he
was escorted to the Music Hall. Aware of Carnegie's role in making
the hall possible, he declared the new symphony space 'a magnificent
building' and there, appropriately, he met Walter Damrosch. The
youthful American conductor, in the midst of rehearsing for the festival, introduced the composer to his orchestra, speaking in German.
As it was only the previous season that the musicians had given the
American premiere of Tchaikovsky's Fourth Symphony, they were
thrilled to meet the eminent musician as well as to find themselves
rehearsing under his direction. The Russian visitor found young Walter

much to his liking and had equally complimentary things to say about the orchestra, which he pronounced 'excellent'.

By this time, the newspapers in and out of New York were all abuzz with news of the Russian composer's arrival. Already the *New York Times* had published a complete listing of the five-day musical program in its issue of 3 May 1891. The audience was to hear several Tchaikovsky pieces: the 'Marche Solennelle', 'Suite No. 3', two a cappella choruses and the 'Concerto No. 3' for piano. There would be works by Beethoven and other composers but it was arranged that Tchaikovsky would conduct his own music, sharing the baton with Damrosch. This highly eventful opening was the leading topic of conversation not only on the east coast but in the far-flung parts of the American nation, with the *Bismarck Daily Tribune* of North Dakota heralding the five-day festival, under date of 3 May 1891, with the headline 'A New Musical Epoch'. The paper went on to praise the majestic proportions of the new Music Hall, noting that the festival would become laudable as much for the music as for the presence of the great Russian composer. This visitor, the paper reported, 'will no doubt be the musical lion of the year.' And he certainly was, for America's music population had for some time basked in the majesty of the composer's creations. Some months before Tchaikovsky's arrival, a New York critic had reviewed a performance of his *Hamlet* overture, writing in the *Evening Post* of 16 February 1891:

This Overture is one of the most important novelties produced here in many years, a composition which indicates that the gifted Russian composer, who is only fifty years old, is destined to become one of the greatest composers of this century. Indeed, his new 'Hamlet' overture would establish his claim to that distinction had he written nothing else. It displays a marvelous mastery of all the technical details of composition and instrumentation – as wonderful in its way as the most brilliant feats of the greatest living pianists. And the music is so dramatically brilliant that it is not difficult to find in it the play after which it is named.

Tchaikovsky barely had time to rehearse the musicians following his arrival, besieged as he was socially on all sides by those responsible for the festival and those who were not. On the opening night of 5 May he was escorted to the hall in a carriage filled to overflowing with attendants, and when he appeared before the orchestra to conduct his 'Marche Solennelle', there was thunderous applause. The composer recorded in his diary with both satisfaction and relief that the 'Marche' went splendidly and was a great success. At first, Tchaikovsky was a little disconcerted by the placing of the orchestra, as reported in *Harper's Weekly* of 16 May 1891. In Europe, he had always been accustomed to the placement of the orchestra members in front of him, arranged in a solid phalanx. Now the placement was elongated to the extreme width of the stage, this having been made necessary by the presence of a chorus. But all was well when young Damrosch promised Tchaikovsky a traditional placement of the orchestra on the stage when the composer himself conducted. *Harper's* further reported that the Russian musician was astonished at the strong performance of the Symphony Society's orchestra and equally delighted with the ensemble work of the chorus. Tchaikovsky in turn was received with tumultuous acclaim and instantly captured the audience when he led the orchestra in the performance of his exhilarating 'Marche Solennelle'. Newspapers the next day could speak of little other than the good fortune of New York in acquiring an impressive music hall and attracting the visit of the wondrously talented Russian composer. the *New York Times* of 6 May 1891 was pleased to announce that the new hall stood the test well, with its 'acoustic properties found to be adequate', and that Tchaikovsky, 'one of the high figures of music to-day, was greeted as he deserved to be and conducted his spirited, militant March Solennelle, in which the theme of the Russian national hymn is admirably employed. He was twice recalled.'

Much less pleased was Tchaikovsky with the remarks of one of Manhattan's leading newspapers, the *New York Herald*, which hazarded the guess the day following the opening concert that the composer was about sixty years of age:

> Tchaikovsky is a man of ample proportions, with rather grey hair, well built, of a pleasing appearance, and about sixty years of age. He seemed rather nervous, and answered the applause with a number of stiff little bows. But as soon as he had taken the baton he was quite master of himself.[7]

Tchaikovsky was horrified not only that his shyness was noticeable in the 'stiff little bows' but that he appeared nearly ten years older than he was. Still, he could confide to his diary following the next two concerts that he and his music received nothing but accolades. 'The Third Suite is praised to the skies,' he wrote, 'and, what is more, my conducting also. Am I really such a good conductor, or do the Americans exaggerate?'[8]

No, the Americans truly did not exaggerate his musical talents, whether as conductor or composer. At this point in his life, Tchaikovsky had composed over 300 works, including a number of operas and five symphonies; Americans knew his work and were thrilled that he honored the New World with his presence. His musical genius, recognized early on, had already become one of the glories of imperial Russia, although that country was a latecomer to the nineteenth-century musical scene. The first Russian musical conservatory did not open until 1862, nor did the profession of musical artist exist at that time in Russia as it did with such éclat in the countries of Germany, Austria, Italy and France. It was at the St. Petersburg Conservatory that the budding musician developed his extraordinary talents (having first attempted a career in law by enrolling for studies in the School of Jurisprudence and working as an official in the Ministry of Justice for four years.) But music was the young nobleman's calling despite the fact that this was not considered a respectable occupation for a member of the Russian aristocracy. Nonetheless, Tchaikovsky pursued it with ardor beginning in 1863 and within three years produced his first symphony. Although he would often travel abroad when invited to conduct, he was always linked in spirit and affection with St. Petersburg and, in time, his music proved to capture the mystery, the power, the flair, and the pervasive sadness of that imperial city. Indeed, 'Tchaikovsky was an imperial composer in several ways,' comments an authority on Russian history:

He shared the imperial mystique, and many of his compositions partook in an imperial idiom epitomized in St. Petersburg. Like the architects of Petersburg, Tchaikovsky engaged in a process of incorporation in his music by introducing Russian folk themes or melodies of his own, recalling folk themes into western, German, formal structures. His genius for doing so was astonishing. Rather than lowering orchestral genres to the level of the popular, he lifted the popular to the stature of the symphonic. He was considered the most European of the Russian composers of the late nineteenth century and endured the obloquy of [Russian] critics who favored indigenous national themes and modes.[9]

Outside the world of music there was scarcely enough time for the composer to play the tourist in New York, whirled about as he was with a round of visits from reporters, composers, librettists, and new acquaintances – not to mention a flurry of dinners and parties. Tchaikovsky had already met Andrew Carnegie on several occasions although this had been amidst a throng of others. Then, on the evening of 10 May, he was invited to the home of the celebrated tycoon for dinner:

> This singular man, Carnegie, who rapidly rose from a telegraph apprentice to be one of the richest men in America, while still remaining quite simple, inspires me with unusual confidence, perhaps because he shows me so much sympathy. During the evening he expressed his liking for me in a very marked manner. He took my hands in his, and declared that, though not crowned, I was a genuine king of music. He embraced me (without kissing me: men do not kiss over here), got on tiptoe and stretched his hand up to indicate my greatness, and finally made the whole company laugh by imitating my conducting. This he did so solemnly, so well, and so like me, that I myself was quite delighted. His wife is also an extremely simple and charming young lady, and showed her interest in me in every possible way.[10]

Tchaikovsky managed a brief stroll along Fifth Avenue where he marveled at what he called 'the palaces' of the rich. (Carnegie's mansion located on Fifth Avenue and 91st Street was then not quite ready for occupancy, but exists to this day in all its splendor, no longer as a residence but as a museum.) Among the many dinners to which he was invited was a luxurious repast at the famous Delmonico's. He was intrigued by his meal in the legendary restaurant where, as he recorded in his diary, he was served oysters with a sauce of small

turtles and cheese. This was a typical dish that New York offered
its nineteenth-century visitors, nearly all of whom remarked on its
uniqueness. The few walks he was able to take on Broadway (where
he bought a hat) led him to pronounce it an extraordinary street where
houses of one and two stories alternate with nine-storied structures.
Further downtown, he found the Broadway buildings 'simply colos-
sal': 'I cannot understand how anyone can live on the thirteenth floor,'
he wrote.[11] As a celebrity visitor to New York it was important that he
pose for a photograph during his stay, so the Russian musician was
taken early in his visit to the prestigious studio of Napoleon Sarony,
famed for his photographs of Oscar Wilde and other celebrities. With
his usual warm response to all new experiences, Tchaikovsky reported
that Sarony received his party

> in a red nightcap. I never came across such a droll fellow. He is a
> parody of Napoleon III. He turned me round and round while he
> looked for the best side of the face – I was photographed in every
> conceivable position during which the old man entertained me with
> all kinds of mechanical toys.[12]

For all of his peculiarities, Sarony was declared by his sitter to be
unusually appealing and cordial 'in the American way'. Then, from the
photographer's studio, Tchaikovsky was escorted on a drive through
Central Park, which he described as 'newly laid out, but very beautiful. There was a crowd of smart ladies and carriages.'[13] The composer
also had the occasion to ride the recently constructed elevated railway,
but mostly he made his way about on foot or in private carriages. He
never saw the profoundly seedy side of the city, either because his
American attendants studiously avoided such contact or because there
was so little time in his hectic schedule. What is surprising is the level
of Tchaikovsky's poise and endurance under the swirl of activity that
marked his Gotham visit. He was by nature a reclusive personality,
uncommonly sensitive and given to bouts of melancholia, all of which
are reflected in his diary entries and just as often in his music. His
American visit was at the tail end of a fairly arduous journey across
Europe lasting three weeks, which had taken him away from the relative tranquility of his home, an environment where he felt he could

work at his best, to several major stops on the European continent including Berlin, Paris and Rouen. Already in Berlin he suffered pangs of homesickness, confiding to his music publisher that 'If I am as wildly homesick as I was on the way here [from Moscow] then I believe I'll never reach America but will flee home in shame half an hour before the ship leaves.'[14] From Rouen on 15 April 1891 he wrote to a friend:

> On the way to America I will scarcely have the opportunity to work. In the first place, my spirits are in an abominable state owing to very intricate reasons upon which I shall not elaborate in order not to tire you. Secondly, the impressions of the sea, the bustle of a ship, no doubt some tossing about and above all the incessant tinkling on the piano by various English misses who will be my companions – all this will bother me. Thirdly, I am already disturbed by emotions awaiting me in America. From the first day in America I must begin to rehearse the four Concerts that I am obliged to conduct. [The performance of] the concerts will come next, along with them, banquets, receptions – In a word various activities incompatible with composing. But there's another matter. For some time the prospect of urgent, tiresome labor has begun to scare me. The realization that the matter [the work being composed] is not proceeding well preys upon me, tortures me, bringing me to tears and afflictions; a painful anxiety constantly gnaws at my heart that it has been a long time since I have felt as unhappy as I do now.[15]

While Tchaikovsky's compositions are both daring and experimental, their often heightened emotional temperature is sometimes said to reflect the composer's own inner turmoil. Yet on arrival in America, he exercised an undeniable charm on everyone with whom he came in contact and showed little of his nervousness: rather, they all spoke of his modesty and graciousness. He in turn was enthusiastic about his first look at the New World and made some perspicacious comments about Manhattan:

> New York, American customs, American hospitality, the very sight of the city, and the unusual comforts of the surroundings – all this is quite to my liking, and if I were younger, I would probably derive

great pleasure from staying in this interesting, youthful country. Everyone here pampers, honors, and entertains me. It turns out that I am ten times better known in America than in Europe. New York itself is a vast city, more strange and original than handsome. The city is situated on a narrow peninsula, surrounded by water on three sides, and can't grow any wider; therefore, it grows up. They say that in 10 years all the buildings will reach at least 10 floors.[16]

Soon after the end of his music-making in New York, the composer paid a visit to Niagara Falls, and then he was off to Philadelphia and Baltimore for further commitments with his baton. Everywhere he went he was enthusiastically received and, as the *Critic: A Weekly Review of Literature and the Arts* wrote in its columns on 16 May 1891, his music everywhere 'wrought the audience to a high pitch of enthusiasm.'

Tchaikovsky was thoroughly elated that his visit to the New World ended on a high note. He reported to his brother that he found American customs and American hospitality much to his taste, and regretted that he was not younger to take it all in. A year following his New York venture, Tchaikovsky met the engaging Walter Damrosch at a celebratory event in England where deference was paid to the composer with an honorary Doctor of Music degree (awarded to four others as well) from Cambridge University. At the banquet following the awards, the two musicians were placed next to each other where Tchaikovsky divulged to Damrosch that he had finished a new symphony and would in time send the score to his American friend. This was Symphony No. 6, the celebrated 'Pathétique'. Damrosch records in his autobiography that on receiving the score, he arranged for its performance soon after; ever since it has been played to thunderous applause the world over.[17]

Tchaikovsky could write with enthusiasm upon his arrival back home in Russia that he 'was most perfectly received in New York.' It had indeed been a charmed visit. Though he planned to make a return engagement, it never materialized: he died two years later. Now, with well over a century passed since he crossed the Atlantic, his music continues to transport his audiences in the New World – as everywhere else – to a high pitch of enthusiasm.

 CHAPTER 15

Henry James
Revisits the New World

O FTEN CITED as one of the nineteenth century's great novelists, Henry James is known as well for the occasionally labyrinthine complexity of his style. Such ornate, if poetic, meandering on the page is employed with great effect in *The American Scene*, a voluminous account by James of his nearly year-long visit to America at the close of the nineteenth century. Having spent more years in Europe than he had in his native America, James finally became a British subject in 1915. His journey to the New World, undertaken in 1904, was his first visit following a spell of over twenty years abroad, so that he could claim in the preface to his account to be endowed 'with much of the freshness of eye, outward and inward, which is commonly held a precious agent of perception'. A question becomes pertinent:

Is he recording his travels as an American or as an Englishman? Ah, the answer is both, and this we are told by James himself, who boldly claims in his preface that he has a great advantage, having had the time to become almost as 'fresh' as an inquiring stranger, but nonetheless not ceasing to feel as acute as a native. Yet, as he favors British spelling throughout, the reader is inclined to believe that here is a subtle, if silent, answer to the question of preferred nationality. Nonetheless, it must be remembered that James had traveled so frequently with his parents on the Continent and in England while still a youngster that he could never claim to have real roots anywhere. Perhaps he should be characterized as a European, though such a notion is countered by a knowing T.S. Eliot, who claimed that while it may be the consummation of many an American to become a European, this is something no person of any European nationality can ever claim to be. What James unquestionably did become was an accomplished man of letters who garnered acclaim in two hemispheres.

It was at the close of the nineteenth century that Henry James had his first look at the expanding country after so long an absence, styling himself throughout the account he penned of his visit in 1904 as 'the restless analyst'. Although it is not mentioned in *The American Scene*, James gave many lectures during the course of his visit, as did Dickens, Thackeray, Wilde and a host of others who crossed the Atlantic from England. Disembarking in New Jersey, the author was to make only a brief stop in New York. There, he found the waterside squalor of the great city too confoundingly familiar, reflecting as it did the barbarisms it had not outlived; yet he admitted that the scenes were sweetened by some shy principle of picturesqueness. Nonetheless, he had become steadily aware of an overwhelming presence on the American continent, or of what he termed a 'consciousness' whose vividness had grown in direct proportion as the ship approached shore:

> The great presence that bristles for him [the visitor] on the sounding dock, and that shakes the planks, the loose boards of its theatric stage to an inordinate unprecedented rumble, is the monstrous form of Democracy, which is thereafter to project its shifting angular shadow, at one time and another, across every inch of the field of his vision. It

is the huge democratic broom that has made the clearance and that one seems to see brandished in the empty sky.[1]

At the very outset, then, James could foresee that reporting on New World conditions would prove to be a matter of prodigious difficulty and selection, in consequence of which the reader might discern a certain recklessness in his surrender to impressions. The author did not tarry in the city, however; he planned to spend a part of the fall following his arrival in New England. There, during a sojourn of several weeks of visits and casual wandering, he let the charms of the autumn season wash over him: he detected the leaves of the forests turning to crimson and gold and a 'strange conscious hush' of the landscape. He found elegance in the commonest objects of nature, and espied the apple tree playing the role of the olive tree in Italy, being both decorative and delicate while scattering autumn colors. So taken was he with the canvas of the New England fall that a solitary maple tree flaming into scarlet prompted him to conjure up the vision of the daughter of an imaginary noble house, dressed for a fancy ball with her whole family of trees. Yet there was another aspect to these tranquil outdoor musings: James found that a sordid, shabby ugliness hung about the New England farms and, above all, about their inmates:

> The teams, the carts, the conveyances in their kinds, the sallow saturnine natives in charge of them, the enclosures, the fences, the gates, the wayside 'bits' of whatever sort, so far as these were referable to human attention or human neglect, kept telling the tale of the difference made, in a land of long winters, by the suppression of the two great factors of the familiar English landscape: the squire and the parson [...] Perpetually, inevitably, moreover, as the restless analyst wandered, the eliminated thing par excellence was the thing most absent to sight – and for which, oh! A thousand times, the small substitutes, the mere multiplication of the signs of theological enterprise, in the tradition and on the scale of commercial and industrial enterprise, had no attenuation worth mentioning.[2]

The author was certain that the ugliness he experienced was due to 'the complete abolition of *forms*' – by which he meant the absence of traditions in America's simplified social order: traditions such as the presence of a parson and a patron in each town, which would uphold tradition and keep ugliness at bay. Indeed, he writes, he 'pounced' on this idea of the abolition of forms to save himself from madness, for then the restless analyst could make the void of such forms responsible for any ugliness he was certain to encounter. Yet, what kind of form could there be in the 'almost sophisticated dinginess of the present destitution', he asked himself, considering that the notion of *Romanitas* – in which virtue is prior to liberty – had been consciously rejected in America, while Europe was forever seeking a new interpretation of it that was suited to modern society?

As he made his way through the northeastern states, James found that the naming of towns was a constant source of irritation: they had designations that seemed to leave on them the smudge of a great vulgar thumb. He did praise Farmington in Connecticut, noteworthy as it was for its old houses showing style, form and proportion. Moreover, such houses were surprisingly numerous, and in the eyes of the visitor all of them bore the charming aspects and high refinements of the older New England domestic architecture. Treading his way toward the familiar region of Boston, James found that the area had become much richer in his absence. What was also taking place in his view was a perpetual rejection of the past, with the will to grow evident everywhere, and to grow at no matter what or whose expense. Were there any limits to this progress, was there anything it would sanction or be sympathetic to? Visiting Cambridge, the author heard great things to come in the rustling of the leaves: Harvard University (which he had briefly attended in his youth) seemed to be in more confident possession of itself and was stretching its long acquisitive arms in many directions. As he watched the students come and go, he wondered to himself: Whose sons are they? He had not yet revisited Ellis Island to catch a glimpse of the ceaseless process of recruiting and enlarging the American race, or what he termed the 'constant plenishing of our huge national pot au feu – of the introduction of fresh – of perpetually fresh so far as it isn't perpetually stale – foreign matter into our heterogeneous system'. But even without that, a haunting wonder as to what might be becoming of us all, 'typically', ethnically, physiognomically, linguistically, personally, was always in order. This issue of America's multi-ethnicity was to rear itself over and over again, particularly since waves of immigrant groups had swelled the population during the author's protracted absence. He was to bring both a passion and an eloquence – as well as ambiguity – to the blurred profile of the future American.

New York City was the next major stop on his itinerary, and although James begins by calling it a 'terrible town', he acknowledges that it has a great scale of space and the beauty of light and air, as well as the open gates of the Hudson River, which are majestic and announce still nobler things. Nonetheless, he finds no trace of the Romantic or of distinction in the city, for New York was not, in his view, among the true flowers of geography, which he proceeds to list in ranking order: Naples, Cape Town, Sydney, Seattle and San Francisco. He found the real appeal of New York to be lodged in its dauntless power:

> The aspect the power wears then is indescribable; it is the power of the most extravagant of cities, rejoicing, as with the voice of the morning, in its might, its fortune, its unsurpassable conditions, and imparting to every object and element […] a diffused, wasted clamour of detonations – something of its sharp free accent and, above all, of its sovereign sense of being 'backed' and able to back. The universal applied passion struck me as shining unprecedentedly out of the composition; in the bigness and bravery and insolence, especially, of everything that rushed and shrieked; in the air of a great intricate frenzied dance, half merry, half desperate, or at least half defiant, performed on the huge watery floor.[3]

As for the rising number of skyscrapers in New York, James found them impudently new, in common with so many other 'terrible' things in America. Because they had no history, no credible potential to accumulate history, and no uses save the commercial, he deemed them 'the most piercing notes in that concert of the expensively provisional into which your supreme sense of New York resolves itself'. Certainly Manhattan's skyscrapers were the last word in economic ingenuity, but the fact was to be deplored that such beautiful, time-honored structures as Trinity Church (dating back to the seventeenth century) were thereby mercilessly deprived of their visibility. James then has Trinity Church itself rise in protest:

> Yes, the wretched figure I am making is as little as you see my fault – it is the fault of the buildings whose very first care is to deprive churches of their visibility. There are but two or three [...] left in New York anyway as you must have noticed, and even they are hideously threatened: a fact at which no one, indeed, appears to be shocked [...] which everyone seems in short to take for granted either with remarkable stupidity or with remarkable cynicism.[4]

The author deplored the fact, as well, that Castle Garden – once a handsome concert hall on the shore of lower Manhattan – was now shrunken, shabby and barely discernible; it had always been a venerable landmark (dating from 1808) and it was there, as a child, that he had heard Adelina Patti sing when she made her acclaimed appearance in the mid century. Were not new landmarks crushing the old just as violent children stamp on caterpillars? That was the reaction of the restless analyst who was, after all, a native New Yorker with great affection for the city, especially for the lower Manhattan neighborhood in which he was born and reared. (His novel *Washington Square* has its setting in his grandmother's elegant townhouse located near that square.) He was glad on a visit to find that the precious stretch of space between Washington Square and 14th Street that marked his boyhood still radiated 'tone'. While the house in which he was born no longer existed he had, in his imagination, erected a permanent commemorative mural tablet, though he was well aware that tablets in New York are 'unthinkable'. A building that drew his unqualified admiration was City Hall, an imposing structure of marble, graced with a rotunda and dome, completed in 1818 and offering a commanding view of the surrounding areas. He found the building – whose interior he toured with the mayor – standing at the very center of that recorded 'assault' of architectural vulgarity, yet never parting with an iota of its noble character. Indeed, he found the edifice a 'shy little case of real refinement'. He admired the Tiffany building because it is only three stories high, as well as the newly erected New York Public Library and the Metropolitan Museum of Art: all of them represented to him a covering of the earth rather than an invasion of the air. Moreover, in his view, none of them paid homage to the great religion of the elevator. These admiring sentiments were not to surface after visiting one of the city's great caravansaries – the Waldorf Astoria. He toured it at length, surprised to find it open to everyone whereas in Europe, he noted, only a few travel in such luxurious conditions. The building loomed in his view as a temple built with clustering chapels and with shrines to an idea he could not define, and which later remained for him a gorgeous, golden blur. Such luxury as the Waldorf flaunted was surely an attempt, he was convinced, to create an aesthetic ideal and make it a synonym for civilization.

Continuing on his tour of the city, James was consistently intrigued with the population of New York, which he pronounced as being characterized by a huge looseness in which it was hard to discern the common element. He deemed this to be true of the dense Italian neighborhoods of the Lower East Side as well as the upper reaches of Fifth and Madison Avenues. It was no less true when he made his way into Central Park, which 'showed the fruit of the foreign tree as shaken down there with a force that smothered everything else' and which led him to comment that he could feel the 'foreign force' in half of everything he ate when dining in the city. As he made his way into Central Park, he admired the nobility of the statue of Civil War general William Tecumseh Sherman by Augustus Saint-Gaudens at its entrance and indeed of the park itself, for he was to remark after his visit to Manhattan's large stretch of green that nowhere in the world does a recreational area play its role so heroically in proportion to the difficulties that are presented. Was it not exhausted by the demands on its resources? The variety of accents with which the air of the park swarmed seemed to raise the question as to whether the park itself or its visitors were most polyglot. He observed untold groups of 'aliens' congregating there in the park's great fields of leisure, creating social scenes in which he felt he had no role. Were this a locale in Europe, he insists, there would be a play of mutual recognition, founded on old familiarities and heredities involving some mutual exchange. Was not such a sense of belonging usually a part of the warmth and intrinsic color of any honest man's rural walk in England, Italy or Germany? Not here in America, he declared. The author then recalled asking a young passerby, sometime earlier in New England, for a direction, and discovering that the man did not understand the question although it was posed in English, French and Italian. He proved to be Armenian, as if, James remarks, this were the most natural thing in the world for a youth in New England to be! As was so often his wont, the restless analyst deeply pondered what he called 'the great ethnic question', apparently learning one basic fact from the many with whom he discussed the issue: there could be no claim to brotherhood with aliens in the first 'grossness' of their alienism, which is to say in the lifetime of his generation.

> Their children are another matter – as in fact the children throughout the United States, are an immense matter, are almost the greatest matter of all; it is the younger generation who will fully profit, rise to the occasion and enter into the privilege. The machinery is colossal – nothing is more characteristic of the country than the development of this machinery, in the form of the political and social habit, the common school and the newspaper; so that there are always millions of little transformed strangers growing up in regard to whom the idea of intimacy of relation may be as freely cherished as you like.[5]

James then asks the question: What type of person is created by such a prodigious amalgam, such a hotchpotch of racial ingredients? What meaning can be ascribed to the term 'the American character'? Still more questions are asked: How was it that manners that took long ages of history to produce had been shed in an hour? Was it conceivable that they would rise again to the surface, affirming their vitality and value and playing their part? On reflection, he felt it best to leave these looming, unanswerable questions alone as being something rather fantastic and 'abracadabrant' (spellbinding). Yet he was loath to do so – or perhaps these unanswerable questions would not leave him – as he toured the Jewish quarter on the Lower East Side with a dignitary who was resident in the neighborhood. His first impression of what he termed a rare experience was that the Jewish scene in lower Manhattan hummed with a truly dense and amazing human presence, dominated conspicuously by children and the elderly and dense beyond any other neighborhood he had ever witnessed. He was prompted to ask: Had one seen with one's own eyes the new Jerusalem on earth? He was amazed at this transfer of a European scene to American shores; it was not only thoroughly intact but, to his astonishment, flourishing. How was that so? How did the transfer of accommodation, of the Yiddish language, of an entire lifestyle come about? Such a very dense population, he learned, was domiciled by way of tenement houses (a term and style of architecture new to him) each of which harbored some five and twenty families. As he strode past the tenements, intensely observing everything he saw, what struck the visitor most acutely in 'the flaring streets (over and beyond the everywhere insistent, defiant, unhumourous, exotic face) was the blaze of shops addressed to the New Jerusalem wants and the splendor with which they were taken for granted.'[6] This intense bustle of life and the immensity of the alien presence in these streets of the Lower East Side struck him as 'climbing higher and higher, into the very light of publicity', making him ponder (as was his wont) the fate of the English language:

> The accent of the very ultimate future, in the States, may be destined to become the most beautiful on the globe and the very music of humanity (here the 'ethnic' synthesis shrouds itself thicker than ever); but whatever we shall know it for, certainly, we shall not know it for English – in any sense for which there is an existing literary measure.[7]

James left the Jewish quarter, pleased that he had had such excellent guides but greatly worried nonetheless – as he was whenever confronting a concentration of immigrants – about what he called the Accent of the Future (the capitals are his). Once again he was wont to say that if the language of Americans is to become the very music of humanity, it would most certainly not be English by any literary measure.

As James continued his tour of New York, he bemoaned the fact, as had many other visitors to the city (as well as scores of residents), that Manhattan did not use her rivers as a scenic waterfront. Still, James found the views of the Hudson offered by Riverside Drive pleasing, as were both the imposing monument to the soldiers and sailors of the Civil War erected there and the tomb of General Ulysses Grant. Nonetheless, the latter memorial prompted a comparison with the tomb of Napoleon in Paris and was found wanting, for it raised the question: Do certain impressions in America represent the absolute extinction of old sensibilities, or do they only represent new forms of them? This was a recurring conundrum in the mind of the restless analyst who, ever obsessed with the lack of 'forms' in America's social structure, concluded that it would be an abuse of ingenuity 'to try to read mere freshness of form into some of the more rank failures of observance'.[8]

A return to the east side of Manhattan led to the observation that uppermost Fifth Avenue is lined with dwellings that seem to be entailed as majestically as red tape can entail them, whereas they are bereft of any such security. Any hint of true entailment was found by the restless analyst to exist only in the 'lurid' light of business and was flagrantly tentative. Invited to an elaborate party in one of the avenue's mansions, where he enjoyed a perfection of setting and service, and where the ladies glittered in gem-studded tiaras, James felt that the evening was so materialistic in tone as to rule out any idea of a sustaining social order. A quite different scene was to present itself for analysis when the author traveled south to the Bowery one winter afternoon to attend a play: in one of the theaters there, a young actor of his acquaintance was playing. He mentions neither the name of the play nor the name of the actor, but was struck by the look of the theater, which he recalled from his youth: it had then been 'the' Bowery Theatre and had been admired – with its imposing Corinthian columns and impressive interior – by no less a critic than the visiting Frances Trollope, who in 1832 had deemed it equal to any theater in London. Now it was little more than a vast dingy edifice and to reach it, James took the streetcar with its typically mixed immigrant population, traveling through the Jewish quarter – or the depth of the Orient, as he termed it – to reach his destination. At the time of his youth, he reminisced, the theater had offered dramatic works following in revered English tradition, but having undergone several tumultuous episodes in its history, including riots and fires, the Bowery was now catering to immigrant tastes, and very often staged Jewish theatricals. As he took his place in the audience, he felt again his aversion to the new and 'alien' American population:

From the corner of the box of my so improved playhouse further down, the very name of which moreover had the cosmopolite lack of point, I made out, in the audience, the usual mere monotony of the richer exoticism. No single face, beginning with those close beside me (for my box was a shared luxury), but referred itself, by my interpretation, to some strange outland form as we had not dreamed of in my day. There they all sat, the representatives of the races we have nothing 'in common' with, as naturally [...] as if the theatre were their constant practice.[9]

The visit to the Bowery was followed by a visit with friends to a beer hall in the downtown east-side neighborhood where the German proprietor had 'omitted' to learn the current American idiom. Still in the company of friends as he toured the crowded downtown neighborhoods, the restless analyst visited a crammed if convivial theater where a Yiddish comedy of manners was being offered. The title again is not mentioned, but what remained from his attendance were snatches of 'alien comedy', with all that the term implied of an esoteric vision on the part of the public that he did not share. The downtown visit continued into the wee hours and impressions of one sort or another were numerous, all of them belonging to 'a world of custom quite away from any mere Delmonico tradition of one's earlier time'. Finally, the continuing romp through a section of New York teeming with immigrants left the author so baffled by a mosaic of impressions that he could only exclaim: 'Remarkable, unspeakable New York!'

Now followed a visit to a city that James knew well and which he loved so much that he feared being unable to describe it: Newport. He found on arrival that the original 'shy sweetness' of the city had been as much as possible bedizened and bedeviled with houses that were monuments to pecuniary power. It had originally been a touchstone of taste, as he remembered it from his youth, a haunt of the refined that had never condescended to give a public account of itself. Indeed, James found it easy to imagine Newport being placed there by nature itself as the high mark of taste, and accordingly to be enjoyed by the few and not the many. He acknowledged that the multiplied houses and population were, of course, a tribute to the value of the place, yet in his youth no such liberties were ever taken precisely because the city was deemed so beautiful, so solitary and so sympathetic. As he wandered happily about this attractive promontory, viewing old haunts with an affectionate eye, the memories of his middle years spent there – when the population danced, drove, rode their horses, wined, dined, dressed, flirted, yachted, polo'd and casino'd – all returned with a welcome grace. James found himself nostalgic, for the Newport of old was to him one of the wonders of the world, with small sea-coves gleaming on its edge like 'barbaric' gems on a mantle. Now it had changed dramatically, and there was nothing to be done about it.

Boston was another familiar area that the author now visited, following his nostalgic tour of Newport. He was to find in the New England city a brutal effacement of much that was related to his past, as though the bottom had fallen out of his biography. Looming large was the polyglot scene that never failed to surprise and bewilder him: the people whom he encountered were 'gross' aliens to him as he toured the city visiting beloved landmarks like the State House and the Boston Athenaeum. Dressed in their Sunday best, the men and women who made up the crowds struck him as laboring wage-earners from whose lips no sound of English was to escape; what the restless analyst heard from perhaps the greater number was a 'rude' form of Italian. To him, the throngs expressed the great cost at which every place on his agenda had become braver and louder while the new population distanced itself from old presumptions and limitations. Was not the original, eighteenth-century town of Boston a city of character and genius, exempt as yet from the 'Irish yoke'? Landmarks long admired were receding into the background. Of course, it was a case, too, of the 'detestable' tall building again: skyscrapers were destroying the quality of everything they overshadowed. The Athenaeum (an exquisite institution in James's view) was accordingly put out of countenance, he declared, by the masses of brute ugliness beside it: one's instinct was to pass by and avert one's head from humiliation! As he continued to draw his portrait of the city, James was pleased to find that the Park Street church had still remained a 'precious public servant' and that there was yet the old charm of Mount Vernon Street. But he pronounced it lamentable that the Boston of history – the Boston of Emerson, Thoreau, Hawthorne, Longfellow, Lowell, Holmes, Ticknor, Prescott and Parkman – could now be seen as almost picturesquely medieval.

The town of Concord, located not far from Boston, was to give the journeying author great pleasure (as it invariably gave to all visitors), not only for its russet beauty but for what James termed its character, its intensity of presence, its preservation of traditions and its constant recall of the genius of Thoreau, Hawthorne and Emerson. He addresses the town with affection, as though it were a close friend:

> The country is colossal and you but a microscopic speck on the hem of its garment; yet there's nothing else like you […] whereas there are vast sprawling, bristling areas, great grey 'centres of population' that spread, on the map, like irremediable grease-spots, which fail utterly of any appeal to our vision […] If you are so thoroughly the opposite of one of these I don't say it's all your superlative merit; it's rather […] the result of the half-dozen happy turns of the wheel in your favour.[10]

The visiting author paused at several other places in New England before making his way south to Philadelphia, a city that didn't 'bristle' in his view, but that offered the traveler the nearest approach to 'companionship' with a city. What was further pleasing there was the absence of the perpendicular (skyscrapers) and the fact that Philadelphia presented itself as a society: it was settled, confirmed and content (unlike New York) and her imagination was at peace. James often viewed the city from the window of the handsome club where he was staying, from where he noted that it could boast a social equilibrium. Conspicuously absent was any sharp note of the outlandish, for in making his or her way about the pedestrian was less likely than in New York to meet the 'grosser aliens', with the attendant shock it was in their power to administer. Not only did he detect a certain local homogeneity, but he held that Philadelphia had a dialect all its own, much as the Venetian dialect is that of Venice and the Neapolitan that of Naples. There was also a note of historic 'decency' in two of the city's monuments, Independence Hall and Carpenters' Hall. James deemed the latter (despite being a 'bedizenment of restoration') to be an elegant structure that could have been found in the city of London. It was of little surprise to James that Philadelphia should strike him as a coherent society, with such an historic figure as Benjamin Franklin dominating the scene through the many far-scattered portraits of him that were to be admired throughout the area:

The sense of life, life the most positive, most human and most miscel-
laneous, expressed in his aged, crumpled, canny face […] represents
a suggestion which succeeding generations may well have found it
all they could do to work out. It is impossible […] after seeing that
portrait, not to feel him still with them, with the genial generations –
even though to-day, in the larger, more mixed cup, the force of his
example may have suffered some dilution.[11]

Baltimore, the next city of comparable size to be visited by James,
offered its visitor from overseas a blurred vision, so that he was
prompted to ask: How am I to make plausible the statement that
Baltimore was interesting? There was, to begin with, the huge shadow
of the Civil War ('It was History in person that hovered') and then there
were repeated vistas of little brick-faced and protrusively door-stepped
houses, which suggested to James rows of quiet old ladies, seated with
their toes tucked up on uniform footstools, under the shaded candle-
sticks of old-fashioned tea parties. The restless analyst meant not to
imply that there was no vice in the city so much as that there was not
even the conception or the imagining of it – and still less any provision
for it. The natural pitch of the city struck him – visually and socially – as
that of disinterested sensibility. Just a few months earlier, Baltimore
had unhappily lost by fire a large part of its business district, but the
disaster was allowed no discussion in the entertainments offered him.
Fortunately, James was able to visit the city's Johns Hopkins University,
as well as its famed University Hospital. A pair of gallant young doc-
tors conducted him through the wards of the latter, underscoring
'the large art, above all, by which, in a place bristling with its terrible
tale, everything was made to seem fair, and fairest even while it most
intimately concurred in the work'.[12]

The nation's capital was next to beckon the restless analyst, and to
him (as to most visitors) the city of Washington presented two faces:
the official and the social. The charm of the city made one forget for
an hour the commercial greed of New York (for nobody he met in
Washington was in 'business'), yet he found that the capital was always
talking about itself – just as London, Berlin and Rome talk about themselves – but with this difference: Washington was in positive quest of
an identity of some sort. He himself was curious to probe the 'real'

sentiments of appointed ambassadors and foreign participants who made their way about the capital, knowing that they were pledged equally to discretion and to a penetration of the city's animus. He found that the American way

> is more different from all other native ways, taking country with country, than any of these latter are different from each other; and the question is of how, each time, the American way will see it through [...] It is inveterately applied but with consequences bewilderingly various. [The restless analyst] has at moments his sense that, in the presence of such vast populations and instilled, emulous demands, there is not, outside the mere economic, enough native history, recorded or current, to go round.[13]

If there was little history to go round, there was much to admire in the architectural aspect of the capital, which James describes as a city of monuments, gardens, symmetries, circles and far 'radiations', with the Potomac for waterpower and for water 'effect'.

And now, as he proceeded further south, how was the sight of Richmond not to strike him potently, the traveler wondered? The former Confederate capital, charged with memories of the Civil War, had loomed in the imagination of the author when he was young as lurid and vividly tragic, the war having invested it with one of the great reverberating names:

> The names hang together on the dreadful page, the cities of the supreme holocaust, the final massacres, the blood, the flames, the tears; they are chalked with the sinister red mark at sight of which the sensitive nerve of association never winces.[14]

Now the city looked simply blank and void to the sophisticated traveler who had long attached some mystic virtue to the very name of Virginia. He had become well acquainted through his readings with the mentality of the mid-century South, which in the very convulsions of its perversity had held on to the conception, almost comic in itself, that was yet so tragically to fail to work, 'that of a world rearranged, a State solidly and comfortably seated and tucked-in, in the interest of slave-produced Cotton'. There was a sense of missing legends in the city as the visitor walked about; they were embedded in the battlefields and in the blood-drenched radius of the city, but in the streets of melancholy Richmond the author found legend thin. He did admire an equestrian statue of the Southern hero Robert E. Lee, but found that it spoke to a cause that could never have been won. In a museum, James met an old lady distinguished for her beauty and good manners, bearing a felicity of the South in her: no little old lady in the North could ever match her, he deemed.

In Charleston, a city much farther to the south, the author found the social scene noticeably wanting forty years after the Civil War: indeed, it was sordid and shabby. The black population outnumbered the white, and in fact there were few white men to be found. There was all about Charleston the suggestion of a social shrinkage, and of an economic blight that was not only unrepaired but irreparable. Had the only focus of life then been slavery? How was it that in such a 'layered society' everything could have so disappeared? Indeed, how could things come to such a pass, he wondered, that the only Southern book of any distinction published for many a year proved to be *The Souls of Black Folk* by Mr. W.E.B. Du Bois, whom James cited as that 'most accomplished of members of the negro race'? The South, concluded the restless analyst, was in the predicament of having to be tragic in order to beguile.

The train carrying the author still farther south had its usual quota of commercial travelers; they struck the tireless analyst as all having the same facial character, the same vocal tone, primal rawness of speech, general accent and attitude. He deemed them exceptionally base and vulgar. What came as a startling surprise in the Southern districts he visited was a marked ineptitude on the part of black workers with regard to any alertness in personal service. He remembered the Southern tradition of a house alive with the scramble of what he termed 'young darkies for the honour of fetching and carrying'. Now the gentry of the South were being exposed to the same ineptitude and he wondered: Was it for this that they had fought and fallen? A stop at Jacksonville in Florida opened up a handsome vista: the charm of the velvet air, the extravagant plants, the palms, the oranges, the cacti, the cheap and easy exoticism. Indeed, the scenes of people al fresco were quite evocative of Naples or of Genoa. Hotel life on that 'romantic' Florida peninsula overwhelmed the surrounding natural world. Comparatively little availed, in his view, 'of the jungle, the air, the sea, the sky, the sunset, the orange, the pineapple, the palm' or even of the 'divine bougainvillea'. He had been promised that of all his destinations Palm Beach would resemble most closely the high society and machinations of Thackeray's *Vanity Fair*; this proved to be true, though high society here was concentrated in one small area, rather than spread out across a town as in Newport. What was further conspicuous in the Florida scene was the dimness of distinctions among the teeming numbers who flocked to the luxurious hotels, yet the distinction least absent was the ability to spend and purchase. Everyone converged in the mid-morning and in the mid-afternoon for drinks, but there was no tea – the only drink James appreciated abroad at that time of day. No signs of 'social' differentiation were to be noted among the occupants of the hotels: the men all appeared to be products of the business world while the women were the indulged ladies of such 'lords'. This neutrality of respectability and scant diversity of social type left the author deprived as a story-seeker or a picture-maker.

> No long time is required, in the States, to make vivid for the visitor the truth that the nation is almost feverishly engaged in producing, with the greatest possible activity and expedition, an 'intellectual' pablum after its own heart, and that not only the arts and ingenuities of the draftsman (called upon to furnish the picturesque background and people it with the 'aristocratic' figure where neither of these revelations ever meets his eye) pay their extravagant tribute, but that those of the journalist, the novelist, the dramatist, the genealogist, the historian, are pressed as well, for dear life, into the service.[15]

It was one of the final dicta of the restless analyst that there was an aesthetic need in America for much greater values, on many levels, than the country and its manners, its aspects and arrangements, its past and present – and perhaps even future – could supply. Could America or would America eventually shed its disordered provincialism and take its place with the honored nations of Europe? Here was a conundrum he had pondered endlessly, and it was now that the palm trees of America's South, which had initially struck the author as dry and taciturn, eventually became as sympathetic to him as so many rows of puzzled philosophers – all disheveled and shock-pated with the riddle of the universe.

Not long after, Henry James left the United States, never to return.

 NOTES

CHAPTER ONE: THE NEW WORLD SOJOURN OF BARON AND
BARONESS HYDE DE NEUVILLE

1   Baron Jean Guillaume Hyde de Neuville, *Mémoires et Souvenirs du Baron Hyde de Neuville* (3 vols, Paris, 1888–92), vol. 1, p. 113. There is an abridged two-volume English edition of the *Mémoires* entitled *Memoirs of Baron Hyde de Neuville*, ed. Frances Jackson (London, 1913).
2   A good deal of obscurity surrounds the birth date of the Baroness, presumably because she was considerably older – perhaps fifteen years or more – than her husband. The Baron's memoirs avoid any indication of the year in which his wife was born.
3   There is no definitive list of the artwork of the baroness. Two publications give a fairly complete account of the more than two hundred sketches and watercolors she executed in America and provide an extensive bibliography with regard to the de Neuvilles on these shores: *American Landscape and Genre Paintings in the New-York Historical Society*, ed. Richard J. Koke (New York and Boston, 1982), vol. 2, pp. 188–217; and Jadviga M. da Costa Nunes, *Baroness Hyde de Neuville: Sketches of America, 1807–1822* (Rutgers and New York, 1984). Drawings by the baroness owned by the New York Public Library are catalogued in Gloria Gilda Deák, *Picturing America 1497–1899* (Princeton, 1988), Nos. 254, 256, 258, 262, 304 and 319. The diminutive watercolor of New York Harbor resides with the New York Historical Society.
4   Hyde de Neuville, *Mémoires*, vol. 1, p. 460. In this connection, see William N. Fenton, 'The Hyde de Neuville portraits of New York savages in 1807–1808', *New-York Historical Society Quarterly*, vol. 38 (April 1954), pp. 118–37.
5   Ibid., pp. 266–8.
6   Francois-Jean, Marquis de Chastellux, *Travels in North America in the Years 1780, 1781 and 1782*, ed. Howard C. Rice, Jr. (2 vols, Chapel Hill, 1963), vol. 2, pp. 536–7.
7   A copy of the statement of regulations issued by the school is held by the New-York Historical Society.
8   Cited in I.N. Phelps Stokes, *The Iconography of Manhattan* (New York, 1927), vol. 5, p. 1552, under the entry for 16 July 1810. In 1810 the school moved from the workshop to Chapel Street.
9   Hyde de Neuville, *Mémoires*, vol. 1, p. 480. The Baron first began the serious study of medicine while still in France, during the years of his condemnation as an outlaw, and he practiced it in the countryside to a limited degree.
10 Ibid., p. 465.
11 Alexis de Tocqueville, *Letters from America*, ed., trans., and with an introduction by Frederick Brown (New Haven and London, 2010), p. 243.
12 The Baroness executed watercolors of the residences of the Simons (Kennedy Galleries), the Crugers (private collection),and Major John Jeremias Van Rensselaer (New-York Historical Society).

13 Hyde de Neuville, *Mémoires*, vol. 1, p. 472.
14 Ibid., p. 486.
15 Ibid., p. 114.
16 Ibid.
17 John Quincy Adams, *The Memoirs of John Quincy Adams, Comprising Portions of his Diary from 1795 to 1848*, ed. Charles Francis Adams (12 vols, Philadelphia, 1875), vol. 5, p. 137. The twelve volumes of the memoirs are a good source of information about the de Neuvilles and the atmosphere in the capital during the period of their diplomatic mission to America.

CHAPTER TWO: FRANCES WRIGHT BRINGS REFORM TO AMERICA

1 *The New-York Columbian*, 18 February 1819.
2 Thomas Jefferson, *Thomas Jefferson Correspondence*, ed. Worthington C. Ford (Boston, 1916), p. 254.
3 Frances Wright, *Views of Society and Manners in America; in a Series of Letters from that Country to a Friend in England, During the Years 1818, 1819, 1820* (London, 1821), pp. 507–8.
4 Ibid., pp. 119–21.
5 *The Eye of Thomas Jefferson*, ed. William Howard Adams (Washington, DC, 1976), p. xi.
6 Frances Wright, *A Plan for the Gradual Abolition of Slavery in the United States without Danger of Loss to the Citizens of the South* (Baltimore, 1825).
7 Robert Dale Owen, *Threading My Way* (New York, 1874), p. 303.
8 James Madison, *Writings*, ed. Gaillard Hunt (9 vols, New York, 1900–10), vol. 9, pp. 310–11.
9 Quoted in Fawn Brodie, *Thomas Jefferson: An Intimate History* (New York, 1975), p. 585.
10 Frances Trollope, *Domestic Manners of the Americans* (2 vols, London, 1832), vol. 1, pp. 33–42.
11 Ibid., pp. 94–8.
12 *New York Evening Post*, 12 January 1829.
13 *The Diary of Philip Hone, 1828–1851*, ed. Allan Nevins (2 vols, New York, 1927), vol. 1, p. 26.
14 Ibid., p. 402.
15 The *New York Courier and Inquirer*, 14 June 1830.

CHAPTER THREE: THE AMERICAN PEREGRINATIONS OF CAPTAIN BASIL HALL

1 Basil Hall, *Travels in North America in the Years 1827 and 1828* (3 vols, Edinburgh, 1833), vol. 1, p. 5.
2 Ibid., vol. 3, p. 149.
3 Ibid., vol. 1, p. 36.
4 Ibid., p. 109.
5 Ibid., vol. 3, pp. 398–9.
6 Ibid., vol. 1, p. 193.
7 Ibid., vol. 2, pp. 120–1.
8 Ibid., p. 158.
9 Ibid., p. 200.
10 Ibid., p. 205.
11 Ibid., pp. 208–9.
12 Ibid., p. 286.

13 Ibid., p. 338.
14 Ibid., vol. 3, p. 49.

CHAPTER FOUR: THE NEW WORLD ENTERPRISE OF FRANCES TROLLOPE

1 Frances Trollope, *Domestic Manners of the Americans* (Barre, Massachusetts, 1969), p. 35. This edition is amply illustrated with sketches executed by David Claypoole Johnston in 1833.
2 Ibid., p. 35.
3 Alexis de Tocqueville, *Letters from America* (New Haven and London, 2010), p. 242.
4 Trollope, *Domestic Manners*, p. 4.
5 Ibid., pp. 8–9.
6 Ibid., p. 13.
7 Ibid., p. 24.
8 Ibid., pp. 36–7.
9 Ibid., pp. 157–8.
10 Ibid., pp. 161–2.
11 Ibid., pp. 174–5.
12 Ibid., p. 181.
13 Ibid., p. 185.
14 Ibid., pp. 218–19.
15 Ibid., p. 294.
16 Ibid., p. 300.
17 Ibid., p. 312.

CHAPTER FIVE: THE POLITICAL MISSION OF THOMAS HAMILTON

1 Thomas Hamilton, *Men and Manners in America*, 2 vols, reprinted as 1 (New York, 1968).
2 Ibid., p. iv.
3 Ibid., pp. 33–4.
4 Ibid., pp. 152–3.
5 Ibid., p. 225.
6 Ibid., pp. 232–5.
7 Ibid., pp. 374–5.
8 Ibid., pp. 60–1.
9 Ibid., pp. 171–2.
10 Ibid., p. 192.
11 Ibid., pp. 244–5.
12 Ibid., pp. 317–18.
13 Ibid., p. 375.
14 Ibid., p. 386.

CHAPTER SIX: THE AMERICAN DEBUT OF FANNY KEMBLE

1 Fanny Kemble [Francis Anne Butler], *Journal* (2 vols, London, 1835), vol. 1, p. 114. Later editions of her work are known by the fuller title *Journal of a Residence in America*.
2 *The Diary of Philip Hone, 1828–1851*, ed. Allan Nevins (2 vols, New York, 1927), vol. 1, pp. 74–5.
3 Kemble, *Journal*, vol. 1, p. 114.

4   Hone, *Diary*, vol. 1, p. 77.
5   Kemble, *Journal*, vol. 1, pp. 116, 111.
6   Ibid., pp. 122, 130, 145, 144.
7   Ibid., p. 132.
8   Ibid., p. 132.
9   Quoted in Margaret Armstrong, *Fanny Kemble: A Passionate Victorian* (New York, 1938), p. 165.
10   William Makepeace Thackeray, *The Letters and Private Papers of William Makepeace Thackeray*, ed. Gordon N. Ray (Cambridge, Massachusetts, 1945), vol. 1, p. clxiii.
11   Kemble, *Journal*, vol. 1, pp. 112–13.
12   Ibid., p. v.
13   Thomas Jefferson, *The Jeffersonian Cyclopedia: A Comprehensive Collection of the Views of Thomas Jefferson* [...], ed. John P. Foley (New York, 1967), vol. 2, p. 634.
14   Kemble, *Journal*, vol. 1, pp. 145–6.
15   Ibid., vol. 1, p. 147.
16   Ibid., vol. 1, pp. 73–4, 60.
17   Hone, *Diary*, vol. 1, p. 76.
18   Kemble, *Journal*, vol. 1, p. 212.
19   Ibid., pp. 61, 65–6, 67.
20   Ibid., pp. 156, 158, 116.
21   Ibid., p. 119.
22   Ibid., pp. 59, 58.
23   Ibid., p. 68.
24   Ibid., p. 56.
25   Quoted in Charles Nevers Holmes, 'The New Park Theatre, New York', *Magazine of History*, vol. 22 (January–June, 1916), p. 73.
26   Frances Anne Kemble, *Records of Later Life* (New York, 1882), p. 1.
27   Pierce Butler, *Mr. Butler's Statement* (Philadelphia, 1850), p. 9.
28   Hone, *Diary*, vol. 2, pp. 862–3.
29   George Templeton Strong, *The Diary of George Templeton Strong*, ed. Allan Nevins and Milton Halse Thomas (New York, 1952), vol. 2, p. 432.
30   Quoted in Armstrong, *Fanny Kemble*, p. 308.
31   Henry James, *Essays in London and Elsewhere* (London, 1893), p. 125.

CHAPTER SEVEN: THE AMERICAN ODYSSEY OF HARRIET MARTINEAU

1   Harriet Martineau, *Retrospect of Western Travel* (3 vols, New York, 1969), vol. 1, p. 42. The work was originally published in 1838.
2   Martineau, *Retrospect*, vol. 1, p. 54.
3   Ibid., p. 151.
4   Ibid., pp. 232–3.
5   Ibid., p. 301.
6   Ibid., pp. 237–8.
7   Ibid., p. 239.
8   Ibid., pp. 266–7.
9   Ibid., p. 138.
10   Martineau, *Retrospect*, vol. 2, p. 66.
11   Harriet Martineau, *Autobiography*, ed. Linda H. Peterson (Ontario, 2007), p. 360.
12   Martineau, *Retrospect*, vol. 3, p. 2.
13   Martineau, *Retrospect*, vol. 2 p. 112.
14   Ibid., p. 231.
15   Harriet Martineau, *Society in America* (Gloucester, Massachusetts, 1968), p. 73.

CHAPTER EIGHT: THE DARING ADVENTURES OF CHARLES AUGUSTUS MURRAY

1   Charles Augustus Murray, *Travels in North America* (2 vols, London, 1839), vol. 1, p. 83.
2   Ibid., pp. 95–6.
3   Ibid., pp. 127–8.
4   Ibid., p. 173.
5   Ibid., pp. 184–5.
6   Ibid., pp. 206–7.
7   Ibid., p. 254.
8   Ibid., p. 303.
9   Murray, *Travels*, Vol. II, p. 118.
10 Ibid., p. 144.
11 Ibid., p. 292.
12 Ibid., p. 293.
13 Ibid., p. 328.
14 Ibid., p. 328.

CHAPTER NINE: THE CLAIRVOYANCE OF THOMAS COLLEY GRATTAN

1   Thomas Colley Grattan, *Civilized America* (2 vols, New York and London, 1969), vol. 1, p. 222. Originally published 1859.
2   Ibid., p. 69.
3   Ibid., pp. 134–5.
4   Ibid., p. 165.
5   Ibid., pp. 234–5.
6   Ibid., p. 233.
7   Ibid., pp. 189, 204.
8   All had been published, however, by 1859, when Consul Grattan published the account of his American visit.
9   Grattan, *Civilized America*, vol. 2, p. 113.
10 Ibid., pp. 393–4.
11 Ibid., p. 312–13.
12 Ibid., p. 246.
13 Ibid., p. 438.
14 Speech in the House of Representatives, 20 January 1827.
15 Treaty of Washington, 9 August 1842, entitled: *To Settle and Define the Boundaries between Her Britannic Majesty in North America and the Territories of the United States.*
16 Grattan, *Civilized America*, vol. 1, p. xi.
17 Ibid., p. v.

CHAPTER TEN: THE FIRST VISIT OF CHARLES DICKENS TO THE NEW WORLD

1   Charles Dickens, *American Notes for General Circulation* (2 vols, London, 1842), vol. 1, pp. 27–8. All quotations from the journal of Dickens are taken from the original 1842 edition.
2   Ibid., p. 64.
3   Ibid., pp. 133–4.
4   George Washington Putnam, 'Four months with Charles Dickens', *Atlantic Monthly* 26 (1870).
5   Quoted in Paul B. Davis, *Dickens and the American Press* (New York, 2007), pp. 58–61.

6   Dickens, *American Notes*, vol. 1, p. 170.
7   The copyright issue between the United States and Great Britain would not be settled until 1891. See the chapter on international copyright in William Glyde Wilkins, *Charles Dickens in America* (New York, 1970), pp. 237–57.
8   Alexis de Tocqueville, *Democracy in America* (New York and London, 1966), p. 438.
9   Quoted in *Abroad in America: Visitors to the New Nation, 1776–1914*, eds. Marc Pachter and Frances Wein (Reading, Massachusetts, 1976), p. 86.
10 Mary Shelley to Claire Clairmont in a letter dated 4 November 1842. Reprinted in *The Letters of Mary Wollstonecraft Shelley,* ed. Betty T. Bennett (Baltimore, 1980), p. 42.
11 Dickens, *American Notes*, vol. 1, p. 209.
12 Ibid., p. 230.
13 Hone, *Diary*, vol. 2, p. 587.
14 Ibid., p. 588.
15 Quoted in ibid., pp. 583–4.
16 Dickens, *American Notes*, vol. 2, p. 69.
17 Ibid., pp. 112–13.
18 Ibid., p. 136.
19 Ibid., p. 177.
20 Ibid., pp. 214–15.

CHAPTER ELEVEN: WILLIAM MAKEPEACE THACKERAY LECTURES IN AMERICA

1   Quoted in Gordon N. Ray, *Thackeray, The Age of Wisdom, 1847–1863* (2 vols, New York, 1958), vol. 1, p. 140.
2   Gordon N. Ray, ed., *The Letters and Private Papers of William Makepeace Thackeray* (4 vols, Cambridge, Massachusetts, 1946), vol. 3, p. 119.
3   Ibid., vol. 3, p. 120.
4   Quoted in James Grant Wilson, *Thackeray in the United States, 1852–3, 1855–6* (2 vols, London, 1894), vol. 1, p. 55. For Thackeray's relationship with Dickens, see Michael Slater, *Charles Dickens* (New Haven and London, 2009), pp. 445–6 et passim.
5   Ray, *Thackeray, The Age of Wisdom*, vol. 2, p. 213.
6   Ray, *Letters and Private Papers*, vol. 3, p. 193.
7   Ibid., p. 227.
8   Ibid., p. 222.
9   Eyre Crowe, *With Thackeray in America* (New York, 1893), p. 148.
10 Ray, *Letters and Private Papers*, vol. 3, p. 254.
11 Ibid., p. 199.
12 Ibid., pp. 580–1.
13 Ibid., p. 579.

CHAPTER TWELVE: EDWARD DICEY, REPORTER EXTRAORDINAIRE

1   Edward Dicey, *Spectator of America*, ed. Herbert Mitgang (Athens and London, 1989), p. 7. Originally published in London, 1863, under the title *Six Months in the Federal States*.
2   Ibid., p. 46.
3   Ibid., p. 44.
4   Ibid., p. 68.
5   Ibid., pp. 91–2.
6   Ibid., pp. 140–1.
7   None of these were enjoyed, alas, by the earlier and more famous British visitor, Frances Trollope. Her resounding denunciation of all things American stemmed

largely from her disappointment in not improving her financial situation while in Cincinnati.

8   Dicey, *Spectator*, pp. 234–5.
9   Ibid., p. 242.
10 Ibid., p. 243.
11 Ibid., pp. 265–6.
12 Ibid., p. 273.

CHAPTER THIRTEEN: OSCAR WILDE BRINGS THE NEW AESTHETICS TO AMERICA

1   How thrilled young Wilde would have been to know that these innovative concepts would one day form the focus of an international exhibit staged in London, Paris and San Francisco from April 2011 to June 2012. The catalogue of the exhibit, entitled *The Cult of Beauty: The Aesthetic Movement 1860–1900*, was issued in both English and French.
2   Donald H. Ericksen, *Oscar Wilde* (Boston, 1977), p. 121.
3   Letter from W.F. Morse dated 8 November 1881, in the Gilbert and Sullivan Collection in New York's Morgan Library.
4   Program for the operetta *Patience* at the Standard Theatre, New York. Gilbert and Sullivan Collection in New York's Morgan Library.
5   Oscar Wilde, 'L'Envoi', in Renell Rodd, *Rose Leaf and Apple Leaf* (Philadelphia, 1882), p. 22.
6   Lloyd Lewis and Henry Justin Smith, *Oscar Wilde Discovers America* (New York, 1936), p. 58.
7   *The Complete Letters of Oscar Wilde*, eds. Merlin Holland and Rupert Hart-Davis (New York, 2000), p. 127.
8   Lewis and Smith, *Wilde Discovers America,* p. 75. See also *Oscar Wilde in America: The Interviews,* Matthew Hofer and Gary Scharnhorst, eds. (Urbana and Chicago, 2010). For the latest detailed account of Wilde in America, see Roy Morris, Jr., *Declaring his Genius: Oscar Wilde in North America* (Cambridge, Massachusetts and London, 2013).
9   Letter from Wilde to George Curzon dated 15 February 1882. British Library Board, London. Held in New York's Morgan Library.
10 See Walter Hamilton, *The Aesthetic Movement in England* (London, 2011), originally published in 1882. The relevant chapter is entitled 'Punch's attacks on the aesthetes'.
11 Holland and Hart-Davis, eds., *Complete Letters of Oscar Wilde*, p. 210.
12 Letter from Wilde to Mrs. Bernard Beere, ca. 22 March 1882. The Morgan Library: Bequest of Gordon N. Ray, 1987; MA 4500.
13 Oscar Wilde, *Impressions of America* (Sunderland, 1906), pp. 26–7.
14 Ericksen, *Oscar Wilde*, p. 211.

CHAPTER FOURTEEN: PETER ILICH TCHAIKOVSKY AND THE BIRTH
OF CARNEGIE HALL

1   Modest Tchaikovsky, ed., *The Life and Letters of Peter Ilich Tchaikovsky* (New York, 1924), pp. 640, 643.
2   Samuel L. Clemens [Mark Twain], *Mark Twain's Travels with Mr. Brown,* collected and edited with an introduction by Franklin Walker and G. Ezra Dane (New York, 1940), pp. 90–1.
3   Edward Dicey, *Spectator of America*, ed. Herbert Mitgang (Athens and London, 1989), p. 138.
4   Piotr Ilich Tchaikovsky, *Letters to His Family: An Autobiography* (New York, 2000), p. 476.

5　Modest Tchaikovsky, *Life and Letters*, p. 566.
6　Ibid., p. 638.
7　Ibid., p. 645.
8　Ibid., p. 648.
9　Richard Wortman, Bryce Professor Emeritus of European Legal History at Columbia University, 'St. Petersburg, the Imperial City, and Peter Tchaikovsky'. Unpublished paper delivered at Carnegie Hall on 15 October 2011, on the occasion of the celebration of the 120th anniversary of the opening of that hall.
10　Modest Tchaikovsky, *Life and Letters*, p. 650.
11　Ibid., p. 640.
12　Ibid., p. 637.
13　Ibid., p. 637.
14　Elkhonon Yoffe, *Tchaikovsky in America* (New York, 1986), p. 27.
15　Ibid., pp. 32–3.
16　Ibid., pp. 62–3.
17　Walter Damrosch, *My Musical Life* (New York, 1924). Damrosch has been recognized for his overwhelming contributions to the musical life of New York by the naming of a park in his honor. This is Damrosch Park located in Lincoln Center, containing an outdoor amphitheater seating three thousand with a traditional band shell.

CHAPTER FIFTEEN: HENRY JAMES REVISITS THE NEW WORLD

1　Henry James, *The American Scene*, with an introduction by W.H. Auden (New York, 1946), pp. 54–5. There are several versions of *The American Scene*; the edition in use here has three very brief chapters added, recording visits to Saratoga, Newport and Niagara. As they were written much earlier, they are not included in the discussion contained in this chapter, which has for its focus the visit of James to the New World in 1904.
2　Ibid., pp. 23–4.
3　Ibid., pp. 74–5.
4　Ibid., pp. 78–9.
5　Ibid., p. 120.
6　Ibid., p. 135.
7　Ibid., p. 139.
8　Ibid., p. 146.
9　Ibid., p. 196.
10　Ibid., p. 257. James had earlier paid warm tribute to Concord in a book-length biography of a fellow novelist entitled *Hawthorne*. While the New Englander Nathaniel Hawthorne (1804–64) was not a native of Concord, he acknowledged that he passed his happiest years there. He also spent seven years abroad, most of them in England.
11　Ibid., p. 296.
12　Ibid., p. 319.
13　Ibid., pp. 357–9.
14　Ibid., p. 369.
15　Ibid., p. 458.

 INDEX